THE
BIG SUR BAKERY
COOKBOOK

Foreword by ERIC SCHLOSSER

THE
BIG SUR BAKERY
COOKBOOK
A YEAR IN THE LIFE OF A RESTAURANT

by MICHELLE AND PHILIP WOJTOWICZ AND MIKE GILSON WITH CATHERINE PRICE

Photography by SARA REMINGTON

WILLIAM MORROW
An Imprint of HarperCollins Publishers

Photographs by Sara Remington, except for the following: pages ii, viii, 193, and 247 by Kodiak Greenwood; page 200 (right) by Heather Engen.

HarperCollins books may be purchased for educational, business, or sales promotional use. For information please write: Special Markets Department, HarperCollins Publishers, 10 East 53rd Street, New York, NY 10022.

Designed by Hatch Design LLC

Library of Congress Cataloging-in-Publication Data

The Big Sur Bakery Cookbook: a year in the life of a restaurant / Michelle Wojtowicz . . . [et al.] ; photographs by Sara Remington.
—1st ed.   p. cm.
Includes index.
ISBN 978-0-06-144148-6
1. Cookery, American. 2. Big Sur Bakery. I. Wojtowicz, Michelle.
TX715.B497485 2009
641.5973—dc22   2008038549

10 11 12 13   ID3/QG   10 9 8 7 6 5 4 3

For our mothers... and Terry

Contents

101

SAN FRANCISCO

SAN JOSE

SANTA CRUZ

MONTEREY

1

BIG SUR

101

SANTA BARBARA

LOS ANGELES

August

September

October

November

December

January

February

Basics

Foreword

"Big Sur has a climate of its own and a character all of its own," Henry Miller wrote. "It is a region where extremes meet, where one is always conscious of weather, of space, of eloquent silence." In the nearly half-century since Miller lived there, Big Sur's extremes have grown more extreme. The droughts have gotten longer; the fires, mudslides, and winter storms, much bigger. And the number of eccentrics roaming the hills—like Miller once did, dragging a wagon full of groceries up steep roads while wearing only a jock-strap—is much smaller.

And yet Big Sur remains so damn beautiful that the most extreme thing about it is its vast difference from just about anywhere else in the United States. There are other spectacular landscapes, but none that like look Big Sur, ending so wildly and abruptly at the coast. In the early-morning light, as mist rises from the sea, the place feels surreal. It's hard to believe that in the twenty-first century, amid the country's most heavily populated state, where the car culture has indelibly left its mark, Big Sur is still remarkably unscathed and pristine.

A lot of people move to Big Sur with high hopes—and leave within a year. Despite its beauty, it isn't an easy place to live. There's a toughness, a strength, and a slightly odd quality to the people who learn to ride out the storms and coexist with the tourists. The unique spirit of the place comes not only from the land but from a community of people who've chosen to live differently from almost everybody else.

Like so many of my favorite spots there, the Big Sur Bakery is hiding in plain sight. You could drive past it a thousand times without noticing it. There's nothing mass-produced about it, nothing predictable or pretentious. The bread and the baked goods are as good as they get; the food leaving the kitchen rivals the best in London and New York, without the attitude. The Big Sur Bakery is a little gem, set beside the road. And it is without question the finest restaurant in America with gasoline pumps out front. Mike, Phil, and Michelle have created a space where anyone is welcome—local, out-of-town, rich, poor, or strange. There's a humility to the whole operation that fits perfectly with the grandeur all around it. I think Henry Miller would've loved it and would've gone there almost every night (as long as someone else was picking up the bill).

Eric Schlosser

ERIC SCHLOSSER

Introduction

All of this wouldn't have happened if it weren't for Mike's pants. If he hadn't been wearing one of his signature pairs of overalls, we might not have noticed him standing on a street corner in Los Angeles, lugging a pair of chain saws on the way back from a landscaping job. If we hadn't noticed him, we wouldn't have pulled over. And if we hadn't stopped to say hello, Mike never would have announced to us that he was moving to Big Sur to open a restaurant, and the Big Sur Bakery would not exist.

Luckily, Mike was wearing overalls.

We pulled over our borrowed car (ours had just been stolen) and asked Mike how he was doing. He told us he was about to sell his house in Topanga and move to the most beautiful place on Earth.

"Where's that?" Phil asked.

"Big Sur," Mike said. "I'm opening a restaurant. Want to come check it out?" It was January 2001 and at that point Michelle didn't even know where Big Sur was. Phil only knew about it from reading Kerouac. As a cook and a baker at Campanile, we loved what we were doing and weren't looking to move or change jobs. Also, even though Mike had been a waiter at Joe's in Venice when Phil was a cook, our friendship had never extended outside the restaurant, let alone into joint business ventures. But Mike was on a mission, and several hours later, we were talking with him over grilled cheese sandwiches at Campanile, learning about Big Sur. It was beautiful, he told us, describing redwoods and dramatic cliffs and the building he was leasing, a 1930s ranch house that was full of potential, despite the fact that its most recent incarnation was as a failed Italian restaurant. Plus, it had a hand-built wood-fired oven. We should come see it—maybe we'd be interested in helping him with the food.

Mike convinced us to come up for a night, and so a couple days later we took a six-hour drive up the coast, carefully navigating Highway 1 as it twisted along the edge of the ocean, trying not to drive off the edge as we stared at the view. For us, two kids born and raised in New Jersey, the panorama of the Pacific was unlike anything we'd ever seen, jaw- and stomach-dropping at the same time.

When we arrived in the early afternoon, Mike and his friend Terry "Hide" Prince—an extraordinarily generous Englishman whom Mike had been visiting in Big Sur for some twenty years—welcomed us into a house-turned-abandoned-restaurant next to a gas stop and a deserted nursery, with a dusty dirt driveway and a pair of outdoor washrooms. Painted purple, orange, and blue, the restaurant had been left in disarray by the former tenant, and the garden was filled with screaming, mud-splattered children. This was no Los Angeles. But Terry put the kettle on, offered us our first installment of his famous homemade Hide bread, and gave us a tour of the restaurant, which had a bunch of bakery equipment and, as promised, a giant hand-built Alan Scott wood-fired oven. Before long we were sipping tea, talking story, and getting some of our first impressions of the place from locals who popped into the restaurant to say hello.

But Michelle was unconvinced. We had great jobs at Campanile and while we dreamed of someday opening up our own place, it was a fantasy that seemed years away from becoming a reality. Heading back down the coast, she bid farewell to Big Sur.

Then she got a look at Phil. He had what she calls his "crazy eyes" and even before he said anything, she knew his mind was made up. Michelle managed to hold him off for a day so that she could meet with Mike again and confirm with friends and family that Phil had, in fact, gone insane. But, as we said, Mike was determined. Two days after we got back, we had quit our jobs. Two weeks later, we were in Big Sur, sleeping on the restaurant's floor because there was nowhere else to rent. It was terrifying, but then again, as Phil kept saying, we were in Big Sur. If we failed, no one would ever know.

As Terry started repainting, we cleaned up the place and Mike headed back down to Los Angeles to sell his house so that we would have funds to open. (Did we mention we didn't have money to start a restaurant?) We slept on the floor until an old-timer named Everett offered us a room in his house. We finally moved the day before we were supposed to open, but Mike kept sleeping in the dining room for several weeks before he found a place. Michelle would come in to start baking and there would be Mike, conked out on an army cot in the dining room. He'd wake up just around the time the pastries were coming out of the oven, tuck away his cot, and get to work serving coffee.

In those days we just offered a sit-down breakfast and baked goods, and besides the two of us, Mike, and Terry, we only had one other employee, our dishwasher. Terry kept us going with strong cups of tea and Hide bread sandwiches and, well, we worked our asses off—which was ironic, given that, as we quickly learned, Big Sur does not attract many people looking for eighty-hour workweeks. People here work to live; they don't live to work—which is a great life philosophy but makes it difficult to find good help. Our staff was always late, and if it was a beautiful day out, it was hard to get them to show up at all. Few of our employees had any restaurant experience, and eventually our rule of thumb boiled down to this: If the person looked "clear eyed," they were hired. One time Mike decided to hire a woman based on the fact that she'd hiked the Appalachian Trail. When Michelle asked what the hell that had to do with the restaurant business, he just said, "Determination." As it turns out, he was right—she ended up being one of the best employees we ever had.

As for us, we were used to working all the time. It's probably in our blood—we both grew up in New Jersey in third-generation-immigrant working-class families and once we'd caught the cooking bug as teenagers, we never stopped. We worked in the kitchen of the Metuchen Inn in New Jersey, we worked our way through the Culinary Institute of America, and when we went to California

for our mandatory eighteen-week externship, we extended it so that we could work for a full year. Once we'd moved out to Los Angeles, Michelle worked in a boutique hotel on Sunset Boulevard and, later, at the Four Seasons and Campanile; Phil started at the Four Oaks restaurant, moved on to Joe's in Venice, then Melisse, Axe, and finally Campanile—all high-pressure, high-quality kitchens run by people who were as serious about their businesses as they were passionate about their food. When we took a summer off to backpack through Europe, we used it as an opportunity to learn as much as we could about different foods and cooking techniques. Back in America, we worked overtime and volunteered at different restaurant gigs. Even when we were working in the same restaurant in Los Angeles, we hardly saw each other—if we got one day off together in an entire month, we were stoked. So adjusting to life in Big Sur was challenging.

Terry and his girlfriend, Rachel, told us we needed to learn how to slow down and enjoy Big Sur. Otherwise, they asked, what's the point of living here? And eventually we began to figure out how to balance our ambition for the restaurant with our desire to enjoy Big Sur. We went on walks together and took our dog to the beach every day. We snuck away in the afternoons, spent time with our new Big Sur friends, and cooked food for countless dinner parties. We were still always busy, but we began to find time to have lives outside of our jobs.

At the same time, we were in the midst of figuring out what to do with our favorite part of the restaurant: the wood-fired oven. You can cook almost anything in a wood-fired oven—these days we use it for our breads, chicken, oysters, leg of lamb, suckling pig, fish, beans, and pizza, to name a few items. But learning to use it is difficult. If it's too hot or too cold, a normal evening at the restaurant can turn into a nightmare. If it's chilly and rainy out, the oven performs differently than it does when it's hot and sunny. Sometimes the wood isn't dry enough. Sometimes our fans go out and smoke floods the kitchen. What's more, it requires a ton of fuel, which means we've basically created a year-round job for our friend Wayne, supplying our oak. We love the pioneer vibe of having a wood-fired oven and cooking with fire, but there are also some nights when we long for something a little less rugged.

As we kept working on the Bakery, we got to know Terry's friends, many of whom we now consider friends of our own. The first person we met—in fact, he stopped by the restaurant on our very first trip up to Big Sur—was Wayne Hyland, a local fisherman, forager, and hunter. And the list has grown since then. There's Forrest, a former commercial fisherman who takes us poke poling for rockfish and helps us split wood for the fireplace. There's Jack the Bee Guy, a machinist and longtime resident who treats us to some of his stash of his local Big Sur honey. A few of our friends are former or current employees, like Eric, a farmer and waiter who now runs a microgreen business with his girlfriend, Jasmine. Marilyn Epp, a former Air Force linguist, started off as our bookkeeper and now is one of Michelle's best friends. Over the years we've also gotten to know our local producers, like Jamie at Serendipity Farms in Carmel, who supplies us with organic vegetables. And thanks to Justin Severino, who worked our pizza station and now makes a living as a butcher, we met Jim Dunlop of TLC Ranch, who provides us with pork and pasture-raised eggs.

In those early days, we also had a parade of locals coming into the restaurant to give us suggestions and remind us that no restaurant had ever survived at our spot. But we managed to make it through that first summer, and at the end of the season, we sat down with Mike to have a powwow about where we wanted the restaurant to go. We decided that if we were going to stay in Big Sur, we had to raise the bar and turn the restaurant into a place where we could serve the kind of food we'd been trained to cook, the kind of food we felt passionate about. So we closed the Bakery for eight weeks and completely revamped it. At that point, we'd just met Erik Seniska, a brilliant artist and designer who's now in charge of everything artistic in the Bakery, and we gave him free reign to reinvent the Bakery's décor. We also switched to serving pastries and coffee during the day, pre-made sandwiches for lunch, and a more upscale dinner menu at night. We lit candles, changed the evening music, and bought wineglasses. Two months and several thousand dollars of debt later, we reopened.

The local response was mixed. We'd developed a following by that point, and some of our regular customers were none too pleased to see wineglasses on the tables and increased prices on the menu. But Phil stuck to his guns and insisted that we needed to cook food that we could be proud of, the kind of food we were taught to make by our teachers at the CIA and by our mentors in Los Angeles. That food required good ingredients, those ingredients cost more, and as a result, we needed to raise our prices. We began working on perfecting our chicken and mashed potatoes, figuring out ways to make fantastic burgers and soups, and devising a pizza that could rival those we grew up with in New Jersey. Eventually, the burger moved to our brunch menu to make room for grilled steaks and fish, the vegetable side category grew, and we began running daily specials. Instead of assigning each entree a specific vegetable side dish, we gave customers the option to choose their own, creating a touch of individuality that we loved.

Through the process, we had a constant desire to expand and grow, to make the Bakery into a restaurant we could be truly proud of. And this process hasn't stopped. Recently a chef friend asked Phil if, after seven years of running the Bakery, he felt he was still learning. After thinking about it for a moment, Phil realized that learning is *all* we do. It's a constant, unending process—and luckily, we love it.

It's good, too, to feel our work is paying off. Our location and the Bakery's unassuming exterior make people feel they've discovered something special when they eat here, a treasure tucked in next to a gas station. That might be part of the reason we've started to have yearly regulars, families who camp in Big Sur every summer who have made dinner at the Bakery into a vacation tradition. And the locals have come around, too. When we first opened, Tony Staude, a ninety-something-year-old local who was an institution in the Big Sur community, complained that our portions were too small and our prices were too high. But it wasn't long before he started eating here regularly, and when he died at ninety-six, he left instructions that we cater his memorial service.

When we were offered a chance to write a cookbook based on the Bakery, it took a while to decide how to structure it. Yes, Big Sur is one of the most beautiful places we've ever seen, but most articles and books about Big Sur give an overly glossy sense of what life here is like. They don't mention that there's only one power line connecting us to Carmel, and when that gets knocked out, we can lose electricity for hours—or days. They don't mention that in the rainy winter season, our business slows to a trickle, our bank accounts run down, and we struggle to make it through to the next summer. They don't mention that Big Sur's wildlife, a draw for many tourists, can also pose a danger, like when a huge mountain lion started eating our neighbors' dogs. And, most importantly, they don't give a sense of the people who actually live here—the eclectic, eccentric community we've come to know and love.

So we decided to keep a journal of twelve months here in Big Sur, starting with March, which marks the beginning of spring and a new year of produce. We also included profiles of some of the friends and community members who have shaped our experience here, not to mention our food. We wanted a way to acknowledge and thank them for all they have done to make the Bakery what it is today.

As for us, we're proud of our lives here in Big Sur. We've taken an abandoned, failed restaurant next to a gas station and turned it into a place that people remember and want to revisit. We're running our own business. We're cooking what we want to. We're working together as partners and have found our places in a community that feels like family. And though it can be difficult to keep all this in mind when business is bad or the electricity is out or small-town life feels suffocating, we're living our dream in one of the most beautiful places in the world. As Terry and Rachel would be happy to remind us, what more, really, could we ask for?

Our Philosophy

If you ask us to describe the type of cooking we do, we always come up with the same three terms: "restore," "mom and pop," and "meat and potatoes."

"Restore" because that's where the word "restaurant" comes from, and it's how we like to think of what we do here at the Bakery: people come in, hungry after a long day, and we restore them with our food. That's what this building has been used for since it was built in 1936, and we like to think that we're keeping up that tradition, but raising the bar.

"Mom and Pop" are, of course, us. We love owning our own place, staking our claim out here on the California coast and taking care of the people who come through our doors. But we're a new generation of mom and pop—cooking with fire, using fresh seasonal ingredients, and serving food that's good not just for the people who eat it, but also for the community that provided it and the land from which it came.

"Meat and potatoes" refers to the food itself. But our overarching goal is to serve simple, rustic food made with the freshest, highest-quality ingredients possible—down to earth, but kicked up a notch. We make everything we can from scratch—no processed foods here—and choose preparation methods that highlight foods' natural flavors without overwhelming them. We might be gourmands ourselves, with years of culinary training under our belts, but we never want our restaurant to feel beyond the reach of how we were raised. That's why we try not to add fancy sauces or sprinkle the menu with esoteric cooking terms. We want to make people feel comfortable and familiar with all the foods we serve—and then blow them away.

Michelle
MICHELLE WOJTOWICZ

Philip
PHILIP WOJTOWICZ

Mike
MIKE GILSON

march

Breakfast at the Bakery

For our customers, mornings at the Bakery begin when we open our doors at 8:00, but the real start time is at 4 a.m., when our morning bakers get here to start the day's bread and pastries. Working in the quiet darkness, they take the preshaped bread out of the refrigerator, remove the ash from the oven, and check the oven temperature—an important task, since it will set the pace of the morning and determine in what order the bread and pastries will be baked. After rolling, filling, and shaping the croissants, they set them near the warm oven to proof; and then bake the muffins, scones, cookies, coffee cakes, quiches, and frittatas; fry the doughnuts; and start the day's bread.

At around 7:00, our morning barista arrives to set up the Bakery and start brewing the coffee, and as the morning sun slides into the valley, our first customers pull in, tires crunching on the driveway's gravel. The room they walk into doesn't look like a restaurant—there are no place settings or candles, no waiters or table service. Instead people line up at the counter for coffee and pastries and thick slices of potato frittata and take their breakfasts outside to the front patio, soaking up the sunshine as they sip their morning dose of caffeine.

The early crowd includes tourists from nearby hotels and campgrounds, filling up on food before starting out on their day. But the morning is also all about the locals. They come in for coffee in a long, leisurely procession, drawn as much by their hunger for gossip as for breakfast. Since there's no actual "town" in Big Sur, people gather at a handful of hangouts to catch up, and the Bakery's front patio has become a popular spot to meet.

As Phil oversees prep work in the kitchen, Michelle helps with the rest of the day's baking—everything from pies, cookies, plated dinner desserts, and homemade ice cream to the occasional wedding cake. When she has a free moment, she hangs out in the front of the house, answering the phone and chatting with the parade of friends who stop by: Eric and Jasmine, dropping off microgreens with their son, Haven, bouncing on Eric's arm. Forrie, taking a break from chopping wood to read the morning paper. Erik, back from his latest decorating adventure, dressed to the nines even though it's barely 9 a.m. Jack the Bee Guy stops by for a soy latte and gives an update on the spring bloom. Wayne drops off some firewood. Marilyn tucks herself into a corner and starts on the day's paperwork. Wrenches in hand, Mike rolls in for a cup of tea on his way to fix a plumbing problem at the Bakery, as a patient wine salesperson he forgot he had an appointment with smiles at him from a nearby table.

From the outside, the day's pace seems leisurely and haphazard, but stick around long enough and you'll realize that there's a predictable rhythm to it all, not to mention a lot of work going on behind the scenes: prepping, baking, accepting deliveries, getting ready for the night ahead. At around 2:00, the last lunchtime sandwiches are sold. As the afternoon sun lights up Mount Manuel, the transition to evening begins.

A Brief History of Big Sur

One of the biggest misconceptions people have about Big Sur is that it's an actual town. It's understandable—with all the hype, you'd think we'd at least have a main street. But no, Big Sur simply refers to the ninety-mile-long piece of land south of Carmel and north of San Luis Obispo. Flanked by the Pacific Ocean to the west and the Santa Lucia Mountains to the east, Big Sur is bisected by a stretch of Highway 1 made famous by its dramatic panoramas and knuckle-whitening curves. The part of Big Sur most tourists visit is a short run of road where the highway ducks back from the ocean into the Big Sur Valley. But as for a main street? Hell, we don't even have a real grocery store.

The history of Big Sur didn't start with the opening of Highway 1, of course. The original inhabitants around here were the Esselen, the Salinan, and a division of the Ohlone called the Rumsien—all nomadic hunter-gatherer Native American tribes who lived in the Big Sur area for centuries before Spanish settlers got here in the 1770s.

Those Spanish didn't do good things for the Native Americans, but they did give Big Sur its name. After snagging some prime beachfront real estate and setting up their capital on the Monterey peninsula, they began referring to the area below them as El Pais Grande del Sur: the Big South Country. They might as well have called it "The Large, Impenetrable Area That Has Great Natural Resources but Is a Pain in the Ass to Get To" since, without a road or a permanent port, Big Sur was basically unreachable.

Still, some settlers managed to set up ranches in the area, and in 1821 Big Sur (along with the rest of California) became a part of Mexico when the Mexicans won their independence from Spain. Things changed again in 1848, when California became part of the United States after the Mexican-American War. For Big Sur residents, the main impact of these various political shifts had to do with land: Mexico gave out land grants; subsequently, the 1862 Homestead Act lured Americans to the area by promising free 160-acre plots to settlers. While still difficult to get to, Big Sur then evolved into the home of a bunch of different businessmen: cattle ranchers, farmers, miners, millers, fishermen, and woodsmen, to name a few. Many of the first settlers' names can still be found all over the area—the Pfeiffers, the Partingtons, the Posts. It wasn't until the completion of Highway 1 in 1937, thanks to money from the New Deal and convict labor, that the area became easily accessible to outsiders. But Big Sur wasn't connected

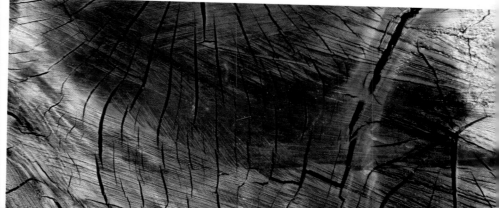

to the California electric grid until the early 1950s, and even today some people proudly live without electricity.

As for the Bakery itself, our building was built around 1936 by Frank Post's daughter Alice (of the famous Post Ranch family) and her husband, Steve Jaeger, who'd come to Big Sur during World War I to break horses. Steve and Alice anticipated that the opening of Highway 1 would bring tourists to Big Sur, so they built a gas station and a ranch house that was divided into two parts: a café, which is now the front of the Bakery, and their home, which is now our dining room. They called it the Loma Vista Inn and opened every season from April to October until sometime in the mid-1970s, when Alice passed away. (The building then went through a few more incarnations before we got here.) Alice and Steve's niece Norma, who lives on the property above us, has tons of black-and-white photographs of the building's beginnings, one of which hangs right inside the Bakery's front door. It shows a group of people gathered around what's now the Bakery's side door, right around the time when Highway 1 first made it easy to travel to Big Sur by car. The caption says "Loma Vista Open House 1937," so the photo was taken about a year after the building was built.

It turned out that Steve and Alice were right: once there was actually a paved road, it was inevitable that tourism (not to mention celebrities) would follow—drawn by the serenity, the natural beauty, and the breathtaking backdrop of the Pacific Ocean. Orson Welles and his then-wife Rita Hayworth bought a cabin on a whim here in 1944 that, rumor has it, they never even stayed in. Henry Miller fell in love with the area when visiting a friend in 1944 and stayed for eighteen years, helping to establish Big Sur's reputation as a bohemian outpost. Other people following in Miller's footsteps included Robinson Jeffers, Edward Weston, Richard Brautigan, Hunter S. Thompson, and Jack Kerouac, whose novel *Big Sur* was published in 1962.

These days, Big Sur is a combination of elements from its past. There are still descendants of the original Native Americans and pioneers hanging around (our own Forrie is related to the Partingtons, and Wayne is part Miwok), but it also draws writers and artists, dreamers and seekers, tons of tourists, a few people on the lam, and the occasional couple looking to start a restaurant.

PROFILE: JIM / PASTURE FARMER

Name: Jim Dunlop   **Occupation:** Farmer

Farm Name: TLC Ranch

Tender Loving Care? Tastes Like Chicken

Date of Birth: February 8, 1969   **Signature:** Jim Dunlop

Pr: No. 1

Are your birds free-range or pasture-raised?
Pasture-raised. Free-range doesn't mean shit.

Explain:
"Free-range" can mean they're raised in a warehouse, as long as they're not in cages. "Pasture-raised" means they're on pasture. I fence my chickens in with electric netting and move the coop every few days to give them new land.

Number of eggs produced per day:
At our highest, two hundred dozen.

Number you personally eat:
If I'm binging, I'll eat four or six at a time. The most I ever had in a week was probably three dozen.

Favorite preparation:
Sunny side up, runny. On toast.

Describe the odor of your pigs:
When sows have piglets, they actually smell like a mixture of earth and caramel and sweetness.

Have you ever been a vegan?
I was a vegetarian for ten years. I care about how animals are treated.

Philosophy on raising animals:
I want to raise them in a way that allows them to display their natural instincts and behaviors. So my chickens can scratch in the dirt and eat bugs and grass. The pigs can run around and roll in the dust and the mud.

Most interesting previous occupations:
After-hours nightclub bouncer in Phoenix. Punk rocker in Manhattan. Ocean lifeguard in South Hampton, New York. Marine corporal, in charge of a machine gun cannon.

How'd you end up out here?
I met a girl. She's now my wife—she's the program director for ALBA, the organization that owns our farm's land. She helps educate aspiring farmers.

Unusual accomplishments:
I hitchhiked 10,000 miles in Australia once. In 1986 some friends and I ran across the United States. My claim to fame, though, is that I set a course record for the Man Against Horse race in Prescott, Arizona. It's fifty miles and you race against endurance horses. I beat all the horses. I was a bad motherfucker back then.

Farthest distance run at one time:
Eighty miles. It took nineteen hours.

What keeps you going?
I'm into coming up with new ways to do things. I like producing really good products and working outdoors. It's funny. . . . First you pretend to be a farmer. Then you keep doing it. And the next thing you know, you actually are one.

Scones

Traditional scone and biscuit recipes often require rolling the dough into a cylinder and slicing off rounds, but those extra steps can make the pastry tough. Instead, we use a method Michelle learned when she was a pastry cook at Campanile: you start out with a shaggy dough that only takes shape when you press it into the cookie cutter. The less you handle the dough the better, so we cut in the butter with a pastry cutter and mix in the buttermilk and fruit by hand. You can avoid another common problem—fruit that breaks up and stains your dough—by starting with fresh fruit but freezing it for a couple hours just before mixing.

As for flavor combinations, the possibilities depend on what's in season. In the summer, we cut up nectarines, plums, peaches, and strawberries; in winter, we rely on dried fruit and candied ginger. Whatever fruits you pick, make sure to give your scones ample space on the cookie sheet, because they'll spread until they've almost doubled in size.

INGREDIENTS

1 cup fresh **huckleberries**
or **blueberries**

1 cup (2 sticks) cold unsalted
butter, cubed

3 1/2 cups **all-purpose flour**

1 cup **granulated sugar**

1 tablespoon **baking powder**

2 teaspoons **baking soda**

1 1/2 teaspoons **kosher salt**

2 tablespoons **vanilla extract**

3/4 cup **buttermilk**

1/4 cup **turbinado sugar**

Makes about 1 dozen scones

About 2 hours before making the scones, scatter the berries on a cookie sheet and put it in the freezer.

Put the cubed butter, flour, granulated sugar, baking powder, baking soda, and salt in a mixing bowl, put the bowl in the freezer, and leave it there for 30 minutes.

Meanwhile, adjust the oven rack to the middle position and preheat the oven to 375°F. Line a baking sheet with parchment paper and set it aside.

Using a pastry cutter, work the chilled ingredients together in the bowl until the butter cubes are the size of peas. Make a well in the center. Combine the vanilla and buttermilk in a separate bowl, and pour the mixture into the well. Mix the ingredients with a wooden spoon to form a shaggy mass. Add the frozen berries and gently mix them in, trying not to crush them.

To shape the scones, place a 3-inch round cookie or biscuit cutter on one corner of the prepared baking sheet. Take a handful of the scone dough and press it into the cutter, patting it down so that the top of the scone is flat. Pull the cutter off the sheet, leaving the scone behind. Repeat this process across the sheet, keeping enough space between the scones for them to double in size, until you've used all the dough. Sprinkle the tops of the scones with the turbinado sugar and bake for 15 to 20 minutes, until they're golden brown along the sides but still tender inside. Transfer the scones to a cooling rack and let them sit for at least 10 minutes before serving.

Potato Frittata

This frittata is available every morning at the Bakery, and it has become a staple for early-morning customers looking for eggs and potatoes. First we parcook the sliced potatoes and then we add just enough eggs to bind them into this hearty breakfast dish. Add bacon if you wish, and serve it with toast. It's also great to take on the go, because it's still delicious when eaten at room temperature.

INGREDIENTS

5 tablespoons **rice bran oil** or **canola oil**

1 small **yellow onion,** sliced

5 **russet potatoes,** peeled and cut into 1/8-inch-thick slices

3 tablespoons **unsalted butter**

Kosher salt

Freshly ground **white pepper**

7 **eggs**

1 tablespoon minced **flat-leaf parsley**

1 tablespoon minced **chives**

2 **whole scallions,** trimmed and thinly sliced

Serves 6 to 8

Adjust the oven rack to the middle position and preheat the oven to 400°F.

Heat a medium sauté pan over medium-high heat and drizzle 2 tablespoons of the oil into it. Add the onions and cook until they're caramelized, 8 to 10 minutes. Deglaze the pan with 1/4 cup water, scraping any brown bits from the bottom with a wooden spoon. Cook until the water evaporates and the onions take on a uniform brown color, about 5 minutes. Transfer the onions to a roasting pan and toss them with the potatoes. Add 1 tablespoon of the butter and the remaining 3 tablespoons oil to the potatoes. Season them generously with salt and white pepper. Cover the pan with aluminum foil and bake for 25 to 30 minutes, until the potatoes are tender. Set them aside to cool for 15 minutes. Reduce the oven temperature to 350°F.

Meanwhile, whisk the eggs, herbs, and scallions together and season them with salt and white pepper.

Add the potatoes and onions to the egg mixture. Heat a 9-inch cast-iron skillet over medium-high heat. Melt the remaining 2 tablespoons butter in the skillet, and add the egg and potato mixture. Cover the skillet with aluminum foil, transfer it to the oven, and bake for 30 minutes. Remove the foil and bake for 10 more minutes.

Slice and serve directly from the skillet, warm or at room temperature.

Breakfast Pizza

This pizza was born on a Saturday morning, right before our brunch service. As the last loaves of bread were coming out of the wood-fired oven, Phil walked into the Bakery hungry for eggs and bacon and decided to fix himself a little pizza with the leftover dough from the night before. He sprinkled it with Parmesan, mozzarella, and bacon pieces, cracked three raw eggs from our chickens right on top, seasoned it with minced herbs, salt, and pepper, and baked it until the egg yolks were set but still soft. It's been a part of our brunch menu ever since.

INGREDIENTS

Bread flour, for dusting

6 **bacon strips**

1 recipe **pizza dough** (see page 235), shaped into 2 balls and refrigerated at least overnight

1/2 cup grated **Parmesan**

2 cups grated **mozzarella**

6 **eggs**

Kosher salt

Freshly ground **black pepper**

2 tablespoons minced **flat-leaf parsley**

2 tablespoons minced **chives**

2 whole **scallions**, trimmed and thinly sliced

1 shallot, **minced**

Makes 2 pizzas (serves 2 to 4)

At least 1 hour before you start baking, adjust the oven rack to the lowest position, put a baking stone on it, and preheat the oven to 450°F.

Generously dust the surface of a pizza peel (a flat wooden or metal shovel with a long handle) with bread flour.

Heat a large sauté pan over medium-high heat, add the bacon strips, and pan-fry until crisp. Put the bacon on a plate lined with paper towels, let it cool, and then chop it into bite-size pieces.

Lightly dust a work surface with bread flour. Working with one ball of pizza dough, dip your hands and the dough in the bread flour to make them less sticky, and pat the dough down into a disk shape with the tips of your fingers. Once the disk is large enough, drape the dough over your fists and carefully start stretching and expanding the dough from underneath to form a round that is 10 to 12 inches in diameter. (If you're feeling lucky, try tossing the dough over your head in a circular motion to stretch it.)

Place the dough on the prepared peel. Sprinkle it with half of the Parmesan, mozzarella, and bacon, and crack 3 eggs over the top. Season with salt and pepper to taste.

Before you put the pizza in the oven, do the "stick test": shake the peel slightly to make sure the pizza is not sticking (if it is, carefully lift the section that is sticking and sprinkle a bit more flour underneath). Then slide the pizza directly onto the baking stone and bake it for 8 to 12 minutes, checking on it after 5 minutes and rotating it if necessary to ensure that it's baking evenly. When the crust is golden, the cheese is melted, and the egg yolks are cooked to medium, use the peel to remove the pizza from the oven and transfer it to a cutting board. Let it cool for 2 minutes and sprinkle with half of the parsley, chives, scallions, and shallots. Slice and serve immediately.

Prepare your second pizza the same way.

Nine-Grain Pancake

Baked in a cast-iron skillet, this is a real pan "cake." At the Bakery, we prepare it in the wood-fired oven, where it puffs up to an inch thick in just a couple minutes. We top it with huckleberries or strawberries, or serve it with maple syrup and butter—or even eat it with a thin European-style yogurt. One pancake should be enough for one person. If you want to serve the pancakes to a group of people, cut them into slices and allow your guests to help themselves.

We buy our nine-grain mix from Giusto's Millers & Bakers out of San Francisco; it's a combination of steel-cut oats, millet, amaranth, barley, soft wheat, winter wheat, rye, flax seeds, and corn grits.

INGREDIENTS

1/4 cup **brown rice**

1/2 cup plus 2 tablespoons **nine-grain mix**

2 tablespoons **flax seeds**

2 tablespoons **sesame seeds**

1/4 cup **sunflower seeds**

1/2 cup plus 3 tablespoons **all-purpose flour**

2 cups **whole-wheat flour**

1 tablespoon plus 1 teaspoon **baking powder**

1 tablespoon plus 1 teaspoon **baking soda**

1 teaspoon **kosher salt**

1/2 cup plus 3 tablespoons **old-fashioned rolled oats**

1/4 cup **molasses**

4 cups **buttermilk**

4 **egg yolks**

6 **egg whites**

4 tablespoons **unsalted butter**

Makes 4 pancakes

Place the brown rice in a small saucepan, add 1 cup water, and bring to a boil over medium-high heat. Reduce the heat and let simmer until the rice is tender, about 30 minutes. Transfer the rice to a separate dish to cool completely.

Combine the nine-grain mix, flax seeds, sesame seeds, and sunflower seeds in a bowl. Bring 1 1/4 cups water to a boil, and pour it over the grains and seeds. Let them soak for 30 minutes or until they're soft.

Place the all-purpose flour, whole-wheat flour, baking powder, baking soda, salt, and oats in a mixing bowl. Stir to combine, and make a well in the center. In a separate bowl, whisk together the molasses, buttermilk, egg yolks, the grain and seed mixture, and 1/2 cup of the cooked brown rice. Pour the liquid mixture into the well, and combine with a wooden spoon.

In an electric mixer fitted with the wire whisk attachment, whisk the egg whites at high speed until soft peaks form. Using a rubber spatula, fold the whites into the flour mixture. (You can hold the batter in the refrigerator until you're ready to use it, but keep in mind that the sooner you bake the pancakes, the lighter they'll be.)

Adjust the oven rack to the middle position and preheat the oven to 350°F.

Preheat two 9-inch cast-iron skillets in the oven for 5 minutes. Add 1 tablespoon of the butter to each pan and swirl it around to coat the pan. Pour one fourth of the batter into each pan, transfer them to the oven, and bake for 15 to 20 minutes. Check the pancakes the same way you would a regular cake: the pancakes are ready when a skewer inserted in the middle comes out clean. Flip each pancake onto a plate, and serve.

Bake the other 2 pancakes the same way.

Meyer Lemon Bars

When Meyer lemons hit Big Sur, they come all at once. We've developed marvelous ways of using them—from marmalades to salad dressings and, of course, our Meyer lemon bars. The crust on these bars is made with pine nuts and cornmeal, and the filling is much thicker than your average bar.

INGREDIENTS

FOR THE DOUGH:

1 cup **unsalted butter**

1/2 cup **pine nuts**

2 3/4 cups **all-purpose flour**

1/3 cup plus 2 tablespoons **sugar**

1/2 cup **yellow cornmeal**

1 teaspoon **kosher salt**

Grated zest of 2 **Meyer lemons**

2 **egg yolks**

2 tablespoons **heavy cream**

FOR THE MEYER LEMON FILLING:

3 1/4 cups **sugar**

1/2 cup **all-purpose flour**

Grated zest of 3 **Meyer lemons**

1 cup **Meyer lemon juice**

1/2 cup **heavy cream**

8 whole **eggs**

5 **egg yolks**

FOR THE TOPPING:

Powdered sugar, for sprinkling

Makes 1 dozen bars

To make the dough, first cut the butter into cubes, spread them out on a plate, and freeze for 30 minutes.

Meanwhile, adjust the oven rack to the middle position and preheat the oven to 350°F.

Scatter the pine nuts on a cookie sheet, and toast them in the oven until they're light brown, about 7 minutes. Let them cool completely.

Pulse the flour, sugar, cornmeal, pine nuts, salt, and lemon zest in a food processor until the pine nuts have been broken into smaller pieces. Add the frozen butter cubes, and pulse until the mixture resembles a coarse meal. Transfer it to a mixing bowl and make a well in the center. Whisk the yolks and cream together in a separate bowl, and pour the mixture into the well. Knead with your hands until the ingredients are fully combined and the dough is uniform and smooth. Flatten it into a disk and wrap it in plastic wrap. Refrigerate for 3 hours.

Roll the chilled dough between two pieces of parchment paper into a 15 by 17 inch rectangle, 1/4 inch thick. Drape the dough inside a 9 by 13-inch baking dish, working it into the corners and up the sides of the dish. Trim off the excess dough with a paring knife, and refrigerate the dish for 30 minutes.

While the crust is chilling, preheat the oven to 350°F.

Bake the crust until it's a rich golden brown, about 20 minutes. Set it aside until completely cool.

Reduce the oven temperature to 325°F.

Make the filling: In an electric mixer fitted with the wire whisk attachment, combine the sugar, flour, Meyer lemon zest and juice, heavy cream, eggs, and egg yolks on high speed until frothy, 2 to 3 minutes. Pour the filling into the cooled crust and bake until the filling is set but not browned, 25 to 30 minutes. Let it cool completely in the baking dish.

Using a chef's knife and wiping the blade clean with a wet towel between cuts, cut into 3-inch squares. Transfer the bars to a platter, sprinkle generously with powdered sugar, and serve.

Date and Quinoa Muffins

We love dates, especially on long road or camping trips. Whenever we heard someone was going to Palm Springs, we used to beg them to bring us a couple cases of Medjool dates. Now we have a small group of friends who pick them up for us when they are down there. We serve these muffins from winter to early spring, when dried fruits are our staple. These started out as a brown sugar muffin but they needed something extra. After a little experimenting, Michelle decided to add dates and orange zest, and when we have candied kumquats, she chops some and folds them in. There's quinoa flour, too, to sneak some whole grains into your diet.

INGREDIENTS

FOR THE STREUSEL TOPPING:

1/4 cup **pecan halves**

1/2 **vanilla bean**

1/4 cup **unsalted butter**

1/4 cup plus 2 tablespoons **all-purpose flour**

1/4 cup (packed) **light** or **dark brown sugar**

1/4 teaspoon **kosher salt**

FOR THE MUFFIN BATTER:

1/2 cup **pecan halves**

1 cup **unsalted butter**, softened, plus extra for coating the pan

1/2 cup **granulated sugar**

1 cup (packed) **light** or **dark brown sugar**

1 tablespoon **baking powder**

1 teaspoon **kosher salt**

2 **eggs**

1 1/2 teaspoons **vanilla extract**

Grated zest from 1 **orange**

1 cup **all-purpose flour**

1 cup **quinoa flour**

1 cup **buttermilk**

10 **dried dates**, pitted and chopped into pieces

Makes 1 dozen muffins

Adjust the oven rack to the middle position and preheat the oven to 375°F.

Scatter the pecans, for both the streusel topping and the muffin batter, on a cookie sheet and toast until they're golden through the center, about 10 minutes. (To check if they're done, cut one open and inspect the color inside.) Let them cool and then roughly chop them. Use 1/4 cup of chopped pecans for the streusel and reserve the rest for the muffin batter. (Leave the oven on.)

To make the streusel topping: Split the vanilla bean lengthwise with a paring knife, scrape out the pulp with the back of the knife, and put the pulp and the pod in a small saucepan. Add the butter and melt over medium-high heat. Cook until the butter separates and the white milk solids start to brown and smell nutty, about 7 minutes. Remove the vanilla bean. Pour the hot brown butter into a dry bowl, place it in the freezer, and leave until solid, about 30 minutes.

Remove the solidified butter from the bowl and chop it into small pieces. Combine the butter, flour, brown sugar, and salt in a bowl and work the mixture with a pastry blender until crumbly. Mix in the chopped pecans and refrigerate the streusel until ready to use.

Butter a 12-cup muffin pan and set it aside.

To make the batter: In an electric mixer fitted with the paddle attachment, cream together the butter, granulated sugar, brown sugar, baking powder, and salt until light and fluffy. Add the eggs, one by one, and mix to incorporate. Mix in the vanilla extract and orange zest. Combine the all-purpose flour and the quinoa flour in a bowl. Then add the combined flours in three batches, alternating with the buttermilk, beginning and ending with flour. Using a rubber spatula, fold in the chopped dates and the reserved pecans.

Fill each prepared muffin cup almost all the way to the top with batter, and sprinkle each muffin with a layer of streusel. Bake for 20 to 25 minutes, or until a cake tester inserted in the middle comes out clean. Let the muffins cool completely in the pan. Then remove them from the pan by running a knife around the edges. Serve.

Doughnuts

Our first roommate in Big Sur was a longtime local named Everett Ma-kowski, who was eighty when he offered to rent us one of the rooms in his big house down in Sycamore Canyon. Everett's nickname was "The Doughnut King" because when he used to commute to work, he some-times ate one or two dozen doughnuts a day—so when we were trying out this recipe at the Bakery, it seemed only natural for him to be our taste tester. Even to this day, we think the doughnuts had something to do with his decision to let us live with him.

We make these doughnuts in a bunch of different ways: sometimes we glaze them, sometimes we fill them with homemade jam and then glaze them. (We make rhubarb, apricot, strawberry, peach, plum, and raspberry jams in the summer and use them in the doughnuts throughout the year.) Sometimes we fill them with vanilla pastry cream and dip them in choco-late glaze. We've also folded caramelized apples into the dough and made apple fritters. Once you have mastered the recipe, feel free to experiment. Just remember to plan ahead: the dough needs to rest overnight.

INGREDIENTS

1 tablespoon plus 1/2 teaspoon **active dry yeast**

2 1/4 cups **bread flour** plus extra, for dusting

1 1/4 cups plus 1 tablespoon **pastry flour**

1 1/2 teaspoons **baking powder**

2 tablespoons **sugar,** plus extra for dusting

1 1/2 teaspoons **kosher salt**

1 1/2 teaspoons **freshly grated nutmeg**

5 tablespoons **powdered milk**

6 tablespoons **unsalted butter,** softened, plus extra for coating the bowl

1 **egg**

Rice bran oil or **canola oil** for frying

Doughnut glaze (recipe follows)

2 cups **rhubarb jam** (see page 28)

Makes 1 dozen jelly or glazed doughnuts

Place 1/4 cup lukewarm water in the bowl of an electric mixer, and sprinkle the yeast over the water. Stir, and then set it aside to activate for 5 minutes.

In another bowl, mix together the bread flour, pastry flour, baking powder, sugar, salt, nutmeg, and powdered milk. Add 1 1/2 cups of this mixture, 3/4 cup cold water, the butter, and the egg to the yeast mixture. Combine in the electric mixer fitted with the dough hook on very low speed for 1 minute. Then, over a 1-minute period, add the remaining flour mixture. Increase the speed to medium and mix for 2 minutes. Stop the mixer, scrape down the sides of the bowl with a rubber spatu-la, and beat on high speed for 2 minutes. Transfer the dough to a large buttered bowl (large enough to let the dough double in size), cover the bowl loosely with a plastic bag (we use plastic garbage bags in various sizes, depending on the size of the pan), and refrigerate it overnight.

The next morning, remove the dough from the refrigerator, turn it onto a floured surface, and roll it down until it's 1/2 inch thick. If you're making jelly-filled dough-nuts, cut out 12 rounds with a 3 1/2 inch round cookie or biscuit cutter. If you want to make glazed doughnuts, cut the same 12 rounds and then turn them into rings by cutting a hole in the center of each one with a 1 inch cutter. Line a cookie sheet with a linen napkin and dust it generously with flour. Place the doughnuts and their holes on the prepared cookie sheet. Put the entire sheet in a plastic bag and tie it loosely. Let the doughnuts rise in a warm part of the kitchen until they double in size, about 30 minutes.

While the doughnuts are rising, fill a large heavy-bottomed pot with oil about 2 inches deep, and heat it over medium heat until the oil reaches 350°F on a deep-fry thermometer.

Working in batches, carefully drop the doughnuts, one by one, into the hot oil without overcrowding the pot. Fry until the doughnuts are golden brown, then flip them over and fry the other side—this should take about 4 minutes total. Test for doneness by picking out a sacrificial doughnut and cutting it right in the middle to see if it's cooked through—this will help you gauge how much more time the doughnuts need. When they're done, remove the doughnuts with a slotted spoon and place them on a plate lined with paper towels. Continue the process with the rest of the doughnuts and the holes (the holes will fry much faster). Let them sit until they're cool enough to handle.

To make glazed doughnuts, dip the top of each doughnut into the glaze until half of the doughnut is coated. Shake off the excess. Put the doughnuts, glaze side up, on a cooling rack and let them dry slightly. Then toss the holes in sugar, place them on top of the doughnuts, and serve.

To make jelly doughnuts, use the handle of a wooden spoon to poke a hole three quarters of the way into each doughnut. Gently move it around to create a nice-size cavern for the jam. Put the jam in a pastry bag fitted with a plain decorating tip. Insert the tip into the doughnut and fill it until it feels heavy. Repeat with the rest of the doughnuts. Dip these in the glaze as well.

Doughnut Glaze

Whisk all the ingredients together in a bowl until a smooth glaze is formed. Keep covered until ready to use.

INGREDIENTS

1 1/2 cups **powdered sugar,** sifted

3 tablespoons **honey**

Grated zest of 1 **lemon**

3 tablespoons **whole milk**

Chocolate Bundt Cake

In her years as a young pastry cook, Michelle made a devil's food cake under every chef she ever worked for—and each one of them had a different opinion about what makes a cake good. One thing they all believe in, though, is using Dutch-process cocoa powder. One of the best is Valrhona cocoa powder, which is wonderfully dark and rich. After many trials, Michelle decided that she likes a very thin layer of frosting and mostly cake.

INGREDIENTS

FOR THE CAKE:

1 tablespoon **unsalted butter,** softened

1 1/4 cups plus 1 tablespoon **brewed coffee**

3/4 cup Dutch-process **cocoa powder**

2 1/4 cups **sugar**

1 1/4 teaspoons **kosher salt**

2 1/2 teaspoons **baking soda**

2 **whole eggs**

1 **egg yolk**

1 1/4 cups plus 1 tablespoon **buttermilk**

1 cup plus 2 tablespoons **rice bran oil** or **canola oil**

1 1/2 teaspoons **vanilla extract**

2 1/2 cups plus 2 tablespoons **all-purpose flour,** sifted

FOR THE ICING:

6 ounces **bittersweet chocolate**

3/4 cup **unsalted butter**

2 cups **powdered sugar**

1/2 cup **sour cream,** at room temperature

1/4 cup **brewed coffee,** cooled (used for Bundt cake only)

Makes one 10-inch Bundt cake or two 9-inch cakes to be layered and iced

Adjust the oven rack to the middle position and preheat the oven to 350°F.

Use the 1 tablespoon butter to thoroughly butter a 10-inch Bundt cake pan, using your fingertips to get into all the ridges. Set it aside. If making a layer cake, butter two 9-inch pans and set them aside.

To make the cake batter: Put the coffee and cocoa powder in a small saucepan and bring to a boil while whisking constantly. Remove from the heat and let it cool to room temperature.

In an electric mixer fitted with the wire whisk attachment, mix together the sugar, salt, baking soda, eggs, and egg yolk on low speed until well combined, 30 seconds. Add the buttermilk, oil, and vanilla extract, and mix for another 30 seconds. Add the flour and mix on medium speed for 2 minutes. Add the cooled cocoa mixture and mix on high speed for 3 minutes. Pour the batter into the prepared cake pan(s) and bake for 1 hour (35 minutes if making cake layers). Let the cake cool completely in the pan. Remove the cake from the pan by inverting it onto a cooling rack.

To make the icing: Chop the chocolate into small pieces, put them in a heatproof bowl (or a double boiler), and set the bowl over a pot of barely simmering water, making sure the bottom of the bowl doesn't touch the water. Remove the bowl from the heat when all the chocolate pieces have melted. Melt the butter in a separate pan, pour it over the melted chocolate, and whisk by hand to incorporate. Sift half of the powdered sugar right into the chocolate mixture, and whisk to combine. Add the sour cream and whisk to combine. Then sift in the remaining powdered sugar and whisk until smooth. The icing should be thick and shiny. Add the coffee and whisk to create a glossy glaze. Pour the glaze over the Bundt cake, covering it completely. Leave it at room temperature until ready to serve.

If you are making a layer cake, omit the coffee when preparing the icing and let the icing sit at room temperature for 2 hours, until it thickens to the consistency of soft cream cheese. To assemble the cake, spread about 1/2 cup of the frosting evenly over the first layer and top with the second layer. Frost the top and sides of the layer cake with the remaining icing. Leave at room temperature until ready to serve.

Brown Butter Rhubarb Bars

Michelle loves rhubarb. She used to think that she was the only one who did, until she started making these bars and realized that if you surround it with brown butter, *everyone* loves rhubarb. There are a few homes in Big Sur with rhubarb patches, and when it comes into season, locals will bring bunches to Michelle as a treat. At that time of year, we still have blood oranges arriving on our doorstep, so we combine them and make a very grown-up bar. The blood oranges give the bars a vibrant red color, and their sweetness balances the tartness of the rhubarb, which in turn helps cut the richness of the buttery crust and filling. These bars are perfect for traveling long distances or packing in a picnic basket—the brown butter will keep them moist. And if your rhubarb is abundant, you can also make a bigger batch of the filling and can it. That way you can make these bars all year 'round. (Be aware that as the jam cooks it will splatter—we recommend wearing long sleeves to prevent burns.)

INGREDIENTS

FOR THE RHUBARB JAM:

1 cup **sugar**

Grated zest and juice of 2 **blood oranges**

1/2 **vanilla bean**

4 **rhubarb stalks,** cut into 1/2-inch pieces

FOR THE CRUST:

1 cup **unsalted butter**

1/2 cup **powdered sugar**

1 1/2 cups **all-purpose flour**

Makes 1 dozen bars

To prepare the rhubarb jam: Place the sugar, blood orange zest and juice in a medium saucepan. Split the vanilla bean lengthwise with a paring knife, scrape out the pulp with the back of the knife, put the pulp and the pod in the pan, and bring the mixture to a boil over high heat. Continue cooking until the faintest bit of caramel color starts to appear around the edge of the pot. Add the rhubarb. Continue to cook, stirring with a wooden spoon, until the rhubarb turns into a smooth jam, 7 to 10 minutes. Transfer the jam (discarding the vanilla bean) to a separate dish to cool while you make the crust and filling.

Make the crust next: Melt the butter in a saucepan over medium-high heat, whisking frequently. Cook until the butter separates and the white milk solids start to brown and smell nutty, about 5 minutes. Pour the hot brown butter into a dry bowl and freeze until solid, about 30 minutes. Place the powdered sugar and flour in a bowl and mix to combine. Take out the frozen butter and cut it into small cubes. Mix the cubes into the flour mixture, using a pastry cutter to break up the butter until large crumbs start to form. Work the crumbs together into a crumbly dough with both hands, and place it in a 9 by 13-inch baking dish. Press the dough firmly with the bottom of a glass to make sure that the crust evenly covers the entire bottom of the dish. Chill the crust in the refrigerator for 30 minutes.

While the crust is chilling, adjust the oven rack to the middle position and preheat the oven to 375°F.

Bake the crust for 15 to 18 minutes, until golden brown. Let it cool before assembling the bars. (Leave the oven on.)

While the crust is cooling, make the brown butter filling: Whisk together the eggs, sugar, orange zest, and flour in a medium bowl. Split and scrape the vanilla bean

FOR THE BROWN BUTTER FILLING:

3 **eggs**

1 1/4 cups **sugar**

Grated zest of 2 **oranges**

3/4 cup plus 2 tablespoons **all-purpose flour**

1/2 **vanilla bean**

1/2 cup plus 2 tablespoons **unsalted butter**

just as you did for the rhubarb jam, and put the pulp and the pod in a medium saucepan. Add the butter and melt over medium-high heat. Cook until the butter separates and the white milk solids start to brown and smell nutty. (Discard the vanilla bean.) Carefully add the warm brown butter to the egg mixture, whisking constantly until all the butter is incorporated.

To assemble the bars, spread half of the brown butter filling over the cooled baked crust. Spoon large dollops of the rhubarb jam over the filling, reserving a quarter of the jam. Spread the remaining brown butter filling over the rhubarb, and finish by spooning smaller dollops of the reserved jam randomly over the top. Bake for 25 to 30 minutes, until the filling is deep golden brown. Remove the dish from the oven and let it cool completely.

Cut into 3-inch squares and serve.

april

Dinnertime

If you stopped by the Bakery at breakfast and again at dinnertime, you could be forgiven for thinking that you'd walked into a different restaurant. In the evening, the casual neighborhood hangout is transformed into a real dining room: candles on the tables, wineglasses, and customers who have come to the Bakery as a treat.

We stay open between lunch and dinner, so throughout the afternoon there's still a stream of passersby stopping in for coffee and any pastries left over from the morning. In the meantime, the servers polish glasses and silverware, fold napkins, replace old menus with new ones, set the tables, and nudge the coffee customers out of the dining room.

Late afternoon at the Bakery is a calm time, in both the front and the back of the house, since most of the chaos has happened between 9:00 and 3:00. The night cooks come in to set up their stations and Phil puts some music on in the kitchen to give everyone something to listen to as they work. The pizza cook stokes the fire, tends the oven, and arranges more wood near the stove in the pizza room so it can dry. Mike reorganizes the wine room and puts together a wine list. Erik comes in to create the flower arrangement. It isn't until around 5 o'clock that things start to heat up and pressure begins to build—the big show is coming.

Our reservation book gives us a general sense of how busy a night will be, but since we get a lot of walk-ins, we can never really predict what's going to happen. When the evening kicks into gear, everyone goes on autopilot. No one talks much in the kitchen, except to explain special orders, which tend to be minimal since Phil doesn't allow many changes to his menu. Our kitchen is so small that it requires a constant dance for people not to run into each other. Pizzas fly, and the pizza room gets hot—very hot. When the night is a good one, you can feel a buzz in the air—everyone totally in their groove, customers sometimes even sticking their heads into the kitchen to give their thanks.

We usually close the kitchen around 9:00 or 10:00, but it takes another hour or so to clean everything up. Once all the guests are gone, we sit at the bar to decompress. Phil challenges someone to a game of chess, or we share a bottle of wine. Eventually Phil locks up the restaurant and we all retreat home to our beds for some much-needed sleep. Five or so hours later, our morning bakers arrive to prepare the morning's pastries, and the cycle begins again.

Honey

If you'd asked us a few years ago how honey was produced, we wouldn't have been able to tell you much. But that was before we met Jack Koch, otherwise known as "Jack the Bee Guy." He's our resident honey expert, and he has taught us everything we know about bees.

Jack keeps his bees in Langstroth hives, which consist of white wooden boxes built without tops or bottoms that stack on top of one another to form a shaft. The bee colony lives in the bottom two boxes and builds the comb from the bottom up. The worker bees (which are all female) gather pollen and nectar from every plant they can—in Big Sur, they have access to a menu that includes huckleberry, dandelion, lupine, rosemary, fennel, and even poison oak. During spring bloom, when fruit trees start to flower, the bees have yet more choices, taking their pick of avocados, apples, berries, and persimmons, to name a few. Jack harvests his honey after each season, as soon as he notices its color start to change. That way the seasons' flavors don't get blended together.

In addition to doing "waggle dances," bees communicate with each other primarily through smell. The queen bee, who sits tight in the center of the hive and can live for more than five years, releases pheromones that dictate the whole mood of the hive. So if she's anxious, it rubs off on all the other bees. Jack says that if you're experienced enough, you can smell the variations too. "It's like the difference between the air freshener you put in a bathroom versus a living room," he says. "It's almost the same, but slightly different—and it triggers the whole hive."

Because bees rely so heavily on their sense of smell, it's important to pay close attention to odor when you're approaching the hive. Jack tries not to wash his hair or use deodorant before he works with the hive because the smell would be, as he puts it, like blasting the bees in the face with a

firehose—the strong smell overwhelms their communication systems, and they get angry. One time, when Jack made the mistake of wearing freshly laundered clothes under his bee suit, the smell of fabric softener on his cuffs got the bees so upset that he ended up with about forty of them swarming around each ankle, stinging. Now, he blows a few puffs of smoke from burnt burlap on himself before working with the bees—for some reason, they don't mind the smell.

To make honey, worker bees fly out of the hive and collect nectar from flowering plants, helping to pollinate them in the meantime. After ingesting and regurgitating the nectar a few times until it is partially digested, they deposit it in the comb's cells. Then the bees in the hive beat their wings to create a breeze to help the water in the honey evaporate. The bees are looking for about an 80/20 ratio of sugar to water—too much sugar and the honey will become solid; too much water and it will ferment into mead. Once they think they've gotten the ratio about right, they cap off each cell with beeswax and allow it to sit, checking on it occasionally to make sure that the ratios are still correct.

So far, Jack's bees haven't succumbed to colony collapse disorder, the mysterious killer of thousands of beehives across the United States. But he still has to deal with natural predators like skunks and ants, both of whom love honey, and blue jays, who like to prey on the bees themselves. Pesticides that are used along the side of Highway 1 knock out thousands of bees, and a dry year with little rain will shorten each season's bloom. In other words, honey takes a lot of work—from bees and beekeeper alike. We're happy that Jack is willing to share his with us.

PROFILE: JACK / BEEKEEPER

Name: Jack Koch
Nickname: Jack The Bee Guy

Day Job: Beekeeper, Machinist, Caretaker, Specializing in Water Systems & Generators.

Date of Birth: June 13, 1954
Signature: *[signature]*

Pr: No. 2

How do the bees fit in?
Beekeeping is a side hobby. It's not an easy thing these days. People think the bee just squeezes honey into the jar, but there's a lot of process there.

Number of hives:
Between five and twenty, depending on the year.

Largest amount of honey produced in a year:
Fifty-five gallons.

Smallest?
Three. There was a drought.

What do you use your honey for?
I eat it with tea, oatmeal, cereal, chai. Oh—and I carry honey on me in the backcountry in case I get cut. It's an antiseptic. As soon as it hits blood, the honey turns to hydrogen peroxide.

Amount personally consumed per year:
If I don't have five gallons of honey, I'm in trouble.

Who gets the leftovers?
It's not commercial—just for local people and people I've known for years. When you get thirty-five people in Big Sur who buy honey, that takes care of a lot of the surplus.

First experience with bees:
I fell into a beehive when I was young and got stung head to toe and didn't die. I was lucky.

What kind of plants do your bees use?
It depends on the time of year. We've got rosemary, sage, thyme, orange trees, avocados, apricots, heather, poison oak. That's just a few. I keep flashcards with lists of each year's blooms.

Favorite honey:
From the spring bloom. It's the soft, delicate end of honey. Crystal clear.

Personality traits necessary for beekeeping:
You have to be really calm. You can't go in with residual feelings from someplace else because the bees will pick up on it. They can smell if you're upset.

Best part of living in Big Sur:
To be able to be familiar with the local community. A lot of times people come through and take what they can get and then leave. So it's nice to be able to add to it.

Best part of beekeeping:
Communicating with nature. If you can keep the hive happy and the queen happy, they reward you.

Grilled Sardines with Frisée and Whole-Grain Mustard Dressing

Our sardines come right out of Monterey Bay and are a real gift with their sweet, rich taste and flavorful skin. Only problem is, they take a long time to clean. A few lucky guests get to eat these, but usually once Phil has finished the tedious task of cleaning them, he asks, "Should we cook some up?" Soon after, our bellies are full—and the sardines never make it to the menu. It's not that often that you see sardines at fish markets, but they're worth searching out. We also love to bake sardines in a cast-iron skillet in the wood-fired oven with a ladleful of tomato sauce and a drizzle of olive oil. Then we put them over toast—they make great open-face sandwiches.

INGREDIENTS

FOR THE FRISÉE:

1 head **frisée**

2 tablespoons minced **chives**

2 tablespoons minced **flat-leaf parsley**

2 tablespoons minced **shallots**

FOR THE WHOLE-GRAIN MUSTARD DRESSING:

1 tablespoon **whole-grain mustard**

1/4 cup **golden (or white) balsamic vinegar**

Kosher salt

Freshly ground **black pepper**

1/2 cup **rice bran oil** or **canola oil**

FOR THE SARDINES:

12 **fresh sardines**, cleaned and butterflied (see sidebar)

¼ cup **rice bran oil** or **canola oil**

Kosher salt

Freshly ground **black pepper**

3 tablespoons minced **flat-leaf parsley**

Serves 4

Start a fire in your grill 30 minutes in advance, burning the wood down until you have a red-hot coal base. You don't want flames touching the fish. (See page 244 for preparing a wood-fired grill.)

Wash the frisée and snip the green tips off the leaves, leaving behind only the white and yellow part of the head. Cut off and discard the core. Tear the remaining leaves into medium pieces. Place the frisée in a bowl, toss in the herbs and shallots, and set it aside, undressed, until ready to serve.

In a medium bowl, whisk the mustard and vinegar with a pinch of salt and pepper until combined. Add the oil in a slow, steady stream until the dressing is thick and emulsified—it should come together pretty quickly. Check the seasoning and add more salt and pepper if necessary. Set the dressing aside.

Brush the sardines on both sides with the oil, season with salt and pepper, and sprinkle with the parsley. Place the fish on the hot grill, skin side down, and cook until their flesh turns opaque, 2 to 3 minutes. Remove the fish from the grill and set them aside on a plate with the skin side up.

Toss the frisée salad lightly with the dressing, add salt and pepper to taste, and arrange the salad on a platter. Place the sardines on top, skin side up.

Cleaning Sardines

Using a sharp knife, slice open the belly of each fish and remove its innards. Cut off the head, open the fish with your fingers, and pull out its spine (this should remove most of the bones, though there may be a few stragglers). Keep the fish butterflied for grilling.

Roasted Leg of Lamb with Pesto

Roasting works well on meat that's attached to the bone because the exterior will caramelize to a crispy crust while the bone will keep the meat moist and red on the inside. To keep the meat as juicy as possible, let it rest for several minutes after taking it out of the oven. How you carve it is also important—always make sure to slice across the grain.

INGREDIENTS

FOR THE LAMB:

2 cups **kosher salt**

2 tablespoons **sugar**

3 **bay leaves**

1 **cinnamon stick**

10 **coffee beans**

5 **black peppercorns**

5 **garlic cloves**

2 **star anise pods**

1 leg of **spring lamb,** bone in, 4 to 5 pounds

8 **rosemary sprigs**

1/4 cup **olive oil**

FOR THE PESTO:

Kosher salt

1 cup (packed) **fresh basil leaves**

1/2 cup flat-leaf **parsley leaves**

1 cup **rice bran oil** or **canola oil**

Freshly ground **black pepper**

Serves 6 to 8

Fill a large pot with 5 quarts water and bring it to a boil over high heat. Turn off the heat and add the salt, sugar, bay leaves, cinnamon stick, coffee beans, peppercorns, garlic, and star anise. Stir until the salt and sugar dissolve. Set the brine aside to cool completely.

Once the brine has cooled, put the lamb leg in it, placing a heavy plate on top of the meat to keep it submerged. Cover the pot with plastic wrap and let it sit overnight (12 to 15 hours) in the refrigerator.

The next day, pull the lamb leg out of the brine, rinse it under cold running water, and pat it dry with paper towels. Discard the brine.

Adjust the oven rack to the middle position and preheat the oven to 375°F.

Trim the excess fat off the lamb, leaving a little to help flavor and moisten the meat. Using a knife, score the surface with long slashes in a diamond-shaped pattern to allow the fat to expand while the meat is cooking. Place 4 rosemary sprigs in a deep roasting pan, and lay the lamb right on top. Remove the leaves from another 4 rosemary sprigs. Rub the meat with the olive oil, and sprinkle the rosemary leaves on top. Roast the lamb until the top is browned, about 40 minutes. Carefully turn the leg over and continue roasting until a meat thermometer inserted near the bone reads 128°F, about 30 minutes.

While the lamb is roasting, prepare the pesto: Fill a medium bowl halfway with water, and put about a dozen ice cubes in it. Set it aside. Bring 2 quarts water to a boil in a large pot. Add 1 tablespoon salt, and blanch the basil and parsley in the boiling water for 10 to 20 seconds, until they're bright green. Immediately strain the herbs through a colander and place the colander in the ice water to cool for 2 minutes (the ice water will stop them from overcooking and will help them retain their color). Drain, and squeeze the herbs dry with a kitchen towel. Combine the herbs and the oil in a blender or food processor, and pulse for a few seconds, until smooth. Season with salt and pepper to taste.

Remove the lamb from the oven and let it sit for 15 minutes before carving.

Slice the lamb and serve it on a platter, accompanied by the pesto.

Ruccola, Endive, and Radicchio Salad with Pine Nuts and Aged Goat Cheese

Endive and radicchio are bitter leaf vegetables that pair well with the rich peppery flavor and leathery texture of ruccola. This is a very sturdy salad that can hold up to the aged goat cheese and the thick dressing, so feel free to dress it heavily. We like to use a goat cheese from Cypress Grove Chevre called the Mad River Roll (see Resources), but any quality goat cheese will do. If you can't find ruccola, you can use arugula—but if you can, try to hold out for the real deal. Ruccola is a peppery, sturdy green with a nice bite to it.

INGREDIENTS

FOR THE BALSAMIC DRESSING:

1/4 cup **pine nuts**

1/4 cup **balsamic vinegar**

1 tablespoon **Dijon mustard**

Kosher salt

Freshly ground **black pepper**

3/4 cup **rice bran oil** or **canola oil**

FOR THE SALAD:

2 tablespoons **pine nuts**

1 small head **radicchio**

2 heads **Belgian endive**

2 handfuls **ruccola**

1 tablespoon minced **flat-leaf parsley**

1 tablespoon minced **chives**

2 whole **scallions,** trimmed and thinly sliced

1 **shallot,** minced

4 ounces **aged goat cheese,** cut into four 1/2-inch-thick rounds

Kosher salt

Freshly ground **black pepper**

Serves 4

Adjust the oven rack to the middle position and preheat the oven to 350°F.

Scatter the pine nuts, for both the dressing and the salad, on a cookie sheet and toast in the oven until golden brown, about 7 minutes. Cool completely (leave the oven on). Set aside 2 tablespoons of the toasted pine nuts for the salad and reserve the rest for the dressing.

To make the balsamic dressing, put the pine nuts, vinegar, mustard, 1 teaspoon salt, and 1/4 teaspoon pepper in a blender and purée until smooth. With the blender running, add the oil in a slow, steady stream until the dressing is thick and emulsified. Check the seasoning and add more salt and pepper if necessary. Set the dressing aside.

To make the salad, pull the leaves off the head of radicchio and discard the core. Cut the leaves into long, thin strips and place them in a large mixing bowl. Carefully pull the leaves off the endive heads and discard the cores. Cut the leaves into long, thin strips and add them to the radicchio. Add the ruccola, parsley, chives, scallions, and shallots, and toss together gently. Keep refrigerated.

Arrange the 4 slices of goat cheese on a baking sheet and place it in the oven. Warm the goat cheese but don't let it melt—check on it after 2 minutes. While the goat cheese is in the oven, generously dress the salad with the balsamic dressing, sprinkle with the reserved 2 tablespoons toasted pine nuts, and season with salt and pepper to taste. Transfer the salad to a platter, arrange the warmed goat cheese on top, and serve immediately.

All three of the following vegetables come into season at around the same time, marking the beginning of spring. We serve these preparations as accompaniments to many of our dishes throughout the season. Their methods of preparation are interchangeable.

Braised Green Garlic

Green garlic, available only in spring, is picked before the garlic's paper-like skin has developed. It has a more delicate flavor than mature garlic and is great raw—but we also like to braise it and add it to any recipe that calls for garlic.

INGREDIENTS

8 **green garlic stalks**

1 tablespoon **rice bran oil** or **canola oil**

1 cup **chicken stock** (see page 241), warmed

1/4 cup **orange juice**

Kosher salt

Freshly ground **black pepper**

Serves 4

Adjust the oven rack to the middle position and preheat the oven to 350°F.

Wash the garlic thoroughly and trim the green stems—they should all be the same length, 4 to 5 inches. Place the garlic in a roasting pan, drizzle with the oil, and add the warm chicken stock and orange juice. Season the garlic with salt and pepper. Cover the pan with aluminum foil and bake for 40 to 45 minutes, until the garlic is tender.

Gently remove the garlic stalks from the pan and reserve then. Transfer the braising liquid to a small saucepan, and reduce it by half over medium-low heat. Check the seasoning, and add salt and pepper if necessary. Arrange the reserved green garlic stalks on a serving dish and spoon the reduced liquid over them.

Roasted
Spring Onions

These onions are young enough to have their greens still intact. Like the garlic, their flavor is more delicate than the adult version. While the terms "scallions" and "green onions" are often used interchangeably, they're actually separate vegetables. Scallions are long and thin with no bulb to speak of, and while their flavor strengthens with age, they don't develop into onions. Spring onions, on the other hand, are baby versions of regular onions, harvested while the bulbs are still small.

INGREDIENTS

4 large or 8 small **spring onions**

1 tablespoon **rice bran oil**
or **canola oil**

1/2 cup **chicken stock**
(see page 239), warmed

Kosher salt

Freshly ground **black pepper**

Serves 4

Adjust the oven rack to the middle position and preheat the oven to 350°F.

Cut the spring onions in half lengthwise and place them in a roasting pan. Add the oil and toss until the onions are evenly coated. Pour in the stock, and season with salt and pepper. Cover the pan with aluminum foil and bake for 30 to 35 minutes, until the onions are tender.

Serve with grilled fish or your favorite vegetable side.

Grilled Ramps

Ramps are Appalachian wild onions that combine the flavors of both garlic and onions. We often treat them like scallions. They have a short season and are delicate enough that they, too, can be eaten raw—but we also love to grill them.

INGREDIENTS

8 **ramps**

2 tablespoons **olive oil**

Kosher salt

Freshly ground **black pepper**

Serves 4

Preheat a grill (see page 244).

Place all the ingredients in a large bowl, toss until the ramps are evenly coated with the oil, and set aside to marinate for 10 minutes.

Arrange the ramps on the hot grill. Watch them carefully, moving them around with a pair of tongs to keep them from burning. The ramps are done when they wilt and soften—it should take only a couple minutes.

Artichokes and Asparagus with Almonds and Grapefruit Dressing

Asparagus and artichokes start showing up in Big Sur around April. Since we can still get ruby red grapefruit then, we like to combine them all into this salad. The flavors go together perfectly. We roast the asparagus in the wood-burning oven, which runs so hot that their flesh gets little char marks and develops a nice nutty flavor. For the baby greens, any kind will do; choose according to what's in season.

INGREDIENTS

FOR THE ARTICHOKES:

4 artichokes

1 lemon

1 medium **yellow onion,** roughly chopped

1 small **carrot, roughly chopped**

1 **celery stalk, roughly chopped**

1 **bay leaf**

1 tablespoon **kosher salt**

FOR THE ALMONDS:

1/2 cup **unblanched almonds**

1 teaspoon **rice bran oil** or **canola oil**

Kosher salt

Freshly ground **black pepper**

FOR THE ASPARAGUS:

8 **asparagus spears,** ends removed

1 tablespoon **rice bran oil** or **canola oil**

1 teaspoon **fresh thyme leaves**

Kosher salt

Freshly ground **black pepper**

Serves 4

Start with the artichokes since they will take the longest to prepare. When cleaning the artichokes your goal is to remove all the exterior leaves, leaving just the heart. To do so, use a serrated knife to cut off one third of the artichokes' tops. Working around each artichoke in a circle, remove the rough green leaves until only soft yellow leaves remain. To clean the stem, peel it with a paring knife and trim off about 1/4 inch at the bottom.

Immediately put the cleaned artichokes in a large pot filled with cold water. Cut the lemon in half, squeeze its juice into the pot, and then toss in the rest of the lemon (this will prevent the artichokes from oxidizing and turning brown). Add the onions, carrots, celery, bay leaf, and salt. Put a heavy plate over the artichokes to keep them submerged as they cook. Bring the liquid to a lazy simmer and cook until you can easily insert a paring knife through the center of an artichoke, about 30 minutes. Let them cool in the pot, keeping them submerged (this helps preserve their color and flavor).

While the artichokes are cooling, adjust the oven rack to the middle position and preheat the oven to 350°F.

Place the almonds on a cookie sheet. Drizzle them with the oil, season with salt and pepper, and toast them until they're golden brown through the center, about 12 minutes. (To check if they're done, cut one open and inspect the color on the inside.) Let the almonds cool, and then roughly chop them.

Increase the oven heat to 450°F. Place the asparagus on a baking sheet, drizzle with the oil, sprinkle with the thyme leaves, and season lightly with salt and pepper. Roast for 8 to 10 minutes, until the asparagus spears are fork-tender. Allow the asparagus to cool to room temperature.

FOR THE GRAPEFRUIT DRESSING:

Juice of 1 **ruby red grapefruit**

1 tablespoon **golden (or white) balsamic vinegar**

1/2 teaspoon **Dijon mustard**

Juice of 1/2 **lemon**

3/4 teaspoon **kosher salt,** or more if needed

1/4 teaspoon freshly **ground black pepper,** or more if needed

6 tablespoons **rice bran oil** or **canola oil**

TO FINISH:

Kosher salt

Freshly ground **black pepper**

2 handfuls **baby greens**

To make the dressing, put the grapefruit juice in a small saucepan. Reduce the juice over high heat until syrupy, 5 to 7 minutes—you should be left with about 1 tablespoon. Whisk together the reduced grapefruit juice, vinegar, mustard, lemon juice, salt, and pepper in a medium bowl until combined. Add the oil in a slow, steady stream, whisking until the dressing is thick and emulsified—it should come together pretty quickly. Check the seasoning and add more salt and pepper if necessary.

Once they've cooled completely, cut the artichokes in half through the stem. Take each half and remove its fibrous center with a spoon, making sure to leave the heart intact. Gently toss the artichoke hearts and the asparagus with about 1/4 cup of the dressing, and season them with salt and pepper. Right before serving, dress the baby greens lightly with a couple of teaspoons of the dressing, and combine with the vegetables. Arrange on a platter and sprinkle with the toasted almonds.

Clovis's Lime Tart with Lime Marmalade and Ginger Ice Cream

Clovis, a Big Sur local who's lived here for more than fifty years, brings us amazing Bearss limes from early November until late April. All the fruit comes from a lime tree that she planted next to her front door thirty-five years ago in hopes that the scent of the blossoms would remind her of her childhood in southern California. Her interest in limes grew after she traveled to Mexico, where she had fresh lime juice in her margaritas.

Clovis keeps a log of the fruit her tree bears, and the record shows that a few years ago her tree produced 200 pounds in one season. She brought them into the Bakery in a woven basket, 20 pounds at a time, and Michelle bought over 160 pounds. Clovis puts the money she earns from her limes into a jar; over time, her lime tree has paid for her vegetable garden and her flower garden.

Bearss limes are different from the conventional limes you see at the grocery store. They have a yellow rind and green flesh and are a bit smaller than a lemon. They're exploding with juice and are absolutely delicious. Buy extra, and you can chase your lime tart with a margarita.

INGREDIENTS

FOR THE SHELL:

2 cups **graham cracker crumbs** (recipe follows)

2 tablespoons **sugar**

2 tablespoons **unsalted butter,** melted, plus more for the pan

FOR THE LIME FILLING:

1 1/2 cups **fresh lime juice** (Bearss preferred)

1 cup **sugar**

6 **eggs**

1 cup **heavy cream**

Makes one 10-inch tart

Adjust the oven rack to the middle position and preheat the oven to 350°F.

To make the shell, combine the graham cracker crumbs, sugar, and melted butter in a bowl. Lightly grease with butter a 10-inch tart pan with a removable bottom. Sprinkle the crumbs over the tart pan, and use the bottom of a glass to press them into a crust, making sure that the crust evenly covers the entire bottom and sides of the pan. Refrigerate for 20 minutes. Then bake for 7 to 10 minutes, until the graham cracker crust starts to smell toasty. Remove from the oven and place on a cooling rack.

Reduce the oven temperature to 325°F.

While the tart shell cools, start the filling by whisking together all the filling ingredients in a medium saucepan. Cook over low heat, stirring constantly with a wooden spoon, until the liquid is thick enough to coat the back of a spoon, 7 to 10 minutes. Pour it into the crust and bake for 10 to 15 minutes, or until the filling is set. (You can tell if it's set by gently touching the center—if it doesn't stick to your finger, it's done.) Let the tart cool to room temperature. Then place it in the freezer until the filling is firm to the touch, about 25 minutes. (This step will prevent the filling from overbaking when you place the tart back in the oven to brown the meringue.)

While the tart is chilling, increase the oven temperature to 400°F.

CONTINUED >>

FOR THE MERINGUE TOPPING:

6 egg whites

1 cup plus 2 tablespoons **sugar**

1/4 teaspoon **kosher salt**

1/4 teaspoon **vanilla extract**

FOR SERVING:

Lime marmalade (recipe follows)

Ginger ice cream (recipe follows)

Graham Cracker Crumbs

INGREDIENTS

3/4 cup **unsalted butter,** softened

1/4 cup **granulated sugar**

1/3 cup plus 1 tablespoon (packed) **light** or **dark brown sugar**

1 tablespoon **honey**

1 1/3 cups **all-purpose flour**

1/2 cup plus 1 tablespoon **whole-wheat flour**

1 teaspoon **kosher salt**

1/2 teaspoon **baking soda**

1 teaspoon **ground cinnamon**

Prepare the meringue: Place the egg whites, sugar, and salt in a heatproof bowl (or double boiler). Place the bowl over a saucepan of barely simmering water, making sure the bowl does not touch the water. Whisk the mixture constantly until the sugar crystals have dissolved (check for sugar granules with your fingers). Remove the bowl from the heat, and whisk the whites with an electric mixer fitted with the wire whisk attachment on high speed until medium peaks form. Add the vanilla extract and whisk to combine.

Remove the tart from the freezer. Spread the meringue over the top of the tart, covering the filling but leaving the edges of the shell uncovered. (You may also pipe the meringue, using a pastry bag fitted with a decorating tip.) Place the tart in the oven and bake until the meringue has browned, 2 to 4 minutes. Refrigerate until ready to serve.

Remove the tart from the pan and transfer it to a platter. To serve, rinse a chef's knife under hot running water, dry it with a kitchen towel, and cut the tart into slices, wiping the blade clean after each cut. Accompany each slice with a dollop of lime marmalade and a scoop of ginger ice cream.

Cream the butter, granulated sugar, brown sugar, and honey in an electric mixer fitted with the paddle attachment until light and fluffy. Add all the remaining ingredients and continue to mix until the dough comes together. Roll the dough out between two pieces of parchment paper until you have a rough 1/4-inch-thick rectangle. Chill it in the refrigerator for at least 30 minutes or as long as three days.

Adjust the oven rack to the middle position and preheat the oven to 375°F.

Peel back the top piece of parchment paper, leaving the one on the bottom, and place the dough on a cookie sheet. Bake it for 20 to 25 minutes, until brown. Let it cool to room temperature. Break the graham cracker into pieces. Put the pieces into a food processor and pulse until fine. Reserve 2 cups of the crumbs for the graham cracker crust. Store the leftovers in an airtight container and keep in the refrigerator for a later use.

Lime
Marmalade

INGREDIENTS

10 Bearss limes,
or 15 conventional limes

4 thumb-size pieces fresh ginger

1 cup freshly squeezed lime juice

2 cups sugar

Makes 2 1/2 cups

Take 3 limes and halve them lengthwise. Place the halves, cut side down, on a cutting board and slice them into 1/8-inch-thick half-moons. Cut off both ends of the remaining fruit with a sharp knife. Place the limes on a cutting board, cut-end down, and following the curve of the fruit, shave off the rind from top to bottom with the knife, revealing the flesh of the citrus and leaving absolutely no pith. Cut each lime into quarters and cut away the core. Throw away the cores and the peels. Place the half-moon slices and the fruit segments in a stainless-steel pot, add 2 1/2 cups water, and bring to a boil. Reduce the heat and simmer until the rinds of the half-moons are soft, about 10 minutes. Remove from the heat.

Peel the ginger with a vegetable peeler or a spoon, and place the pieces in a small pot. Add water to cover and bring to a boil. Strain, and rinse the ginger under cold water. Place the ginger in a blender, add the lime juice, and blend until the ginger is completely puréed. Add the ginger mixture to the cooked lime and mix to combine. Refrigerate overnight or until very cold.

Add the sugar to the lime mixture and bring it to a boil. Reduce the heat to a simmer and cook until the mixture registers 219°F. To determine if the marmalade is done, spoon a dollop onto a chilled plate. If it doesn't spread, it's ready.

Ginger
Ice Cream

INGREDIENTS

4 thumb-size pieces fresh ginger

2 cups whole milk

2 cups heavy cream

1/2 cup honey

2 cups sugar

12 egg yolks

Makes 6 cups

Peel the ginger with a vegetable peeler or a spoon, and cut it into slices. Place the slices in a saucepan, add just enough cold water to cover, and bring it to a boil. Strain, and rinse the ginger under cold running water. Combine the ginger and 1 cup of the milk in a blender, and purée until smooth. Combine the ginger mixture with the cream, the remaining 1 cup milk, the honey, and half of the sugar in a medium saucepan and bring to a boil. Remove the mixture from the heat and let it steep for 10 minutes.

Meanwhile, whisk the egg yolks with the remaining 1 cup sugar in a large bowl until smooth.

Bring the cream mixture back to a boil and temper the hot liquid into the egg yolks by adding it to the yolks a ladle at a time while whisking vigorously. Strain the liquid through a fine-mesh sieve into a bowl. Discard the ginger, and return the liquid to the pan. Cook over very low heat, stirring constantly with a wooden spoon, until the liquid is thick enough to coat the back of the spoon. Refrigerate until it's cold. Freeze the mixture in an ice cream maker, according to the manufacturer's directions.

May

Fishing in Monterey

Today Monterey is probably best known for sea otters and John Steinbeck (his novel *Cannery Row* was set in Monterey). But for us, Monterey is all about fish.

Located about thirty miles north of Big Sur, Monterey's history of commercial fishing began in the mid-1800s when Chinese settlers started harvesting abalone, yellowtail, sardines, squid, and shark, among other creatures, from the bay's deep waters. By the beginning of the 20th century, Monterey was best known for its vast production of canned sardines—and in fact the sardine frenzy was so intense that by the end of World War II, the region's supplies had been depleted. In 1945, John Steinbeck published *Cannery Row*, and Monterey began its evolution into what it is today: a spot still known as a commercial fishery, but with a downtown devoted primarily to tourism.

The Monterey Bay Aquarium represents both worlds. People come from all over the globe to check out its exhibits (and, yes, otters), but it also has become a leader in the sustainable fishing movement. Its Seafood Watch program helps protect the ocean's fish stocks by recommending which varieties to buy or to avoid, depending on the health of fish populations and the methods that are being used to catch or farm them.

One repercussion of the sustainability movement is that it has become much more difficult to fish commercially. These days, the California Department of Fish and Game has an ever-growing list of regulations governing what species you can fish (and for that matter, how you can fish them). The regulations are stringent enough that some fishermen have left the area in search of less restrictive waters—and those who stick around sometimes have to call the department daily to stay abreast of the latest rules.

But of course there are reasons for the regulations. Take, for example, the mysterious disappearance of the Sacramento River fall-run Chinook salmon, which usually make up the bulk of the salmon caught in the Sacramento River system and off the California and southern Oregon coast. The situation was so bad in 2008 that the California Department of Fish and Game canceled the commercial and recreational ocean salmon fishing seasons.

We don't have the necessary licenses to serve our own catches at the restaurant, but we still try to stock our menu with choices that are both sustainable and local. Luckily, even with all its restrictions (or perhaps because of them), Monterey Bay provides a continuous abundance of seafood for our menus.

The Mountain Lion

May—or more specifically, Memorial Day weekend—marks the real start of the tourist season in Big Sur. After a winter's worth of Sunday afternoons off and quiet morning coffee with the locals, our quiet hamlet turns into sudden chaos. The parking lot fills with strangers' cars, many of whom are expecting to get sucked into another tourist trap—and it's always a thrill to see their looks of surprise when they realize that, despite being next to a gas station, we're not a greasy spoon. Lucky them—and lucky us. Locals might call the tourists "tourons" and complain about having to share the highway with RVs, but it doesn't take long for our business sense to kick in.

This May was dramatic for reasons that had nothing to do with tourists: a mountain lion began stalking and attacking local dogs. One night, Wayne Hyland's son Rowan's mother watched as the lion grabbed their dog by the neck after she had let it out for the night and killed it. Several nights later, their second dog met the same fate. Now, when a wild animal starts attacking domestic ones, people in Big Sur start to get a little nervous. When a wild animal starts grabbing them twenty feet away from their owners, people get hysterical. They put out traps; they called the game warden. Parents became worried about letting their kids play outside—after all, a toddler would be easier prey than a golden retriever. Michelle stopped taking walks on the ranch at morning and nightfall, and eventually stopped altogether. Over the course of four months, the same mountain lion killed fifteen dogs.

All this played out just as the tourists started to flow. Ironically, they were attracted to the natural beauty of Big Sur at the same time that a part of Big Sur's nature started eating our pets. Thank god, then, for Wayne Hyland. Wayne's an essential part of our lives at the Bakery, helping with maintenance, taking us fishing, foraging for mushrooms—and he's also an amazing hunter and outdoorsman. Even before Rowan's second dog was eaten, Wayne took matters into his own hands. He tracked the lion, learning where it buried its prey and came back to feed. And then one night at midnight, as the fog rolled in off the ocean, he went out to hunt the lion. He could hear the sounds of it feeding as he approached—ripping muscle and tendon from bone—but he still snuck closer. He told us later that the lion knew he was there but was too engrossed in its meal to care.

It took only one shot. Wayne fired directly into the lion's heart, killing it as it fed. That might sound heartless and cruel, but this lion had become a threat, not just to dogs, but to humans too. Wayne, who believes that people in general have moved too far away from nature, made the neighbors come and see the lion after he killed it, so that people could appreciate how large it was. He'd told us when he shot it that it was big enough to take out a grown man, and when people saw its carcass, it was clear that he was right. Life subsequently went back to normal—complaints about the busy roads, stress about covering all the Bakery's shifts—but when we went home at night, we slept better than we had in weeks.

Names: ERIC FRANKS AND JASMINE RICHARDSON

Occupations: MICROGREEN FARMER, ASSISTANTS TO THE

ASSISTANT TO NO ONE

Signatures:

Pr: No. 3

Microgreens grown:
Watercress, arugula, daikon, endive, pea shoots, basil,
cilantro, radish, broccoli, cabbage, celery, beet—a lot
of different types.

How'd you get into microgreens?
We were farming in Maine, where in the winter there's less
than seven or eight hours of light a day. We were trying to
find things to do and realized you can always make seeds
germinate because it doesn't take light.

How many pounds do you sell each week?
About five to ten pounds' worth of four-ounce packets.

Where do you grow your greens?
On a deck outside of our rented house in Big Sur. It's
porch farming.

How big is your porch?
Twenty-five feet by ten feet.

Square footage of microgreens grown on porch:
Fifty square feet.

Pounds of seed used per year:
Seventy pounds.

What's your usual schedule?
We sow, harvest, and deliver twice a week.

**Approximate number of hours between
picking and delivery:**
Between six and ten.

Why microgreens?
Because we only have a porch.

How'd you learn to farm?
We spent seven years going from Pennsylvania to Maine,
working on different farms and learning traditional
techniques—like working with draft horses.

How do you harvest the greens?
We cut them with scissors. Then Jasmine washes
them and we set them out on towels and use fans to
dry them. They're way too delicate for a crank dryer.

What can you use microgreens for?
You can use them in place of any raw greens. They
add flavor and aesthetics—they're a way to get
a really intense flavor from a tiny little thing.

Strangest things you've farmed:
Micro corn shoots.

What makes your business rewarding?
That it's ours—and it's a unique setup that's successful.
We're using the skills we learned as farmers to grow
stuff without land.

Braised Rabbit with White Wine, Scallions, Mustard Seeds, and Ham-Wrapped Roasted Loin

Butchers usually don't like to sell rabbit parts, so when you go shopping for rabbit, you're likely to be stuck with the whole animal. (Do ask your butcher to cut up the rabbit for you, though.) This recipe allows you to prepare the quarters and loins separately, using the method that's most appropriate for each one. Braising the rabbit fore- and hindquarters a day ahead of time gives them a wonderful flavor. Shortly before serving, the loins are wrapped in jamón serrano and quickly roasted.

INGREDIENTS

2 tablespoons **mustard seeds**

2 whole **rabbits**, butchered into 4 forequarters, 4 loins, and 4 hindquarters

1 cup **white wine**

1 cup **orange juice**

3 whole **scallions**, trimmed and thinly sliced

Kosher salt

Freshly ground **black pepper**

2 tablespoons **rice bran oil** or **canola oil**

2 cups **chicken stock** (see page 239)

8 slices **jamón serrano (serrano ham)** or **prosciutto**

Serves 4

One day ahead, prepare the quarters: Toast the mustard seeds in a small sauté pan over medium heat, tossing the pan frequently, until the seeds start to release their mustard aroma, 2 minutes. Remove from the heat.

Place the fore- and hindquarters in a deep dish, and add the white wine, orange juice, toasted mustard seeds, and scallions. Season lightly with salt and pepper. Cover and refrigerate for 6 hours.

Adjust the oven rack to the middle position and preheat the oven to 300°F.

Remove the quarters from the marinade and pat them dry (reserve the marinade). Heat a large sauté pan over high heat and drizzle 1 tablespoon of the oil into it. Sear the quarters until they're golden brown, about 3 minutes, then flip them over and sear the other side for another 3 minutes. Place the quarters in a roasting pan that is large enough to fit them comfortably. Deglaze the sauté pan with the reserved marinade, scraping any brown bits from the bottom with a wooden spoon. Cook the marinade over medium heat until it reduces by half, 12 to 15 minutes. Then add this to the rabbit quarters.

Warm up the chicken stock in the same sauté pan and add it to the roasting pan. Cover the roasting pan with aluminum foil and place it in the oven. Braise until the quarters are soft and incredibly tender, 45 minutes to 1 hour. The meat should almost fall off the bone. Remove the pan from the oven and let the quarters cool in the braising liquid to room temperature; then cover and refrigerate overnight.

The next day, about half an hour before serving, adjust the oven rack to the middle position and preheat the oven to 350°F.

Season the rabbit loins generously with salt and pepper. Arrange 2 pieces of the jamón serrano on a flat surface so that their edges overlap—you want to create a strip that's long enough to wrap around a loin. Place a loin on top of the jamón serrano, and starting at one edge, roll the ham tightly around the loin until the loin is completely covered. Repeat with the rest of the ham and loins.

Place the roasting pan with the braised quarters in the oven to reheat, 10 to 15 minutes.

Meanwhile, heat a large ovenproof sauté pan over high heat, and drizzle the remaining 1 tablespoon oil into it. Sear the loins on one side until the ham is crispy. Then turn them over, transfer the pan to the oven, and roast until the meat is cooked through but isn't well done, 8 to 10 minutes.

Serve the braised quarters with the loin.

Note

The leftover forequarters (if there are any) can be turned into a spread, which you can serve on toast for lunch the next day. Just pick the meat off the bone and pulse until smooth in a food processor.

Spring Risotto

Risotto calls for a short-grain rice, usually Arborio or Carnaroli, that's cooked with a flavorful liquid until some of the risotto's starch breaks down to create the dish's trademark creaminess. It's important to cook your rice in a richly seasoned stock so the risotto will absorb its flavor while it cooks. To add more flavor, just pick whatever's fresh and in season. Peas in spring, corn in summer, squash in fall, carrots in winter—feel free to experiment.

INGREDIENTS

Kosher salt

1 1/4 cups shelled English peas

1 1/4 cups shelled fava beans

1 cup fresh corn kernels

4 tablespoons unsalted butter

1 medium yellow onion, finely chopped

Freshly ground black pepper

1 1/2 cups Arborio or Carnaroli rice

1/4 cup dry white wine

3 1/2 cups chicken stock (see page 239), warmed

2 whole scallions, trimmed and thinly sliced

2 ounces Parmesan, grated (about 1/4 cup)

2 cups rich beef broth (recipe follows)

Serves 4

Fill a medium bowl halfway with water, and put about a dozen ice cubes in it. Set it aside.

Bring a quart of water to a boil in a medium saucepan. Add 1 tablespoon salt, and blanch the peas in the boiling water until they're bright green and tender, about 3 minutes. Immediately strain out the peas (reserving the hot water for the other vegetables) and use a colander to place them in the ice water (the ice water will stop them from overcooking and help them retain their color). Let them cool for 2 minutes. Reserve the peas and repeat the same process with the fava beans (3 minutes in the boiling water) and corn kernels (5 to 7 minutes in the boiling water).

Melt 3 tablespoons of the butter in a medium saucepan over medium-low heat, and add the onions. Season them lightly with salt and pepper, and sweat until the onions are translucent, about 5 minutes. Add the rice, and stir to coat with the butter. Cook for 2 to 3 minutes to "sear" the grain—this step will ensure that the risotto will have a bite to it. Deglaze the pan with the wine, and simmer until it has evaporated. Then add 3 cups of the warm chicken stock and cook, stirring continuously, until the risotto is tender, about 15 minutes. If necessary, continue cooking, adding the remaining 1/2 cup stock if the risotto starts to dry out. The risotto is ready when it's al dente, with a thick and creamy consistency.

Stir in the blanched peas, fava beans, and corn kernels, along with the scallions, Parmesan, and remaining 1 tablespoon butter. Check the seasoning, and add more salt and pepper if necessary. Place the risotto in individual bowls, ladle the beef broth around it, and serve.

Rich Beef Broth

INGREDIENTS

1 quart beef broth

1/2 onion

1/2 carrot

1/2 celery stalk

1/2 red bell pepper

1/2 garlic clove

1 bay leaf

1 flat-leaf parsley stem

Kosher salt and black pepper

Makes 2 cups

Combine all the ingredients except the salt and pepper in a medium saucepan and bring to a boil. Reduce the heat and let simmer for 40 minutes.

Strain, put the liquid back into the saucepan, and reduce by half. Season with salt and pepper.

House-Cured Salmon

The idea of home-curing your own salmon sounds old-fashioned and complicated, but it's actually really easy. This salmon is great served in omelets, scrambled eggs, and sandwiches, not to mention on top of bagels or pizza (once it's come out of the oven). What's more, cured salmon keeps far longer than fresh fish, and has a different flavor and texture than a typical salmon steak. We make ours salty and sweet and add peppercorns and dill, but if you've got other favorite herbs and spices—or even liquors—feel free to throw those in as well. The only crucial thing is to cure the fish in salt long enough to remove most of its moisture (moist environments foster bacteria that may cause spoilage). The thickness of the fish will determine the length of the curing time; after two days, check to see if the salmon is ready by pressing it with your finger. If it feels springy, let it cure for one more day. If it gets too salty, a quick rinse with water will help. That's about it. Just remember, as always, to start with fresh wild fish from a reputable source.

INGREDIENTS

2 tablespoons **black peppercorns**

3 cups **kosher salt**

1/2 cup **sugar**

1 **salmon side,** 2 to 3 pounds, skin on, thin bones removed

1 bunch **fresh dill**

Makes 2 to 3 pounds of cured salmon

Crack the peppercorns by putting them on a flat surface, like a cutting board, and pressing them with the flat bottom of a heavy pan until they split into pieces.

Mix the salt and sugar together and pour half of the mixture into a plastic or ceramic container that's big enough to hold the salmon lying flat. Place the salmon, skin side down, on top of the sugar/salt mixture, and completely cover it with the dill, peppercorns, and the remaining salt/sugar mixture. Cover the container with plastic wrap, put it in the refrigerator, and leave the salmon to cure for 2 to 3 days.

To check if the salmon is done, press the fillet right in the middle (where it's thickest) with your index finger: it should feel firm to the touch and it shouldn't spring back. When it is ready, rinse the salmon under cold running water and pat it dry with paper towels. Slice thin shavings off the salmon by cutting strips at a 20-degree angle with a very sharp knife. Serve right away (we love it with eggs or sandwiches) or reserve for up to a week in the refrigerator.

Grilled Salmon with Meyer Lemon Dressing

In Big Sur, we go half the year without salmon, so when the salmon fishing season opens in Monterey Bay, we get pretty excited. There are tons of ways to prepare salmon, but this is one of our favorites—it's simple and fast, with a Meyer lemon dressing that highlights the natural flavor of the fish.

INGREDIENTS

4 salmon fillets,
6 to 8 ounces each

2 tablespoons **rice bran oil**
or **canola oil**

3 tablespoons minced
flat-leaf parsley

Kosher salt

Freshly ground **black pepper**

1 cup **Meyer lemon dressing**
(see page 237)

Serves 4

Preheat your grill 30 minutes in advance, burning the wood down until you have a red-hot coal base. (See page 244 for instructions on preparing a wood-fired grill.)

Brush the salmon fillets with the oil on both sides, sprinkle them with the parsley, and season them generously with salt and pepper. Place the salmon on the grill, skin side down. When you can see that the fish has distinct grill marks, flip the fillets over and cook them to your desired doneness—we recommend medium-rare to medium. To determine when the salmon is cooked to medium-rare, cut it in the middle and check to see if the center of the fillet is still tender and glossy.

Arrange the salmon on a platter, drizzle generously with the Meyer lemon dressing.

Strawberry and Rose Geranium Shake

Rose geranium, which is cultivated for the perfume industry, can also be used to flavor ice cream. It's one of Michelle's all-time favorite flavors, especially when paired with strawberries. Phil says it's too feminine a flavor for him, but we've seen many a man sipping on this pink shake at the Bakery. We grow the geranium on the property and use the leaves to flavor the ice cream. This shake has a subtle rose flavor and is divine on a hot summer day.

INGREDIENTS

FOR THE STRAWBERRY SORBET:

1/4 cup **sugar**

2 pints **strawberries,** quartered

Few drops **lemon juice**

FOR THE ROSE GERANIUM ICE CREAM:

4 cups **heavy cream**

1 cup **sugar**

15 large pesticide-free **rose geranium leaves**

8 **egg yolks**

FOR THE SHAKES:

1 cup **heavy cream**

1 teaspoon **sugar**

1 pint **strawberries,** quartered

1 cup **milk**

Makes 6 shakes

Start with the sorbet: Put the sugar in a small saucepan, add 1/4 cup water, and bring to a boil. Remove from the heat and set aside to cool completely.

Place the strawberries in a blender, add the cooled sugar syrup and a few drops of lemon juice, and purée until smooth. Pour the purée through a fine-mesh sieve into a bowl. Take half of the pulp that was trapped in the sieve and add it to the strained purée. Discard the remainder of the pulp. Freeze the mixture in an ice cream maker according to the manufacturer's directions.

To make the rose geranium ice cream, combine the cream with half of the sugar and all the rose geranium leaves in a medium nonreactive saucepan. Bring the mixture to a boil, remove it from the heat, and let it steep for 30 minutes. Meanwhile, whisk the egg yolks with the remaining 1/2 cup sugar in a large bowl until smooth.

Bring the cream mixture back to a boil and temper the hot liquid into the yolks by adding it a ladle at a time while whisking vigorously. Strain the liquid through a fine-mesh sieve into a bowl, discard the geranium leaves, and return the strained liquid to the saucepan. Cook over very low heat, stirring constantly with a wooden spoon, until the liquid is thick enough to coat the back of the spoon. Refrigerate until it's cold. Freeze the mixture in an ice cream maker according to the manufacturer's directions.

When you're ready to make the shakes, chill six glasses in the freezer for about 15 minutes. Combine the cream and the sugar in a bowl, and whip until soft peaks form. (You want the cream to be a little bit runny.) Refrigerate until ready to use.

Put half of the strawberries, half of the rose geranium ice cream, and 1/2 cup of the milk in a blender and purée until smooth. Pour into three glasses and repeat to make three more shakes. Add a scoop of strawberry sorbet to each glass, and top with a dollop of whipped cream. Serve immediately, with a long straw and a spoon.

Peppermint Ice Cream Sundae

This is Mike's favorite combination of dessert flavors—he loves how the coolness of the peppermint offsets the chocolate's richness. It's easy to find spearmint in the supermarket, but hold out for peppermint. Cocoa nibs are tiny, unrefined pieces of roasted cocoa beans.

INGREDIENTS

FOR THE PEPPERMINT ICE CREAM:

1 1/4 cups **heavy cream**

3/4 cup **whole milk**

1 bunch **peppermint**, leaves only (about 1 cup)

2 tablespoons **honey**

1/2 cup **sugar**

6 **egg yolks**

FOR THE CHOCOLATE COOKIES:

2 tablespoons **cocoa nibs**

1 1/2 cups **powdered sugar**

1/4 cup Dutch-process **cocoa powder**

1/4 teaspoon **kosher salt**

2 **egg whites**

1 1/2 teaspoons **vanilla extract**

Serves 4 to 6, with leftovers

Start with the peppermint ice cream: Combine the cream, milk, peppermint leaves, honey, and half of the sugar in a medium nonreactive saucepan, and bring to a boil. Remove it from the heat and let the mixture steep for 30 minutes. Meanwhile, whisk the egg yolks with the remaining 1/4 cup sugar in a large bowl until smooth.

Bring the cream mixture back to a boil and temper the hot liquid into the yolks by adding it one ladle at a time while whisking vigorously. Pour the liquid through a fine-mesh strainer into a bowl, discard the leaves, and return the strained liquid to the saucepan. Cook over very low heat, stirring with a wooden spoon, until the liquid is thick enough to coat the back of the spoon. Refrigerate until it's cold. Freeze the mixture in an ice cream maker according to the manufacturer's directions.

Meanwhile, make the chocolate cookies: Adjust the oven rack to the middle position and preheat the oven to 350°F.

Line a cookie sheet with parchment paper. Grind the cocoa nibs in a mini food processor or coffee grinder until they have the consistency of coffee grounds; set aside. Sift the powdered sugar and cocoa powder together into a bowl, and add the salt. In an electric mixer fitted with the wire whisk attachment, whip the egg whites until they form soft peaks. Fold the powdered sugar mixture into the egg whites, then the vanilla, and finally the ground cocoa nibs. Using a pastry bag fitted with a plain decorating tip, pipe the batter onto the prepared cookie sheet, making rounds roughly the size of a nickel. (If you don't have a piping bag, you can drop little teaspoons of batter onto the sheet, but the cookies won't be nearly as pretty!) Bake the cookies for 12 minutes—they should be shiny and firm on top but still stick to the sheet. (You want to slightly underbake the cookies to keep them soft and chewy.) Let them cool completely, and then peel the cookies off the parchment paper with the aid of a metal spatula.

FOR THE CHOCOLATE SAUCE:

4 ounces **bittersweet chocolate,** chopped into small pieces

1 tablespoon Dutch-process **cocoa powder**

2 tablespoons **sugar**

2 tablespoons **honey**

1 tablespoon **unsalted butter,** softened

FOR THE WHIPPED CREAM:

1 cup **heavy cream**

1 teaspoon **sugar**

To make the chocolate sauce, put the chocolate pieces in a heatproof bowl (or a double boiler), set it over a pot of barely simmering water (making sure the bottom of the bowl doesn't touch the water), and melt the chocolate. Remove the bowl from the heat when all the chocolate pieces have melted, and set it aside. Combine the cocoa, sugar, honey, and 1/2 cup water in a small saucepan, and bring the mixture to a boil while stirring constantly. Add this cocoa mixture to the melted chocolate, stirring until combined. Add the butter and stir until it has melted. Keep the sauce in a warm place until ready to serve.

To serve, chill four sundae dishes in the freezer. Whip the cream with the sugar in a bowl until it forms soft peaks. (You want the cream to still be a little bit runny.) Build the sundaes by layering chocolate cookies between scoops of peppermint ice cream. Drizzle each sundae with chocolate sauce and top with whipped cream. Serve with more cookies on the side.

June

Pork and
Beer Dinner

If you're friends with a pig farmer and a butcher and a couple of beer connoisseurs, at some point you've got to have a party. Father's Day happened to be the first Sunday of the season that we were open in the evening, and we decided that there'd be no better way to kick off summer than by hosting a Pork and Beer Dinner.

In Big Sur, it seems that everyone knows someone who knows someone who does something interesting with food, like raise pork on pasture, or make blood sausage by hand. In our case, that someone is Justin Severino, a former pizza cook at the Bakery who moved up to Santa Cruz and opened a butcher's shop called Severino's Community Butcher. Justin introduced us to Jim Dunlop, who raises pigs out in the pastures of TLC Ranch, his farm in Prunedale, and supplies Justin with fresh pork for his store. (These days, Jim also provides the Bakery's eggs.)

Two of our other friends, Bill and Danielle, run a pub down the road. They're serious beer people and have always wanted to do an event at the restaurant where they designed beer pairings to go with our food. So we thought, why not combine two of the greatest things in life—pork and beer—and put together an amazing dinner where every dish has something in it from the pig?

Another chef friend (who's also the singer in Phil's band), Todd Williamson, jumped on board too. Together with Todd and Justin, we came up with a pork-infused menu, and Bill and Danielle picked out beer pairings for each dish. The result was plans for a hearty, meaty meal that would drive vegetarians away screaming—but that would make a true carnivore (and beer-lover) drool.

Justin took care of the appetizers: cured salami, pork rinds, pork belly salad, and blood sausage—everyone's non-favorite until we actually tasted it. Todd did slow-roasted pork with wonton soup. Phil made a grilled confit of pork shoulder with Chuckie's homemade barbecue sauce and baked beans, and Michelle finished things off with a blueberry pie that had a crust made with lard.

CLOSED
FOR
PRIVATE
PARTY

At first we were worried about selling enough seats—we'd made the mistake of putting the price on the flier but no menu, and right up until a week before the event, the locals didn't bite. It's a bad feeling to think that you're going to end up with pork confit for fifty and no one to eat it, and we couldn't change the quantity of meat because we'd already paid for it. But a few days before Sunday, people started signing up, and by the time we got ready to serve the first course, we had sixty-eight people at the restaurant, eighteen more than we'd aimed for. There were friends and acquaintances, neighbors and former employees—practically no one that we didn't somehow know.

That Sunday was a perfect night, fogless and warm, and the temperature stayed in the seventies all the way until nightfall. We sat outside at long redwood tables with cloth draped overhead for shade and strings of white lights to illuminate the scene as the sun went down. When the meal began, Jim got up and described his farm and how he raised his pigs, and each chef talked about what they'd made. Then came the food—and music, provided by one of our favorite local bands, a group called Sex Farm that includes a couple of tattoo artists and is led by a guy named Rosebud. They played old-fashioned rock and roll outside as we ate, changing some of the lyrics and song titles to include references to pork.

As the band performed and food was served, kids ran around wearing plastic pig noses that we'd bought as favors, and Bill and Danielle poured glass after glass of beer—we had two varieties for each of the four courses. Soon the tabletops were covered with mismatched glasses and plates of food, with all our friends gathered around laughing and eating. Despite the fact that we were at our restaurant, it felt different from even our best and busiest nights. Surrounded by friends, it was as if we'd invited people into our home to cook and eat and have fun together. And even though it was stressful—worrying about selling the seats, preparing and plating food for sixty-eight people at once—everything worked out. But that's the thing. Somehow, it always does.

TLC Ranch

Jim Dunlop and his wife, Becky, run the TLC Ranch in Prunedale, where they raise pigs, chickens, cows, and lambs on organic pasture. We already knew about the farm—Justin had been giving us sausage made from their pigs as he developed his recipes, and we order their organic, pasture-raised eggs for the Bakery. But we'd never been to the farm ourselves, so when Jim invited us to check it out in person, we jumped at the chance.

When we arrived, Jim greeted us at the ranch house and led us off into the fields so that we could meet our sausage firsthand. Unlike pigs at typical commercial farms, Jim's pigs are pretty much free-range (he keeps different groups in different areas of the farm, but other than that, they're free to roam), so you never know when you'll turn a corner and find a huge sow rooting around in the dirt, or a lost piglet squealing for its mother. Following Jim, we hopped into a fenced-off area where fifty or so young pigs were grazing. Once they'd noticed us, several came up to investigate, but they quickly got distracted by food and let us pet their heads as they nibbled on the greens near our feet.

Jim introduced us to the pigs' parents—they'd all been produced from one large boar and a huge sow who lived in her own pen and had ears that smelled, no joke, like sweet caramel. Then we walked on dirt roads through fields of artichokes and blackberries, stopping to check out the chickens and pointing out pigs along the way. It was like Wilbur-gone-wild—pigs roamed all over the place, munching on crops and cabbage heads, and scratching their heads on wooden posts. And they weren't all your stereotypically pink piglets, either; some had spots that made them look like somewhere along the line they'd crossed genes with a Dalmatian.

Jim's ranch is actually owned by a nonprofit organization called ALBA that helps train people in organic farming, so once we'd had our fill of the pigs, he led us around the rest of the property, pointing out a newly planted field of rye and pea shoots that he planned to move the pigs onto once they were finished with their current pasture. We tried a couple of the pea shoots and came to the conclusion that as farm animals go, these were some pretty lucky pigs.

After the tour we met up with Becky, cracked open a bottle of Italian wine, and snacked on pork tacos while chatting and watching their daughter play. It was a wonderful evening in and of itself, but it was especially nice to talk with other people who so wholeheartedly believe in what they are doing. Our businesses are hard, we all work long hours with little financial reward, and yet as we looked around the table everyone seemed optimistic and happy.

When we got back in the car, Michelle turned to Phil and said, "They're living the dream, aren't they?"

"Sure," he said. "If the dream is to work really hard for no money."

(We can always count on Phil for a reality check.)

But even so, visiting the ranch completed a circle that we've been trying to close for a long time: meeting farmers in person so that we know, firsthand, where the food we serve is coming from.

PROFILE: JUSTIN / BUTCHER

Name: Justin Severino   **Bestsellers:** Pork chops and bacon

Occupation: Owner, Severino's Community Butcher, Inc.

Relationship with Big Sur Bakery: Friend, enthusiast, former pizza cook

Signature: Justin Severino

Pr: No. 4

Current products:
Sausage, salami, prosciutto, guanciale, lardo, pâtés, and fresh cuts of pork, beef, and lamb.

First butcher in the family:
My grandfather, Eugen Sandella.

Equipment used?
Heavy cleavers, sharp knives. I cut everything by hand.

Favorite part of pig to eat?
Cheek.

To touch:
Right behind the ears.

Weirdest part of the pig you've eaten:
Snout.

Personal goal:
Being the first small producer of artisan, pasture-raised prosciutto in the country and actually making a dollar or two.

Biggest challenge:
The USDA makes small producers follow the same rules as huge producers, which isn't cost-effective. The rules also make it hard for small producers to raise and slaughter their animals themselves.

Worst reaction to your shop:
Vegans slashed my tires.

Who loves pigs more—you, or vegans?
Me.

Why?
We have a similar goal: wanting to make sure the pigs are raised as ethically as possible. But instead of just talking about it, I'm doing it.

Grilled Pork Confit with Chuck's Barbecue Sauce

Our good friends Dan and Roxana served this pork at our wedding and we loved it. Typically, confit recipes call for animal fat, but we find that using a neutral vegetable oil helps preserve the meat's natural flavor. It might seem crazy to simmer meat in oil, but don't worry—the pork doesn't actually absorb the fat. You're basically steaming a large portion of meat in the oil, getting it to release moisture while breaking down its tissue. That's why it's important to use a sturdy cut of meat: something like a loin would dry out. It's a great way to handle large cuts of meat because once it's cooked and put in oil, the meat keeps for a while. (We usually eat ours within a week.) The first thing we do with it is cut it into thick pieces, grill it until crispy, and serve it with this fantastic sauce that was brought to us by Chuck, our former sous-chef and a Texas native. We also like to thinly slice the pork confit and eat it on sandwiches with mustard aïoli.

You'll need to start this preparation two days ahead.

INGREDIENTS

FOR THE PORK CONFIT:

1 cup **kosher salt**

1 cup **sugar**

4 **garlic cloves,** crushed

4 **thyme sprigs**

2 1/2 to 3 pounds **boneless pork shoulder**

Rice bran oil or **canola oil**

Serves 4

Fill a large pot with 4 quarts water and bring it to a boil. Remove from the heat. Add the salt, sugar, garlic, and thyme sprigs and stir until the salt and sugar are fully dissolved. Set the brine aside to cool completely.

Put the pork shoulder in the cooled brine, and place a heavy plate on top of the meat to keep it submerged. Cover the pot with plastic wrap and let it sit overnight (12 to 15 hours) in the refrigerator.

The next day, pull the pork shoulder out of the brine, rinse it under cold running water, and pat it dry with paper towels. Discard the brine.

Adjust the oven rack to the lower position and preheat the oven to 300°F.

Put the pork in a large baking dish (a Dutch oven works great) and add enough oil to cover the meat by 1 inch. Place a heavy plate on top of the meat to keep it submerged. Put the dish in the oven and cook for 3 1/2 to 4 hours, until the pork is fork-tender.

Remove the dish from the oven and let the pork cool to room temperature in the oil. Then refrigerate the whole pot (yes, pork and oil) overnight. (Once it has chilled overnight, the pork confit is ready to be used however you like.)

FOR CHUCK'S BARBECUE SAUCE:

2 tablespoons **rice bran oil**
or **canola oil**

1 **red bell pepper**, roughly chopped

1 **yellow onion**, roughly chopped

1 **red onion**, roughly chopped

6 **garlic cloves**

1/2 cup **red wine vinegar**

1/4 cup (packed) **light** or **dark
brown sugar**

1/2 cup **Worcestershire sauce**

2 cups **tomato sauce**
(see page 238)

2 tablespoons **Dijon mustard**

Kosher salt

Freshly ground **black pepper**

2 tablespoons minced
flat-leaf parsley

The next day, start by making the barbecue sauce: Heat a medium saucepan over medium heat, and drizzle the oil into it. Add the bell peppers and onions and cook until they're very tender and the onions are starting to caramelize, about 15 minutes. Add the garlic, red wine vinegar, brown sugar, Worcestershire sauce, tomato sauce, and mustard, and bring the mixture to a simmer. Cook for 10 minutes over medium heat, until the sauce is as thick as ketchup. Purée the sauce in a food processor or blender until smooth. Strain it into a serving bowl, and season it with salt and pepper to taste.

Preheat your grill 30 minutes in advance, burning the wood down until you have a red-hot coal base. (See page 244 for preparing a wood-fired grill.)

Take the meat out of the oil, wipe off the oil, and slice the meat into 1-inch-thick pieces. Sprinkle black pepper and parsley on each piece before grilling. Put the slices of pork confit on the grill. When the exterior starts to get brown and crisp, flip the slices over and cook until the meat crisps up on the other side. Serve immediately, with Chuck's barbecue sauce alongside.

Pork Belly Pizza with Barbecue Sauce and Sweet Corn

This pizza combines three of our favorite things: cured pork belly, Chuck's barbecue sauce, and sweet corn. It takes a while to cure a pork belly (five days in the refrigerator!), but when it's done, damn, is it good.

INGREDIENTS

FOR THE PORK BELLY:

2 cups **kosher salt**

1/2 cup (firmly packed) **light brown sugar**

1 pound **pork belly,** skin removed

Makes 2 pizzas; serves 4 to 6

Five days ahead, cure the pork belly: Mix the salt and brown sugar together in a bowl. Spread half of the mixture in a container that's large enough to hold the pork belly, lay the pork belly on top, and cover it with the remaining mixture. Place a piece of plastic wrap over it, and weight it down with a heavy plate to keep pressure on the belly. Refrigerate for 5 days. To ensure that it will cure evenly, flip the belly over once a day and cover it again with the curing mixture, remembering to weight it down with the heavy plate.

At the end of the fifth day, 1 hour before you are ready to bake the pizzas, adjust the oven rack to the middle position, place a baking stone on it, and preheat the oven to 450°F.

While the baking stone is heating, remove the pork belly from the cure, rinse it under cold running water, and pat it dry with paper towels. Set it aside to come to room temperature.

Meanwhile, fill a medium bowl halfway with water and put about 2 dozen ice cubes in it; set it aside. Bring 2 quarts water to a boil in a large pot over high heat. Add 1 tablespoon salt and cook the corn until it is tender, about 2 minutes. Immediately strain the corn through a colander, place the colander in the ice water, and let the corn cool for 2 minutes (the ice water will stop the corn from overcooking). Drain the corn thoroughly.

Cut the pork belly into bite-size rectangles, approximately ¼ inch by 1 inch, until you have 1 cup. (Store the leftover belly, wrapped in plastic wrap, in the refrigerator for another use.)

Generously dust the surface of a pizza peel (a flat wooden or metal shovel with a long handle) with bread flour. Lightly flour a work surface.

FOR THE PIZZA:

Kosher salt

1 cup fresh **corn kernels**

Bread flour, for dusting

1 recipe **pizza dough** (see page 235), shaped into 2 balls and refrigerated at least overnight

1 1/2 cups **Chuck's barbecue sauce** (see page 77)

1 1/2 cups grated **low-moisture mozzarella**

1/2 cup grated **Parmesan**

2 whole **scallions,** trimmed and thinly sliced

Freshly ground **black pepper**

Working with one ball of pizza dough, dip your hands and the dough in the bread flour to make them less sticky, and pat the dough down into a disk shape with the tips of your fingers. Once the disk is large enough, drape the dough over your fists and carefully start stretching and expanding the dough from underneath to form a round that is 10 to 12 inches in diameter. (If you're feeling lucky, try tossing the dough over your head in a circular motion to stretch the dough.)

Place the dough on the prepared peel and spread 3/4 cup of the barbecue sauce evenly over the surface of the dough, leaving a 1/2-inch border uncovered. Sprinkle the pizza with half of the mozzarella, Parmesan, pork belly pieces, corn, and scallions. Season the pizza to taste with salt and pepper.

Before you put the pizza in the oven, do the "stick test": shake the peel slightly to make sure the pizza is not sticking (if it is, carefully lift the section that is sticking and sprinkle a bit more flour underneath). Then slide the pizza directly onto the baking stone and bake it for 8 to 12 minutes, checking on it after 5 minutes and rotating it if necessary to ensure that it's baking evenly. When the crust is golden and the cheese is bubbly, use the peel to remove the pizza and transfer it to a cutting board. Let it cool for 2 minutes. Then slice and serve immediately.

Prepare your second pizza the same way.

Baked Beans

Phil grew up on traditional baked beans from a can, but this is a fresher, cleaner version that makes a great accompaniment for pork. At the Bakery, we combine navy beans, red beans, and cranberry beans. Since the beans differ in size and density, they must be cooked separately—which means three pots of beans simmering away at the same time. Feel free to do the same if you'd like, but to simplify this recipe, we decided to stick to one type of bean.

INGREDIENTS

1 pound dried **navy, red, or cranberry beans**

1 small **onion,** halved

1 small **carrot**

1 **celery stalk**

1 **bay leaf**

2 **garlic cloves**

1 quart **chicken stock** (see page 239)

3 ounces (about 3 slices) **bacon,** diced

3 tablespoons **whole-grain mustard**

3 tablespoons **light** or **dark brown sugar**

1 teaspoon freshly ground **coffee beans**

1 teaspoon freshly ground **black pepper**

1 teaspoon **kosher salt**

2 tablespoons minced **flat-leaf parsley**

1 tablespoon minced **fresh oregano**

1 tablespoon **fresh thyme leaves**

Serves 6 to 8

Put the beans in a large bowl, add water to cover, and let them soak at room temperature overnight. (Add plenty of water. Dry beans can absorb great amounts of liquid.)

The next day, drain the beans, transfer them to a medium pot, and add the onion, carrot, celery, bay leaf, garlic, chicken stock, and bacon. Bring to a boil. Then reduce the heat and simmer until the beans are tender but not mushy (they'll cook further when you bake them), 30 to 45 minutes. (As the beans cook, skim off any foam that forms.)

Strain the beans, reserving the cooking liquid (you'll use it for the sauce). Discard the onion, carrot, celery, and bay leaf, and set the beans aside.

Adjust the oven rack to the middle position and preheat the oven to 350°F.

Combine the mustard, brown sugar, ground coffee, pepper, and salt in a bowl and stir in the reserved cooking liquid. Combine the sauce and the beans in a baking dish large enough to hold the beans, cover with aluminum foil, and bake for 1 1/2 to 2 hours, until the beans have absorbed most of the liquid.

Remove from the oven, stir in the fresh herbs, and serve.

Blueberry Pie

If you've ever wondered what made your grandmother's pie crust taste so good, we'll give you a hint: she probably used lard. We get our lard from TLC Ranch's pasture-raised pork, and the result is an incredibly flaky pie crust that would make any grandma proud. We like to use a combination of fresh blueberries and frozen huckleberries for this pie. (Huckleberries, which arrive sporadically throughout the season, are one of the few fruits that we find stand up well to freezing.) We love the tart dimension huckleberries add to this pie. Don't worry if you can't find them, though—the pie will turn out fine with all blueberries. Serve it with a dollop of whipped cream or a scoop of vanilla ice cream.

INGREDIENTS

FOR THE PIE DOUGH:

3 1/4 cups **all-purpose flour**

1/2 cup cold **unsalted butter,** cut into cubes

3/4 cup cold **lard**

1 1/4 teaspoons **kosher salt**

2/3 cup **ice water**

1 **egg,** beaten

FOR THE FILLING:

4 cups fresh **blueberries**

2 cups frozen **huckleberries**

3/4 cup **sugar**

1/4 teaspoon **freshly grated nutmeg**

Grated zest of 1 **lemon**

3 tablespoons **all-purpose flour**

1/4 cup **crème fraîche**

1 tablespoon **unsalted butter,** cut up

FOR THE TOP CRUST:

1 **egg,** beaten

2 tablespoons **sugar**

Makes one 9-inch pie

To make the dough, combine the flour, butter, lard, and salt in a bowl, put the bowl in the freezer, and chill for 30 minutes.

Remove the flour mixture from the freezer and use a pastry cutter to break up the butter and lard into pieces the size of a dime. Make a well in the center, and pour in the ice water and the egg. Mix with your hands until the dough comes together, but don't worry about getting it too smooth; bits of butter should still be visible in it. Cut the dough in half and flatten each half into a disk. Wrap each one with plastic wrap, and refrigerate them for at least 30 minutes or as long as 3 days.

Adjust the oven rack to the middle position and preheat the oven to 450°F.

To make the filling, combine the berries, sugar, nutmeg, and lemon zest in a bowl. Cover it with plastic wrap and set aside at room temperature for 30 minutes.

Toss the berry mixture with the flour. Add the crème fraîche and mix until the berries are coated.

Roll out the pie dough on a lightly floured surface to form two rounds about 12 inches in diameter. Pick up one round by rolling the dough onto the rolling pin, and lay it in a 9-inch pie pan. Gently press the dough over the bottom of the pan and up the sides, leaving a lip around the edge.

Spoon the berry mixture into the pie shell and dot with the butter. Place the round of dough over the filling. Trim the excess dough just to the border of the pie pan and crimp the edges (or seal the pie by pressing the edges with a fork). Brush the top of the pie with the beaten egg and sprinkle it with the sugar. Cut slits in the top crust to allow steam to escape.

Bake the pie for 15 minutes. Then reduce the oven temperature to 375°F and bake it for another 45 minutes, until the crust is very golden brown and the filling is bubbling in the center. Let the pie cool for at least 1 hour before slicing.

Hazelnut Flan with Roasted Cherries

Not quite as rich as traditional crème brûlée or pot de crème, flan is an appropriate ending to a hearty meal. What sets flan apart from these other kinds of custard is that there's a thin layer of caramel at the bottom of each ramekin. As the custard bakes, the caramel layer becomes a light amber-colored sauce that surrounds the flan when you invert it onto a plate.

Our flan is subtly flavored with hazelnuts. We serve it with cherries that have been drizzled with Banyuls (a sweet wine produced in the South of France) and roasted at very high temperature.

INGREDIENTS

FOR THE CARAMEL LAYER:

3/4 cup **sugar**

FOR THE CUSTARD:

1 cup **hazelnuts**

2 cups **whole milk**

2 cups **heavy cream**

3/4 cup **sugar**

1/2 teaspoon **kosher salt**

3 **whole eggs**

5 **egg yolks**

Makes 8 individual flans

Start by making the caramel to coat the ramekins: Place the sugar and 1/4 cup water in a small saucepan, cover with a lid, and bring to a boil over high heat. Cook, covered, for 5 minutes. Then remove the lid and continue cooking over high heat until the sugar caramelizes to a dark amber color. (Really dark is great.) This will take 5 to 7 minutes. Carefully divide the warm caramel among eight small ramekins, swirling each one until the bottom is completely covered. Let the caramel cool until it's completely set, about 10 minutes.

Adjust the oven rack to the middle position and preheat the oven to 350°F.

Scatter the hazelnuts on a cookie sheet and toast them in the oven until they are very light brown, about 10 minutes. Let them cool completely. Roughly chop them.

Reduce the oven temperature to 300°F.

Combine the milk, cream, half the sugar, the salt, and the hazelnuts in a medium saucepan, and bring to a boil over medium-high heat. Remove the pan from the heat and let the mixture steep for 30 minutes.

Whisk together the eggs, yolks, and the remaining sugar in a mixing bowl. Bring the cream mixture back to a boil, and temper the hot liquid into the eggs by adding it, a ladle at a time, while whisking vigorously. Strain the liquid through a fine-mesh sieve into a bowl. Discard the hazelnuts and return the liquid to the saucepan. Cook over very low heat, stirring constantly, until the liquid is thick enough to coat the back of the spoon, 5 to 7 minutes.

Place the caramel-coated ramekins in a roasting pan and fill them all the way to the top with the custard. Carefully add enough warm water to the roasting pan to reach

FOR THE ROASTED CHERRIES:

24 fresh **cherries**, with stems on

3 tablespoons **sugar**

Pinch of **kosher salt**

Pinch of freshly ground **black pepper**

2 tablespoons **Banyuls Rimage** (a sweet red dessert wine)

halfway up the sides of the ramekins. Cover the pan with aluminum foil, carefully transfer it to the oven, and bake for 30 minutes. Remove the foil and bake for another 10 to 15 minutes, until the flan is completely set.

Let the pan cool for 15 minutes, or until you're able to handle the ramekins easily. Remove the ramekins from the water bath and refrigerate the flans, covered with plastic, overnight.

About an hour before serving the flans, adjust the oven rack to the top position and preheat the oven to 450°F.

Arrange the cherries in a single layer in a roasting pan. Sprinkle with the sugar, salt, and pepper. Roast the cherries for 10 to 15 minutes, until the sugar starts to caramelize and the cherries begin to release their juice.

Remove the pan from the oven and deglaze the pan with the Banyuls Rimage. Toss to coat the cherries with the wine. Return the pan to the oven and roast for another 5 to 7 minutes. Deglaze once again, this time with 2 tablespoons water, and toss the cherries in the sauce. Let the cherries cool slightly.

To unmold the flans, run a knife along the edge of each ramekin and invert it onto a plate, allowing the caramel to pool on top of and around the flan. Garnish the flans with the warm cherries, and serve.

July

Heat

July is, hands down, the most intense month at the Bakery. Not only is tourist season in full swing, but all our summer produce is hitting its peak, we've got a bigger staff than at any other time of the year, and we're open six days a week, including lunch and brunch. It's hot, it's hectic, and Phil loves it.

Out on the floor of the restaurant, we keep the atmosphere calm. Back in the kitchen, though, it's nonstop action, the room filled with the frenetic energy that comes from cooking orders for a full house.

The tough part about busy nights is that we've got a small kitchen and only three stations, and any time an order comes in it can hit any one of us—salads and appetizers, pizza, or the entree station. We do some of our meats in the wood-fired oven as well, so one second our pizza guy is making a pie, and the next minute Phil's shouting out for him to throw in a chicken. It's crazy to begin with, and then we'll get an "order fire"—an entree without an appetizer—and Phil has to figure out a way to make it work. Can we push their order up higher? Do we need to get a waiter to send out some olives? It's like the adrenaline icing on a cake—the masochistic thrill that you can experience only in a kitchen. You either hate it or you love it.

Since we don't use heat lamps, we try to keep plates on the "runway"— the stainless steel table where we put finished dishes—for as short a time as possible. The runway itself stays mostly clear: salt and pepper, a wet cloth to wipe the dishes, and another cloth so that waiters don't burn their hands. Before each entree goes out, we "green-light" it, which means drizzling it with some sort of infused oil, usually basil, as a fresh, bright green signal that the food's ready. A ring of the cowbell tells servers in the dining room to drop what they're doing and pick it up.

When we first started putting together menus for the Bakery, they were traditionally composed—we matched each entree with a specific side dish. But we broke away from that model and now let customers do the choosing.

Any one of our entrees can come with any one of our side dishes, so you could come to the Bakery and have tuna five nights in a row with five different sides. Who knows if our customers really notice the difference, but to us, it's something that makes us special.

Depending on the night, Phil could be working any of the stations, but his favorite place to be is by the stove, his back facing west. It makes him feel like he's at the very edge of the country, and it also lets him look out over the kitchen, through the doors, and see a bit of what's going on in the front of the house. It's not that he doesn't enjoy going out on the floor and interacting with the customers. But Phil's job and goal is to cook things as perfectly as he can, which means, as he puts it, that he has a better relationship with the chicken than he does with the people.

Running a kitchen—any kitchen—is like rock and roll. It's anarchy and pure excitement. Every night is a performance. People come in, they give you money, and they expect a good show. It's up to us to deliver it. If you ask Phil what it's like, he'll say he feels like he's going a hundred miles an hour, down on sleep and high on coffee, and there are fifty things going on during the day and fifty things at night and it just never ends. Any cook who has run a kitchen will have the same story: the adrenaline is going nonstop. But that's what Phil loves about it: the pressure of being put through a test every evening and going to sleep feeling that he's done a hard day's work. And no matter what happens, by the end of the night, the evening's stress has already been forgotten. After cleaning up the kitchen and putting in some food orders, he treats himself to a glass of wine and a game of chess, and heads home to bed. Before you know it, it's another day.

July Fourth

Considering the fact that most tourists come to Big Sur to relax, it's surprising how many people show up totally stressed out. Maybe it's from driving on Highway 1 (it's beautiful, but it's also windy, narrow, and has a sheer drop to the ocean on one side). Maybe it's being trapped in a car for too many hours, or the result of too much quality "family time." Whatever the reason, we get some pretty frazzled people in the Bakery, and it's nice to watch the effect that good food, good music, and a break from the road usually have on their moods.

The key word there is "usually," and it excludes certain days. Like, for example, the Fourth of July. That day is jinxed, and this year was no exception. Not only did we have our usual crowds of hungry, impatient families (people who travel on major holidays tend to be in a hurry) but in the middle of our lunchtime rush, we lost our electricity. If you want a guaranteed way to make people look at you like you're crazy, try telling them, on a perfectly sunny, calm day, that the power's out.

Since we have a wood-fired grill and oven, we could still cook, but we no longer had functioning registers, credit card machines, lights, or music. We also didn't have power for the exhaust fan that sucks the smoke from the wood-fired grill out of the kitchen. So there was a smoky kitchen full of stressed-out employees and a restaurant floor packed with confused, irritable, impatient, hungry customers. What's more, Mike and Phil were both unreachable, which meant that Michelle had to try to pacify the customers, deal with the staff, and figure out how to get the generator on—and while she's talented in many areas, she'll tell you herself that fixing generators is not one of her strengths. Eventually she succeeded, but it didn't even solve the problem; we share its power with the gas station next door, and it's not strong enough to provide energy for both of us, so the power still kept going in and out.

It was the sort of experience that didn't make sense—no electricity on a sunny summer day in 21st-century America—until you realize that we're twenty-seven miles from the nearest city and there's basically one power line that runs down from Carmel. An auto accident, a single tree branch—it doesn't take much to knock out our electricity.

The only option was to close the restaurant, but as soon as the staff had gotten excited about the idea of an unexpected afternoon off, the power suddenly went back on and the day went back to normal. It all worked out, but it still prompts the question: The Fourth of July is a "barbecue holiday" that should be spent on the beach, where it doesn't matter if you have electricity, so why the hell are we open?

Name: _Jamie Collins_ **Occupation:** _ORganic Row Crop FarmeR_

Favorite food that you don't personally grow: _Artisan Cheese,_

The stinkier the better !

Date of Birth: _May 3, 1973_ **Signature:** _[signature]_

Pr: No. 5

Describe Serendipity Farms:
Our main farm in Carmel started in the 1920s as the Odello Artichoke Ranch, run by Italian sharecroppers. The Odellos kept this farm going until the disastrous El Niño flooding in the winter of '97–98. I have a great relationship with them. They're thrilled to see the land in production again.

What do you raise?
Heirloom tomatoes, artichokes, strawberries, raspberries, and various greens, herbs, and root crops—whatever will flourish on the Monterey peninsula, except asparagus and fruit trees.

Why?
Asparagus is a weeding hell. And fruit trees don't come into commercial production for eight to ten years, which isn't practical for us because we lease our land.

Favorite ways to eat tomatoes:
Sliced on toasted Asiago sourdough bread with a scrambled egg, greens, mayo, and sea salt—the breakfast of champions. You also can't beat a Caprese salad.

Benefits of being a female farmer:
Women farmers are rare, so it helps Serendipity Farms to stand out. Lots of women like to support other women working in typically male-dominated careers. I do, too—I just heard that the Carmel Valley fire chief is a woman and I was like, "Right on, firewoman!"

Favorite part of farming:
Being able to harvest the freshest produce possible and share it with others. I also like to work really hard during the season, then take time off in the winter to travel.

Hardest part:
Making the money last until harvest. I can't help but add more to the farm or try something new every year. This year we got two beehives, and our seven Nubian goats just gave birth.

Any family history of farming?
Nope. I grew up in the concrete jungle of L.A., where no one has a clue where their food came from. I had to get the hell out of there.

Plans for the future:
Goat cheese, honey, summer farming camp for kids, historical interpretive center based on the artichoke fields where we are now farming . . . the list goes on.

How do you control pests?
We have never sprayed anything, organic or otherwise, to control pests. Biological control is best. We plant diverse crops and rotate them often to avoid pest buildup. We plant beneficial hedgerows and allow crops to flower to attract good bugs to the field.

Favorite tomato:
It changes. One year I was really in love with Aunt Ruby's German Green, which has a clean cucumber taste. Last year it was Persimmon, a bright orange, meaty tomato. This year it may be the new variety, Cherokee Chocolate.

Burgers with House-Made Buns, Pickles, and Fries

There's hardly any food more stereotypically American than hamburgers, but all too frequently, we Americans screw them up. We decided to build our own version of a burger to reclaim what we consider to be a great thing. We take our burgers seriously at the Bakery and serve them with our own house-made buns, pickles, and fries—but feel free to set your own priorities, and resort to store-bought supplies as you see fit.

INGREDIENTS

FOR THE BURGER PATTIES:

2 pounds **ground chuck** from a reputable source

Kosher salt

Freshly ground **black pepper**

FOR THE BURGERS:

4 **buns** (recipe follows)

8 ounces **white Vermont cheddar,** sliced 1/4 inch thick

Marinated onions (recipe follows)

Homemade mayonnaise (see page 236)

4 **heirloom tomato** slices

4 **butter lettuce leaves**

Ketchup

Yellow mustard

4 **pickles** (recipe follows)

French fries (recipe follows)

Serves 4

Preheat the grill 30 minutes in advance, burning the wood down until you have a red-hot coal base. (See page 244 for preparing a wood-fired grill.)

Divide the meat into four portions and shape them into patties. Season both sides of the patties heavily with salt and pepper, and place them on the grill. Then leave them alone—you want to let the outside caramelize, and moving the burgers too early can rupture their surface and allow the juice to leak out. Once the burgers move easily when gently prodded, flip them over. Cook to your desired doneness—rare is great!

To serve, encourage your guests to build their own burgers on a bun with the sliced white cheddar and their choice of marinated onions, mayonnaise, tomato slices, lettuce, ketchup, and/or mustard. Don't forget the pickles and the fries!

House-Made Buns

INGREDIENTS

1 cup plus 2 tablespoons
whole milk

1 1/2 tablespoons **active dry yeast**

2 tablespoons **unsalted butter,**
softened, plus extra for coating
the bowl

3 1/4 cups plus 2 tablespoons
all-purpose flour, plus extra
for dusting

2 1/2 tablespoons **sugar**

2 teaspoons **kosher salt**

1 **egg**

1 tablespoon **sesame seeds**

Makes 6 or 7 buns

Put the milk in a small saucepan and warm it over very low heat until lukewarm. Remove the pan from the heat. Sprinkle the yeast over the milk, stir, and set it aside for 5 minutes to activate.

Butter a large bowl and set it aside.

In an electric mixer fitted with the dough hook attachment, combine the yeast mixture with half the flour on low speed. Then, over a 1-minute period, add the remaining flour along with the sugar, salt, egg, and butter. Increase the speed to medium and mix for 2 minutes. Then turn the speed to high and mix for 2 minutes more. Transfer the dough to the prepared bowl, cover it loosely with plastic wrap, and set it aside in a warm area for 45 minutes to 1 hour, until the dough has doubled in size.

Turn the dough out onto a floured surface. Divide it into 6 or 7 equal pieces, and arrange them in a row on the surface. Keeping the other portions covered with a kitchen towel so they won't dry out, roll each piece into a ball. Leave them, covered, on the surface for another 10 minutes to relax the gluten. Then, using a rolling pin, flatten the balls into rounds that are 3 1/2 to 4 inches in diameter. Place the buns on a baking sheet lined with parchment paper, put the baking sheet inside a large plastic bag, and tie the open end closed. Place the pan in a warm area of the kitchen and let the buns rise until they have doubled in size, 30 to 45 minutes.

Meanwhile, preheat the oven to 375°F.

Remove the sheet pan from the bag, brush each bun with water, and then sprinkle the sesame seeds on top. Bake the buns for 20 to 25 minutes, until golden brown. Let them cool for at least 10 minutes before serving. Slice in half and serve.

French Fries

INGREDIENTS

4 medium **russet potatoes**

Rice bran oil or **canola oil**

Kosher salt

Freshly ground **black pepper**

1 tablespoon minced
flat-leaf parsley

1 tablespoon minced **chives**

1 whole **scallion,** trimmed and
thinly sliced

Makes 24 steak fries

Adjust the oven rack to the middle position and preheat the oven to 350°F.

Wash and scrub the potatoes. Place them on a baking sheet and bake them until they can be easily pierced with a paring knife, 45 minutes to 1 hour.

Remove the potatoes from the oven, let them cool to room temperature, and then refrigerate them overnight.

The next day, cut each potato in half lengthwise. Lay each potato half on its flat side; cut it lengthwise into 3 wedges.

Fill a large pot with oil about 2 inches deep. Heat the oil over medium-high heat until it reaches 375°F on a deep-fry thermometer. Working in batches, fry the potatoes until they're golden brown, about 3 minutes. Drain them on a plate lined with paper towels.

Season the potatoes generously with salt and pepper. Sprinkle the parsley, chives, and scallions over them, and serve immediately.

Pickles

INGREDIENTS

FOR THE PICKLES:

8 small to medium **pickling cucumbers**

1/2 cup **kosher salt**

FOR THE PICKLING BRINE:

1 quart **champagne vinegar**

6 **garlic cloves**, crushed

2 **shallots**, sliced

1/4 cup **kosher salt**

1 tablespoon **sugar**

1 tablespoon **mustard seeds**

1 tablespoon **fennel seeds**

1 tablespoon **black peppercorns**

1 tablespoon **hot red pepper flakes**

2 **bay leaves**

Makes 8 pickles

Wash the cucumbers and dry them with paper towels. Dissolve the salt in 2 quarts hot water. Pour the salted water into a large glass container, and submerge the cucumbers in it. Put a plate on top to prevent the cucumbers from floating to the surface. Refrigerate for 24 hours.

The next day, take the cucumbers out of the salted water and rinse them off.

Make the pickling brine: Put the vinegar, garlic, shallots, salt, sugar, and 1 quart water in a medium pot. Combine the mustard and fennel seeds, peppercorns, red pepper flakes, and bay leaves in a sauté pan, and toast over medium-low heat until they start to release their aroma, about 3 minutes. Add the toasted spices to the vinegar mixture and bring it to a boil. Then lower the heat and let the brine simmer for 10 minutes.

Place the cucumbers in a clean, dry glass or ceramic container, and pour the hot brine over them. Use a plate to keep the pickles submerged in the liquid, and place the container, uncovered, in the refrigerator; leave it until the brine cools down. Then cover the container with a lid and refrigerate for 1 week. (The pickles will be good to eat in a week and great in a month. Store them in the refrigerator.)

Marinated Onions

INGREDIENTS

1 medium **yellow onion,** sliced into thin rings

Ice water

Juice of 1 **lemon**

1/4 cup **champagne vinegar**

1 tablespoon minced **flat-leaf parsley**

1 tablespoon minced **chives**

1 whole **scallion**, trimmed and thinly sliced

1/4 cup **olive oil**

1/2 teaspoon **kosher salt**

1/8 teaspoon freshly ground **black pepper**

Makes about 1 cup

Soak the onion slices in a bowl of ice water for 15 minutes. Drain the onions, place them in a nonreactive bowl, and drizzle the lemon juice and champagne vinegar over them. Toss in the parsley, chives, and scallions. Drizzle with the olive oil, and season with the salt and pepper. Marinate at room temperature for at least 30 minutes. The marinated onions can be made up to 8 hours in advance.

Succotash

Succotash is a Native American dish that traditionally consists of corn and lima beans. Our version includes multiple climbing beans, peas, dried cranberries, and sautéed mushrooms—enough variety for a satisfying summertime meal.

INGREDIENTS

Kosher salt

2 cups fresh **corn kernels**

1 cup shelled **English peas**

1 cup **string beans**, stem ends removed, cut into thirds

1 cup shelled **fava beans**

4 tablespoons **rice bran oil** or **canola oil**

4 tablespoons **unsalted butter**

1 cup quartered **cremini mushrooms**

1 cup quartered **white button mushrooms**

2 tablespoons **dry white wine**

1/2 cup **vegetable stock**

1/4 cup **unsweetened dried cranberries**

Freshly ground **black pepper**

Serves 4

Fill a large bowl halfway with water, and put about 2 dozen ice cubes in it; set it aside.

Bring 4 quarts water to a boil in a large pot. Add 2 tablespoons salt and cook the corn kernels in the boiling water until they're bright yellow and tender, 5 to 7 minutes. Immediately remove the corn from the water with a slotted spoon, place it in the ice water, and let it cool for 2 minutes (the ice water will keep the corn from overcooking and help it retain its color). Remove the corn kernels from the ice water and set them aside. Repeat the blanching process with the peas, string beans, and fava beans, about 2 minutes each.

Heat a large sauté pan over high heat, and drizzle 2 tablespoons of the oil into it. Add 1 tablespoon of the butter and both kinds of mushrooms, and sauté until they begin to soften, about 5 minutes. Deglaze the sauté pan with the wine, scraping any brown bits from the bottom with a wooden spoon. Transfer the mushrooms to a plate to cool.

Heat a large saucepan over medium heat and drizzle the remaining 2 tablespoons oil into it. Add 1 tablespoon of the butter and sauté the corn until warmed, about 2 minutes. Stir in the remaining blanched vegetables, the sautéed mushrooms, the vegetable stock, and the dried cranberries. Cook for another 2 minutes. Add the remaining 2 tablespoons butter, season with salt and pepper to taste, and serve.

Blue Cheese–Stuffed Figs with a Balsamic Reduction

Figs hold a special place in the heart of every Californian. Each year, when the local black Mission fig trees explode into season, people bring them by and we prepare this dish—it's our version of the traditional combination of sweet fruit and salty cheese. It's also easy: just stuff the figs and roast them in the oven until they are soft and melty. Make sure to choose figs at the peak of their ripeness.

But you don't always need to serve figs with cheese. We also use them in stuffed pork loin (you can substitute them for the peaches), and Michelle likes to roast them with honey and serve them warm with lavender ice cream. And even when figs are no longer in season, our wood-fired grill is often lit with fig wood.

INGREDIENTS

12 ripe **black Mission figs**

4 ounces **Spanish blue cheese,** such as Valdeón or Cabrales

4 bamboo or metal **skewers**

1/4 cup **rice bran oil** or **canola oil**

Kosher salt

Freshly ground **black pepper**

1/2 cup **balsamic vinegar**

1 handful **baby arugula**

Serves 4

Adjust the oven rack to the top position and preheat the oven to 450°F.

Trim the stems off the figs and cut an X three-quarters of the way into the top of each fig. Stuff each fig with 1 to 2 teaspoons of the blue cheese, and then press the fruit back into place to close. Place 3 stuffed figs on each skewer. Brush the figs with the oil, season lightly with salt and pepper, and arrange the skewers on a cookie sheet lined with aluminum foil. Roast until the figs are soft and warmed through (they should be oozing juices and slightly caramelized), about 10 minutes. Remove the figs from the skewers.

While the figs are roasting, put the balsamic vinegar in a small saucepan and simmer over medium heat until it is reduced to the thickness of honey. You'll know it's done when large bubbles start to form. Keep it warm until ready to use.

Arrange the arugula on a serving platter, place the warm figs on top, and drizzle with the warm balsamic syrup. Serve immediately.

Lemon Verbena, Mulberry, and Biscuit Trifle

We serve this trifle every summer in a deep glass dish. With layers of cream, berries, and drop biscuits, not only does it make a beautiful presentation for outdoor parties, but it gives us an opportunity to highlight the summer berries and lemon verbena grown on Partington Ridge here in Big Sur. To make the custard, we infuse crème anglaise with lemon verbena, combine it with whipped cream, and stabilize the mixture with gelatin. Mulberries are a complex berry with distinctive spicy undertones; if you can't find them, use organic blackberries instead. As for the drop biscuits, they got their name because instead of being cut in a particular size and shape, they're simply dropped onto a cookie sheet right before baking.

INGREDIENTS

FOR THE LEMON VERBENA CUSTARD:

3 cups **heavy cream**

2 cups **milk**

20 **fresh lemon verbena leaves**

1/2 cup **honey**

12 **egg yolks**

1/4 cup **sugar**

1 teaspoon **kosher salt**

1 tablespoon plus 1 teaspoon powdered **gelatin**

FOR THE DROP BISCUITS:

1 cup plus 2 tablespoons **all-purpose flour**

1/4 cup **sugar**

1 1/2 teaspoons **baking powder**

1/4 teaspoon **kosher salt**

1/4 cup cold **unsalted butter**, cubed

1/2 cup plus 2 tablespoons **heavy cream**

1/4 cup **turbinado sugar**

Serves 8 to 10

Start with the custard: Combine 2 cups of the cream with the milk, lemon verbena leaves, and honey in a medium nonreactive saucepan, and bring to a boil. Remove the pan from the heat and let the mixture steep for 30 minutes.

Meanwhile, whisk the egg yolks with the sugar and salt in a large bowl until smooth.

Bring the cream mixture back to a boil and temper the hot liquid into the yolks by adding it, one ladle at a time, while whisking vigorously. Strain the mixture through a fine-mesh sieve into a bowl, and return the strained liquid to the pan (discard the lemon verbena). Cook over very low heat, stirring constantly, until the liquid is thick enough to coat the back of the spoon. Transfer it to a clean bowl, let it cool completely.

Place the gelatin in a medium saucepan and whisk in 2 tablespoons cold water. Let it sit undisturbed until the gelatin absorbs all the liquid and resembles applesauce; this will take a few minutes. Meanwhile, whip the remaining 1 cup cream in a mixing bowl until soft peaks form; refrigerate the whipped cream until you're ready to use it.

Warm the gelatin over very low heat until it melts. Immediately remove it from the heat and slowly whisk in half of the cooled custard; then add the rest. Fold in the chilled whipped cream, and pour the mixture into a chilled bowl. Refrigerate until cold.

While the custard is chilling, bake the drop biscuits: Preheat the oven to 350°F.

Place the flour, sugar, baking powder, and salt in a bowl and toss to combine. Cut the cubed butter into the flour mixture with a pastry cutter until pea-size crumbles start to form. Add the cream and mix with a wooden spoon until combined. Drop walnut-size spoonfuls of the biscuit mixture onto a parchment lined cookie sheet.

FOR THE BERRIES:

4 pints mulberries or blackberries

1/4 cup sugar

FOR THE SWEETENED WHIPPED CREAM:

1 1/2 cups heavy cream

2 tablespoons sugar

Sprinkle the biscuits with the turbinado sugar and bake for 10 to 15 minutes, until they're golden brown. Let them cool completely on the sheet.

About 30 minutes before serving, toss the berries and sugar in a bowl, and set it aside. (The berries will start to release their juices.)

Prepare the sweetened whipped cream by whisking the cream with the sugar until soft peaks form. (You want the cream to be a little bit runny.)

To build the trifle, spoon the lemon verbena custard into a large trifle bowl, top it with the macerated berries, and then sprinkle the biscuits over the berries. Finish the trifle with the sweetened whipped cream. Scoop the trifle into individual bowls and serve immediately.

Roasted Apricots

Apricots handle roasting remarkably well. Their sweetness concentrates, and you can get a really special flavor by adding a sprig of lavender or a vanilla bean to the roasting pan. Our favorite variety is the Blenheim apricot because it has the perfect balance of sweetness and tartness and tends to be a little smaller than other varieties. Serve these apricots with whipped cream and shortbread cookies.

INGREDIENTS

4 **Blenheim apricots,** halved lengthwise and pitted

2 fresh **lavender sprigs**

2 tablespoons **sugar**

2 tablespoons **sweet wine,** such as Sauternes

2 tablespoons **honey**

Serves 4

Adjust the oven rack to the top position and preheat the oven to 350°F.

Place the apricots, cut side up, in a cast-iron skillet. Add the lavender sprigs and sprinkle with the sugar. Bake in the oven for 10 to 12 minutes, until the apricots start to soften and release their juice.

While they're still warm, drizzle the apricots with the sweet wine and the honey. Let them sit for 3 minutes, remove the lavender sprigs, and then serve. (You can also let the apricots cool completely and serve them at room temperature.)

August

Fishing with Wayne

August is such a busy month that when Wayne offered to take us out fishing, we jumped at the chance. What better way is there to spend a day off, after all, than bouncing around the Pacific Ocean in a fourteen-foot aluminum skiff?

After driving up to the crest of the bluff overlooking the ocean, we hopped out of his truck, making sure to avoid the poison oak that grows everywhere this time of year, and got ready to head down to the private beach. Wayne likes to be self-sufficient, so he has rigged up all sorts of systems to make it possible for him to function solo, like a zipline with a pulley that we used to lower our bag of sandwiches and cooler of beer. It's powered by an old exercise bike set up at the edge of the cliff, so every time you want to send something to the beach (or bring it back up) someone has to sit down, gaze out across the Pacific, and pedal. It's got the nicest view of any gym we've seen.

Down on the beach, Wayne uses another pulley system to lower his boat down from the rocks where he's propped it and then sets up a series of driftwood logs to roll it toward the water. Sometimes you can just hop right in, but this time there was a series of large swells coming in. We sat in the shade of the rocks and ate lunch, waiting for a calm spell so that we could launch.

We had to abort once, but on our second try we made it out onto the ocean, navigating through a passageway of rocks. Despite the fact that it was August, the water was freezing—Michelle had on a wetsuit—and we could see our breath in the air even as the sun warmed our backs. (Wayne, however, went shirtless.) The water was blue-green and clear, and as Wayne motored us toward one of his favorite fishing spots, we could see kelp forests beneath

the boat and jellyfish floating by. There was even an otter, relaxing on its back above the seaweed, that looked at us suspiciously and then ducked off for a more private place to swim.

Before this starts sounding too romantic, though, we should point out that we're not fishing people. We grew up in New Jersey. Not the pretty, rural part of New Jersey, but the suburbs right outside of New York. Fishing—and anything about "country life"—was not in the picture. And we're also too impatient to ever really get into the idea of fishing the way most people think of it: casting a line, sitting around, and waiting for hours for a bite.

But that's not a problem with Wayne. He knows spots where there are so many fish that you can see them swarming under the surface of the water, and you can barely get a line down to the bottom without catching something. Fishing this way makes us feel like kids, probably because there's no real effort or waiting involved. Drop a line, catch a fish. Drop the line again, catch another. Floating on a skiff off the Pacific coast, looking up at the cliffs that most people only gaze down from, it's exhilarating.

It'd be easy to get carried away, but since we were just fishing for our own dinner, it didn't make sense to catch too many. Eventually we motored and rowed our way back toward shore and cracked open a few beers as Phil and Wayne cleaned the fish right on the beach, putting the meat into a cooler that we then pedaled up the hill.

Back at the Bakery, we threw together a tomato and avocado salad, sliced some fresh buffalo mozzarella, and served up the fish. That evening, faces flushed from the sun, still giddy from bouncing around on the water, we sat down to a fresh-caught feast.

Our Wood-Fired Pizza

We grew up with thin-crust, Neapolitan-style pizza, and our cheese pizza, our most basic pie, is a tribute to those we ate at our neighborhood parlors—crispy, with the perfect blend of tomato sauce and mozzarella. When designing our less traditional pies, we use the same approach we take toward the rest of our food: carefully pairing fresh, seasonal vegetables with complementary cheeses, sauces, and meats to create pizzas that are just as composed as the other items on our menu.

Our heirloom tomato version represents our love for Italian pizza, and our prosciutto and sage pie is our California-coming-of-age pizza. In August we like to take advantage of the local heirloom tomatoes, but the variety of local produce means that we can mix up toppings all year long. Instead of just adding things to a traditional cheese pie—the normal approach in every pizza shop in Jersey—we change the sauces to create pizzas that are more sophisticated. Our eggplant pizza has an eggplant sauce, dollops of tomato sauce, roasted eggplant cubes, and goat cheese, for example, and our long-cooked broccoli and broccolini pizza uses preserved garlic and oil as the sauce.

You can always just top a traditional cheese pizza with sausage, pepperoni, or the California favorite of ham, pineapple, and jalapeño peppers. But once you start experimenting, there's no end to the possible combinations. We do a breakfast pizza year-round, and regularly feature seasonal toppings like chanterelles and squash (butternut goes great with Parmesan, mozzarella, prosciutto, and sage brown butter). Our suggestion: Make a couple of pizza doughs, check out what's in season, and create your own.

PROFILE: FORREST / *Poke Pole Fisherman*

Name: Forrest Millington   **Hometown:** Pacific Grove

Last time you drove a car: In the late 70's

Miles walked per year: Upwards of 2,000

Date of Birth: MAY 9, 1964   **Signature:** Forrest Millington

Pr: No. 6

What do you love about living in Big Sur?
What don't I love? The landscapes. The mountains. How easily you can find quietness and solitude.

Worst part of living here:
Everything's uphill.

Why Big Sur?
My great-great-grandfather was John Partington—he pioneered Partington's Ridge in Big Sur. Even though my family doesn't have any land here, I wanted to come down and check out Big Sur because it was part of my heritage.

How many times have you been out of California?
Twice. Once to Idaho and once to Hawaii last year. That was my first plane ride. I didn't like flying at all.

Total siblings:
Nine—there are five boys and four girls. I'm the youngest boy.

How long have you been fishing for rockfish?
Since I was a kid. We lived a block from the ocean, so I grew up fishing. I did twenty years of commercial fishing out of Monterey, working the Big Sur coast.

Why do you go poke pole fishing?
Lately there's been a lot of restrictions on where you can and can't go fishing. But poke pole fishing is allowed pretty much 24/7, even when there might be restrictions on boats.

Who taught you?
When I was young I saw an old guy doing it back in Cannery Row. That gave me the idea to do it myself because it's a good way to gather food—you get mussels, crabs, abalones all at once down there.

Role at the Bakery:
Self-appointed daytime manager. I split firewood. I clean tables now and again when they're busy, or start fires for them in the pizza oven. I landscape around the Bakery.

Yearly income:
It's . . . unstable. Is that a good answer?

Why the barter system?
It's less complicated than running around in the rat race where people are stressed out about their lives and are miserable. I figured I'd just keep it simple.

Life philosophy:
I try to keep things as mellow and peaceful as possible. I try to make a difference every day, whether it's picking up trash on the side of the road or helping someone for free and not expecting something back.

What's under the hat:
Hair. Normal hair!

Heirloom Tomato Pizza

If you've never seen the huge selection of wonderful and colorful heirloom tomato varieties out there, then you need to get out to the market. We think of our pizza Margherita as the Italian flag in a psychedelic mood—and when you've got fresh basil and perfectly ripe tomatoes, it's a quintessential summertime meal. Add the tomatoes after par-baking the pizza so they just warm up but don't release too much juice. We buy our heirloom tomatoes from Serendipity Farms in Carmel Valley, which grows over twenty different varieties. We like a selection of Brandywine, Green Zebra, and Sungold—and the list keeps growing.

INGREDIENTS

Bread flour, for dusting

1 recipe **pizza dough** (see page 235), shaped into 2 balls and refrigerated at least overnight

4 tablespoons **tomato sauce** (see page 238)

4 tablespoons grated **Parmesan**

3 medium assorted **heirloom tomatoes,** sliced

8 ounces (2 to 3 balls) **buffalo mozzarella,** sliced into rounds

Kosher salt

Freshly ground **black pepper**

6 fresh **basil leaves,** julienned

Makes 2 pizzas

One hour before you start baking, adjust the oven rack to the lower position, put a baking stone on it, and preheat the oven to 450°F.

Generously dust the surface of a pizza peel (a flat wooden or metal shovel with a long handle) with bread flour. Lightly flour a work surface.

Working with one ball of pizza dough, dip your hands and the dough in the bread flour to make them less sticky, and pat the dough down into a disk shape with the palm of your hand. Once the disk is large enough, drape the dough over your fists and carefully start stretching and expanding the dough from underneath to form a round that is 10 to 12 inches in diameter. (If you're feeling lucky, try tossing the dough over your head in a circular motion to stretch the dough.)

Place the dough on the prepared peel and spread 2 tablespoons of the tomato sauce evenly over the surface, leaving a 1/2-inch border uncovered. Sprinkle 2 tablespoons of the Parmesan over the tomato sauce.

Before you put the pizza in the oven, do the "stick test": shake the peel slightly to make sure the pizza is not sticking (if it is, carefully lift the section that is sticking and sprinkle a bit more flour underneath). Then slide the pizza directly onto the baking stone and bake it for 4 to 6 minutes, until the pizza is slightly browned.

Using the peel, remove the pizza from the oven. Arrange half of the sliced tomatoes on top of the pizza, and then arrange half of the sliced mozzarella over the tomatoes. Season with salt and pepper, put it back in the oven, and bake for another 4 to 6 minutes—the mozzarella should melt but still maintain its shape and the tomatoes should be just warmed through. (Do not overbake—the tomatoes will start to release too much juice and the pizza will be soggy.)

Use the peel to remove the pizza and place it on a cutting board. Let it cool for 2 minutes. Then top it with half of the basil, slice, and serve immediately.

Prepare your second pizza the same way.

Rockfish Scampi and Flatbread

When you hear the word *scampi*, you usually think of shrimp. But since Wayne and Forrest are always bringing in rockfish, we decided to come up with our own version of this old-school favorite.

INGREDIENTS

FOR THE FLATBREAD:

Bread flour, for dusting

1 recipe **pizza dough** (see page 235), shaped into 2 balls and refrigerated at least overnight

1/4 cup **olive oil**

Kosher salt

Freshly ground **black pepper**

FOR THE SCAMPI:

2 tablespoons **rice bran oil** or **canola oil**

1/2 **yellow onion,** finely chopped

1/2 **carrot,** finely chopped

1 small **celery stalk,** finely chopped

4 **rockfish fillets,** about 5 ounces each (rockfish is usually labeled "rock cod" in the grocery store; see page 114 for alternatives)

2 tablespoons **preserved garlic** (see page 234)

1 tablespoon minced **flat-leaf parsley**

1 tablespoon minced **chives**

1 whole **scallion,** trimmed and thinly sliced

Kosher salt

Freshly ground **black pepper**

1/4 cup **dry white wine**

1/2 cup **chicken stock** (see page 239)

1/4 cup **unsalted butter,** cut into pieces

Serves 4

One hour before you start baking, adjust the oven rack to the lower position, place a baking stone on it, and preheat the oven to 450°F.

Generously dust the surface of a pizza peel (a flat wooden or metal shovel with a long handle) with bread flour. Lightly flour a work surface.

Working with one ball of dough, dip your hands and the dough in the bread flour to make them less sticky, and pat the dough down into a disk shape with the tips of your fingers. Once the disk is large enough, drape the dough over your fists and carefully start stretching and expanding the dough from underneath to form a round that is about 14 inches in diameter. (If you're feeling lucky, try tossing the dough over your head in a circular motion to stretch the dough.)

Place the dough on the floured peel and make a rectangle by cutting off the edge with a pizza cutter or a sharp knife. (You can bake the edge into breadsticks.) With the tip of a sharp knife, prick the dough all over to prevent it from bubbling. Then slide the dough directly onto the baking stone and bake it for 7 minutes, checking on it after 5 minutes and rotating it if necessary to ensure that it's baking evenly. When the flatbread is golden, use the peel to remove it from the oven and place it on a cutting board. Brush it with half of the olive oil, and season it with salt and pepper. Let it cool for 1 minute. Then slice it into chip-size pieces and keep them covered in a warm area of the kitchen.

Prepare the second flatbread the same way.

When you are ready to cook the fish, adjust the oven rack to the middle position and reduce the oven temperature to 350°F.

Heat a large sauté pan over medium heat and drizzle the rice bran oil or canola oil into it. Add the onions, carrots, and celery and sweat until the vegetables are soft, 5 to 7 minutes. Transfer the vegetables to a separate plate to cool.

Cut the rockfish into 1-inch cubes. Place the fish in a medium bowl, add the cooked vegetables and the preserved garlic, parsley, chives, and scallions. Mix to combine. Season generously with salt and pepper. Transfer the mixture into a cast-iron skillet, and add the white wine, chicken stock, and butter. Bake until the fish is opaque, 10 to 12 minutes.

To serve, leave the "scampi" in the cast-iron skillet. Bring it out to the table along with the flatbread chips to scoop it up.

Whole Rockfish, Scored and Charred

We pull these rockfish right out of the waters of Big Sur. There are many ways to prepare rockfish (which is called "rock cod" in the grocery store), but this is our favorite: seasoned simply with lemon and thyme and roasted in the wood-fired oven. If your kitchen doesn't have a wood-fired oven, use your broiler to char the fish (be careful not to totally burn it!). If rockfish is not available in your area, try using any two-pound whole whitefish—just make sure that it's sustainably caught. Check the Monterey Bay Aquarium in the Resources for a list of recommended fish.

INGREDIENTS

1 tablespoon **black peppercorns**

4 whole **rockfish** (or alternative), about 2 pounds each, scaled, gutted, fins removed

Coarse sea salt

12 **thyme sprigs**

1 **lemon,** halved lengthwise and then sliced into half-moons

4 **garlic cloves,** sliced

1/4 to 1/2 cup **olive oil**

Serves 4

Preheat the broiler.

Crack the peppercorns by placing them on a flat surface, like a cutting board, and pressing them with the flat bottom of a heavy pan until they split into pieces.

Season the gut cavity of each fish generously with sea salt and cracked pepper, and stuff them with 3 thyme sprigs each. Using a sharp knife, score the skin of the fish with three diagonal slashes on each side. Tuck a lemon slice and a few garlic slices into each incision (this will help infuse the flavors into the flesh as the fish cooks). Brush olive oil over both sides of the fish, and season with additional sea salt and cracked pepper.

Brush a large roasting pan (large enough to hold the 4 whole fish) with olive oil and set it aside.

Heat a large sauté pan over medium-high heat and drizzle 2 tablespoons olive oil into it. Put 1 fish in the hot pan and sear one side until the skin browns, about 4 minutes. Then carefully transfer the fish to the prepared roasting pan, laying the fish seared side down. (You must sear the fish on one side first because the broiler will impart direct heat only on the opposite side, and you want to make sure that both sides are properly cooked.) Repeat the process with the remaining oil and fish.

Put the roasting pan under the broiler and cook the fish for 10 to 12 minutes, until the skin starts to char. Check for doneness in the center of the fish, since that takes the longest to cook. The fish is done when you can easily flake the flesh away from the bones with a fork. Keep in mind that any fish that is cooked whole will take longer than you think; be patient and don't worry too much about dryness—the bones will keep the fish moist.

Remove the roasting pan from the oven and let the fish rest for 4 minutes. Discard the thyme sprigs. Gently transfer the fish to a platter or individual plates, and serve.

Fish and Chips, Big Sur Style

Our British friend Terry lives for fish and chips. Between Wayne and Forrest, we're bombarded with loads of fresh rockfish during the summer, so one day we decided to listen to Terry's request and came up with this dish. We couldn't bring ourselves to drop the fish into the deep-fat fryer, though. Instead we opted for lightly breading and pan-frying our fillets. This simple preparation makes a great lunch, and for dinner you could serve the fish with succotash (see page 98) instead of the chips (just don't tell Terry).

INGREDIENTS

FOR THE TARTAR SAUCE:

3/4 cup **homemade mayonnaise** (see page 236)

1 **pickle** (see page 97), minced

Juice and grated zest of 1 **lemon**

2 teaspoons **capers**, minced

1 tablespoon minced **flat-leaf parsley**

1 tablespoon minced **chives**

1 whole **scallion**, trimmed and thinly sliced

1 small **shallot**, minced

Kosher salt

Freshly ground **black pepper**

FOR THE CHIPS:

4 medium **russet potatoes**

Rice bran oil or **canola oil**

Kosher salt

Freshly ground **black pepper**

1 tablespoon minced **flat-leaf parsley**

1 tablespoon minced **chives**

1 whole **scallion**, trimmed and thinly sliced

Serves 4

To make the tartar sauce, put the mayonnaise, pickle, lemon juice and zest, capers, parsley, chives, scallions, and shallots in a bowl and mix until well combined. Season the tartar sauce with salt and pepper to taste. Transfer it to a plastic container or glass jar, and refrigerate until ready to use.

To make the chips, adjust the oven rack to the middle position and preheat the oven to 350°F. Wash and scrub the potatoes. Place them on a baking sheet and bake them until they can be easily pierced with a paring knife, 45 minutes to 1 hour.

Remove the potatoes from the oven, let them cool to room temperature, and then refrigerate them for at least 30 minutes.

Cut each potato in half lengthwise, and laying the potato half on its flat side, cut it lengthwise into 3 wedges.

Fill a large pot with oil about 2 inches deep. Heat the oil over medium-high heat until it reaches 375°F on a deep-fry thermometer. Working in batches, fry the potatoes until they're golden brown, about 3 minutes. Drain them on a plate lined with paper towels, and then season them generously with salt and pepper. Sprinkle with the minced parsley, chives, and scallions. Reserve the chips in a warm spot.

For the fish, combine the breadcrumbs, grated Pecorino, parsley, and thyme in a food processor and pulse until the mixture resembles a very fine meal.

FOR THE FISH:

1 cup **breadcrumbs**

2 tablespoons finely grated **Pecorino Romano**

1 tablespoon **flat-leaf parsley leaves**

1 tablespoon **fresh thyme leaves**

4 **rockfish fillets,** 5 to 6 ounces each (rockfish will usually be labeled "rock cod" in the grocery store; see page 114 for alternatives)

Kosher salt

Freshly ground **black pepper**

1/2 cup **all-purpose flour**

1 **egg,** beaten

1/4 cup **rice bran oil** or **canola oil**

2 tablespoons **unsalted butter**

Season both sides of the fish fillets generously with salt and pepper. Put the flour, egg, and the breadcrumb mixture in separate shallow bowls. Dredge each fillet in flour and tap off the excess. Then dip in the beaten egg and let the excess run off. Finally coat it with breadcrumbs, making sure the surface is completely coated. Set the fillets aside on a plate.

Heat a cast-iron skillet over medium-high heat, and drizzle the oil into it. Add the butter, and wait until it melts. Without overcrowding, fry the fillets in the skillet until they're golden, 2 to 3 minutes on the first side. Flip the fillets over and cook until the other side is golden as well, another 2 minutes. Place the fish on a plate lined with paper towels.

Serve the fish and chips immediately, with the tartar sauce on the side.

Creamless Chowder with Clams and Mussels

Anybody can use cream to make a rich chowder—Monterey's wharf is full of the stick-to-your-stomach, served-in-a-bread-bowl variety. That's fine on a cold, stormy day, but we prefer this healthier version that's thickened with a puréed vegetable base instead. The key ingredient to any chowder is the fish stock. For us this is an easy preparation because the guys at the Wharf practically give away the whitefish bones. To ensure that your fishmonger will put some aside for you, call to order them early in the day (that's when they butcher most of their fish) and pick them up later that afternoon. Serve the chowder with toasted slices of sourdough bread.

INGREDIENTS

FOR THE CREAMLESS BASE:

1/2 **leek**

2 tablespoons **rice bran oil** or **canola oil**

1 small **yellow onion,** roughly chopped

1/2 **fennel bulb,** roughly chopped

1 **russet potato,** peeled and cubed

1/2 cup roughly chopped **white button mushrooms**

1 **celery stalk,** roughly chopped

4 **garlic cloves,** roughly chopped

Kosher salt

Freshly ground **black pepper**

5 cups **fish stock** (recipe follows)

FOR THE CHOWDER:

2 ounces **pancetta,** cut into small dice

4 tablespoons **rice bran oil** or **canola oil**

1 small **yellow onion,** finely chopped

1 small **carrot,** finely chopped

1 **celery stalk,** finely chopped

20 Manila clams, scrubbed

20 **mussels,** scrubbed and debearded

1 cup **dry white wine**

Serves 6

Start with the base: Cut off the dark green end of the leek, leaving behind its white bulb and the beginnings of its green stem. Slice it into thin half-moons, and thoroughly wash them in a bowl of cold water. Drain off the water, wash them again, and drain.

Heat a large pot over medium-low heat and drizzle the oil into it. Add the leeks, onions, fennel, potatoes, mushrooms, celery, and garlic. Season lightly with salt and pepper, and sweat the vegetables until they are soft but have no color, about 30 minutes. Add the fish stock and simmer for 25 minutes.

Reserve 1 cup of the cooking liquid (to adjust the consistency of the base if necessary). Purée the remaining base mixture in a blender until smooth. If it is too thick, add some of the reserved cooking liquid. Set it aside—this is your creamless base.

Start the chowder by cooking the pancetta in a large sauté pan over medium-low heat until the fat starts to melt and the pancetta is crisp and golden brown, 5 to 7 minutes. Remove the pancetta from the pan with a slotted spoon, and put it on a plate lined with paper towels. Place the pan back on the stove, add 2 tablespoons of the oil to the fat released by the pancetta, and sauté the onions, carrots, and celery over medium-low heat until the vegetables are tender, about 10 minutes. Set the cooked vegetables aside.

Heat a pot that is large enough to hold all the shellfish over high heat, and drizzle the remaining 2 tablespoons oil into it. Add the clams, mussels, and wine. Season with salt and pepper, and immediately cover the pan so the shellfish can steam. Cook until the shells open, 2 to 4 minutes. As the shells open, remove them with a pair of tongs and put them in a serving tureen or divide them among individual soup bowls. Discard any unopened shells.

Adjust the oven rack to the top position and preheat the oven to 350°F.

Make the toasts: Melt the butter in a small saucepan. Brush both sides of the bread slices with the melted butter, place them on a cookie sheet, and toast them in the oven until golden brown, about 10 minutes.

Kosher salt

Freshly ground **black pepper**

3 tablespoons minced **flat-leaf parsley**

3 tablespoons minced **chives**

3 whole **scallions,** trimmed and thinly sliced

FOR THE SOURDOUGH TOASTS:

2 tablespoons **unsalted butter**

6 slices **sourdough bread,** cut 1/2 inch thick

To finish the chowder, pour the creamless base into the pot you cooked the shellfish in, add the pancetta and the cooked vegetables, and warm the mixture over high heat. Stir in the parsley, chives, and scallions, and season with salt and pepper to taste. Pour the warm chowder over the shellfish, and serve with the slices of toasted country bread.

Fish Stock

Makes 4 quarts

INGREDIENTS

1 **leek**

5 pounds **whitefish bones** (such as halibut)

2 **flat-leaf parsley stems,** roughly chopped

1 medium **yellow onion,** roughly chopped

2 **celery stalks,** roughly chopped

1/2 cup chopped **white button mushrooms**

1 small **fennel bulb,** roughly chopped

1 **lemon,** cut in half

2 cups **dry white wine**

Cut off the dark green end of the leek, leaving behind its white bulb and the beginnings of its green stem. Then roughly slice the halves, and thoroughly wash the slices in a bowl of cold water. Drain off the water, wash them again, and drain.

Rinse the fish bones thoroughly under cold running water. Place the leeks, the fish bones, and all the remaining ingredients in a large pot. Add 4 quarts water, bring to a simmer over medium-low heat, and cook for 40 minutes, skimming the surface with a spoon or a ladle every once in a while to remove the foam that forms.

Strain the stock into a large plastic container, and discard the solid ingredients. Cover, and store in the refrigerator for up to 3 days.

Fresh Garbanzo-Bean Stew

Tender fresh garbanzo beans, fingerling potato confit, sautéed onions, and roasted red bell peppers come together in this colorful, textured stew. It tastes so good because of the combination of cooking techniques—each adds to the stew's richness. It might be tempting to use dried or canned garbanzo beans (a.k.a. chickpeas), but this recipe calls for beans fresh off the vine, which are available during warmer months at some farmers' markets or grocery stores with good produce sections. When no fresh garbanzos are available, use dried garbanzo beans—but be aware that dried beans take more than twice as long to cook.

INGREDIENTS

6 tablespoons **rice bran oil** or **canola oil**

3 small **yellow onions**: 1 roughly chopped, 2 sliced

1 **carrot**, roughly chopped

1 **celery stalk**, roughly chopped

1 quart **chicken stock** (see page 239)

2 cups shelled **fresh garbanzo beans** or 1 cup **dried garbanzo beans**, soaked in water overnight and drained

2 **flat-leaf parsley stems**

1 **bay leaf**

Kosher salt

3 **red bell peppers**

2 tablespoons **unsalted butter**

Freshly ground **black pepper**

2 cups **fingerling potato confit** (see page 234), potatoes cut in half lengthwise

Minced **flat-leaf parsley**, for garnish

Serves 6

Start with the garbanzo beans: Heat a medium pot over medium-high heat, and drizzle 3 tablespoons of the oil into it. Add the chopped onion, carrot, and celery, and brown the vegetables slightly, about 5 minutes. Add the stock, garbanzo beans, parsley stems, bay leaf, and 1 teaspoon salt. Simmer until the beans are tender, 10 to 15 minutes (fresh beans cook considerably faster than dried; if using dried garbanzo beans, cook for 45 minutes to 1 hour).

Remove the pot from the heat, strain the liquid into a bowl, and reserve the beans separately (discard the bay leaf and parsley stems). Reserve the cooking liquid—you'll need it later on.

(If you are cooking dried garbanzos, go ahead and prepare the peppers and onions while they are cooking.) To roast the bell peppers: Place the peppers directly on the open flame of a gas burner or a grill, and roast until the skins are charred, using tongs to turn the peppers so that they char evenly. Once they are blackened all over, place the peppers in a bowl, cover tightly with plastic wrap, and allow the peppers to steam for 5 minutes. Then peel off the skins (they should come off easily), remove the stems and seeds, and slice the peppers into 1/3-inch-wide strips.

Next, prepare the onions: Heat a large sauté pan over medium-high heat and drizzle 2 tablespoons of the oil into it. Add 1 tablespoon of the butter and the onions. Season them lightly with salt and pepper, and sauté until brown, about 5 to 7 minutes. Deglaze the sauté pan with 1/3 cup water, scraping any brown bits from the bottom with a wooden spoon. Cook until all the liquid evaporates. Deglaze the pan again with another 1/3 cup water, and cook until the liquid evaporates. (The extra round of deglazing will deepen the flavor.) Set the onions aside.

To put the stew together, heat a large saucepan over medium-high heat and drizzle the remaining 1 tablespoon oil into it. Add the remaining tablespoon of butter and the potatoes, cut side down. Cook until golden, about 2 minutes. Reduce the heat to medium. Add the peppers and onions and sauté slightly, about 1 minute. Add the garbanzo beans and their cooking liquid; cook until the stew is slightly thickened, 8 to 10 minutes. Season with salt and pepper to taste, stir in the minced parsley, and serve. Like most stews, this one will taste even better the next day.

Honey and Chamomile Ice Cream Terrine

Chamomile is one of Michelle's favorite teas, especially with honey and milk. She loves to have it after a meal or before she leaves the restaurant for the evening. This ice cream recipe produces a creamy terrine that is great served with sliced peaches. Buy dried chamomile flowers in bulk for the best flavor.

INGREDIENTS

10 raw **hazelnuts**

Unsalted butter, for the loaf pan

2 cups **heavy cream**

2 cups **whole milk**

1 1/2 cups **honey**

1 cup loose **chamomile tea** (flowers)

12 **egg yolks**

2 ripe **peaches**

1 tablespoon **sugar**

Makes 1 terrine; serves 8 to 10

Adjust the oven rack to the middle position and preheat the oven to 350°F.

Scatter the hazelnuts on a cookie sheet and toast in the oven until they're golden through the center, about 10 minutes. (To check if they're done, cut one open and inspect the color inside.) Chop them roughly.

Butter an 8 1/2 by 4 1/2 by 2 3/4-inch loaf pan and line it with plastic wrap, leaving the excess flaps hanging over the sides of the pan. Place the pan in the freezer until ready to use.

Combine the cream, milk, and honey in a medium nonreactive saucepan and bring to a boil. Remove the pan from the heat, add the chamomile tea, and let it steep for 10 minutes. Then pour the mixture through a fine-mesh sieve into a bowl. Discard the tea leaves. Return the strained mixture to the saucepan.

Whisk the egg yolks in a large bowl until smooth. Bring the cream mixture back to a boil, and temper the hot liquid into the yolks by adding it, a ladle at a time, while whisking vigorously. Return the mixture to the pan and cook over very low heat, stirring with a wooden spoon, until the liquid is thick enough to coat the back of the spoon. Strain the liquid through a fine-mesh sieve one more time, and refrigerate until it's cold. Freeze the mixture in an ice cream maker according to the manufacturer's directions.

Pull the loaf pan from the freezer and fill it one third of the way with the chamomile ice cream. Sprinkle a third of the hazelnuts over the ice cream, and fill the pan another third of the way with ice cream. Sprinkle with a third of the nuts, and top with enough ice cream to fill the pan completely. (Reserve the leftover ice cream in the freezer for a later use.) Sprinkle the remaining nuts over the top. Tap the loaf pan on the counter to even it out and remove any air bubbles. Cover the top with the plastic flaps, and freeze overnight.

About 10 minutes before serving, slice the peaches and put them in a bowl. Sprinkle with the sugar and let them macerate (the peaches will start to release their juices).

To serve, remove the terrine from the loaf pan by inverting the pan onto a plate. While holding the plastic wrap liner, pull the loaf pan off. Rinse a chef's knife under hot running water, and cut 1-inch-thick slices of the terrine. Serve each slice with some of the macerated peaches.

September

Gary, Bacchus

We met Gary Pisoni because of wine. Food Network was shooting a show featuring his wine, and for some reason Michelle got invited to make a pizza in Gary's little wood-fired oven out in his vineyard. But our real connection developed because he and Mike both love studying astrology. They became quick friends, and one night in September, just before the harvest, we arranged to have a dinner at his vineyard. We'd bring the food, he'd provide the wine, and we'd have an excuse to see what life is like on the other side of the mountains.

Gary's vineyard, 1,300 feet above sea level in the San Lucia Highlands, is basically due east from Big Sur—but since there's no direct road over the mountains, it takes over an hour and a half to drive there. And you need to know where you're going—there's no sign at the side of the road, just a number on a telephone poll and a series of dirt roads winding up toward the vineyard itself. But if you don't get lost in the rows of pinot noir, eventually you'll reach a small waterfall and a wooden deck that Gary built, complete with an outdoor bar, a huge grill, and a wood-fired oven.

We invited about twenty friends and brought huge platters of food, arriving early enough in the afternoon to have a chance to tour the vineyard and still have plenty of time to cook. Gary, always eager to show off his vineyards, wasted no time in breaking open a few bottles of wine and herding us into his 1969 open-air Jeep.

That's when things got crazy. Gary is frequently called a "maverick" when people write profiles about him, but he drives more like a madman. One hand on the wheel, one hand gesturing in the air, and one foot firmly on the gas pedal, he roars along the steep dirt roads of his vineyard at speeds so fast that you have to hold on so you don't bounce out. He loves slamming to a stop next to particularly succulent-looking bunches of grapes, reaching out to grab a handful, and offering it to the people in the Jeep. But there's no delicate sampling when Gary is involved. "You've gotta take monkey bites!" he instructs, chomping into the grapes and spitting the seeds out through his teeth. Before you can manage your own bite, Gary's taken off again through the vineyard.

His parents—Eddie and Jane, both vegetable farmers—bought the land in 1979 to use as a horse and cattle ranch, but when Gary saw the soil, he became obsessed with pinot noir. Despite the fact that he couldn't find any water, he started planting grapes in 1982, trucking water up from the valley. After five dry wells, he hit water in 1991, and he and his sons, Mark and Jeff, released their first batch of Pisoni Estate Pinot Noir in 1998. Now they sell grapes to about eight other winemakers, with all their deals brokered on a handshake. Their wine is revered by serious pinot noir enthusiasts around the world.

When people returned from Gary's vineyard tour, they needed a few minutes to settle their stomachs. Eventually we all flocked to the cave Gary had created a short way uphill from the deck, embedded into a hillside with only its entrance exposed. Gary uses it for entertaining and, on long nights of wine tasting, as a place to crash when he doesn't want to drive home. Windowless, damp, it's in the shape of an H, with two makeshift bedrooms at the back and a long banquet hall at the front, complete with a stereo system and a huge fireplace. We piled our plates with food—mackerel, tomato salad, lamb—filled our glasses with pinot noir, and gathered around the table, illuminated only by candles and the fire, as Harry Belafonte played in the background.

Gary kept the wine coming. After offering up a toast to Michelle and Phil, he poured glass after glass, his voice echoing through the room in staccato sentences, interrupted by his own laughter. Gary's the sort of person who goes up to eleven—he's full of a frenetic enthusiasm that catches other people up in it—so that as the night wore on (and the glasses continued to be filled), we became just as loud as he was.

The greatest thing about Gary, when it comes to wine, is that he insists on celebration. There's nothing pretentious or snooty about him—this is a man who takes his enjoyment of his wine just as seriously as he does the wine itself. The first time he came into the Bakery, he and Mike drank wine out of canning jars, and Mike likes to say that Gary looked happier drinking out of that jar than most people do sipping wine from the fanciest stemware.

The Hospitality Business

In addition to running the front of the house, Mike's in charge of the Bakery's wines. Some people refer to him as sommelier, but he prefers the title "wine guy" since it sounds less snobbish. Regardless of what he's called, though, Mike has a big responsibility: selecting wines that will complement the menu, season by season, day by day.

The resulting list is pretty long: we stock anywhere from about 50 wines in the slow winter months to 150 during the summer high season. Mike picks wine from all over the globe, but he places a strong emphasis on vintages from the central coast of California. We tend to have a good selection of Grüner Veltliner and Rhone varietals—and we also like to keep a variety of local pinot noirs on hand.

Mike first started getting into wines back when he was a waiter at Joe's Restaurant in Venice, California. The manager used to let the waiters go in on a bottle of wine at wholesale cost as the evening wound down, which gave the waiters a great education and provided the restaurant with a knowledgeable sales force. So Mike does something similar here in Big Sur: wine reps come by on Thursday with samples, and later in the evening, once the restaurant's closed, we pull out some bread and cheese and olives and taste wines together. That way everyone learns about the wines on our list firsthand, and Mike has a chance to get second opinions on those he's thinking of buying.

But actually, Mike's relationship with Big Sur hospitality and wine goes back years before the Bakery was started—before Phil and Michelle had even heard of Big Sur. He's been traveling up here since the early '80s to visit Terry, whom he met nearly thirty years ago in Manhattan Beach. Since then, their paths have crossed in places as far away as New Zealand and Thailand, and Terry has always had his door open for Mike, greeting him with a boisterous shout of "kettle on!" An eccentric Englishman, sandalmaker, master storyteller, and eternal optimist, Terry loves the Big Sur tradition of trading goods and services rather than exchanging money. Every time Mike showed up, Terry would have some fresh-caught local fish he'd gotten in exchange for repairing someone's sandals, or fruits and vegetables from a garden he was caretaking, and a fresh loaf of his legendary Hide bread.

Mike started off trying to reciprocate by bringing food too, but soon realized that whatever local products Terry had on hand always seemed better than anything he could come up with. Rare cheeses from France? "Try this from over the hill, Gilly," Hide would say, putting a little local honey in their tea as Mike bit into the freshest, tangiest goat cheese imaginable. The one gift Terry really appreciated—and didn't already have—was good wine. So Mike, using the knowledge he was gleaning from his experience at Joe's, would bring a few bottles and offer up a glass as he helped cook whatever foods Terry had gathered. Mike likes to say that those visits with Terry—spent belly-laughing over endless cups of tea, drinking wine out of coffee mugs, serving up whatever food there was to whomever showed up—taught him more about hospitality than any other experience.

PROFILE: MIKE / HOST

Pr: No. 7

Name: Michael Gilson   **Everyday Nickname:** Gilly

Why did you open the Bakery? For a number of reasons, none of which had anything to do with money.

Date of Birth: Dec. 28, 1960   **Signature:** Michael Gilson

Job description:
You name it and then some. I like to say that it's to remain optimistic at all times, but in a more practical sense, my time is split between customer service and wine stuff. Most days I'm also a handyman. Do you know how many pieces of equipment can go down in a restaurant at one time?

Weirdest handyman experience:
Standing on the roof above the wood grill holding a dying exhaust fan in place with a broomstick so that the kitchen wouldn't fill up with smoke while Phil finished the night's cooking.

Previous encounters with Phil and Michelle:
I worked as a waiter at Joe's Restaurant in Venice, California, where Phil was a cook. I was impressed with the passion and confidence Phil exuded in the kitchen— plus, he had a '64 Ford Ranchero, just like mine. Michelle always dressed beautifully and would wait at the bar for Phil to get off work.

Favorite part of the Bakery:
Taste testing. I also really enjoy making people happy. And people get happy about this place. They really do.

How is the restaurant business in your blood?
My relatives in Croatia have a wood-grill oceanfront seafood restaurant in Hvar, Croatia, where they catch the fish and make wine themselves. My brother has a hotel with a wine bar in Paso Robles, and my dad was quite the restaurant critic.

Best Bakery meal:
My birthday dinner when Phil made me a grilled lobster and Michelle made chocolate mint ice cream cake.

Oddest Bakery responsibility:
I have made every business card for the Bakery by hand.

Factors considered when hiring people:
People say I check their astrology charts, but actually I just check to see if they have any felonies.

Roasted Beets with Beet Greens and Goat-Cheese Crostini

When Phil was a kid, the only beets he'd eaten came from a can, and despite his dad's insistence that they were loaded with vitamins and minerals, Phil never really liked them. It wasn't until he moved to California and was introduced to baby beets that beets became his thing. We've been working with organic baby beets for over ten years now and still love them—Phil's dad proved to be right after all. We consider this recipe a "maximum utilization" dish, because we use the beet greens as well.

INGREDIENTS

FOR THE BEETS AND BEET GREENS:

24 assorted **baby beets, greens** attached

Kosher salt

Freshly ground **black pepper**

6 tablespoons **olive oil**

1/2 small **yellow onion,** sliced

2 **garlic cloves,** sliced

Pinch of **hot red pepper flakes**

3 tablespoons plus 1 teaspoon **red wine vinegar**

FOR THE GOAT CHEESE CROSTINI:

4 slices **sourdough** or **country bread,** cut about 1/2-inch thick

2 tablespoons **olive oil**

1 tablespoon minced **flat-leaf parsley**

Kosher salt

Freshly ground **black pepper**

2 to 3 ounces **soft goat cheese**

Serves 4

Adjust the oven rack to the middle position and preheat the oven to 350°F.

Trim the stems off the beets. Roughly chop the greens (you want 2 cups chopped), and wash them. Set the greens aside.

Wash the beets, making sure not to puncture their skin. Arrange them in a single layer in a roasting pan, season with salt and pepper, and drizzle with 2 tablespoons of the olive oil and about 1/2 cup water. Cover the pan with aluminum foil and roast the beets until they are fork-tender, 35 to 45 minutes, depending on their size.

While the beets are roasting, prepare the greens: Heat a large sauté pan over medium heat and drizzle 2 tablespoons of the olive oil into it. Add the onions, garlic, and red pepper flakes, and cook slowly until the onions are translucent, about 4 minutes. Add the reserved beet greens, season them with salt and pepper, and cook, stirring occasionally, for 8 to 10 minutes, until the stems are tender. Remove from the heat, stir in the 1 teaspoon vinegar, and transfer the greens to a dish to cool.

When the beets are tender, carefully remove them from the roasting pan while they're still warm and use a kitchen towel to rub off the skins. (Choose your towel carefully—it'll get stained.) Cut the beets in half, put them in a large sauté pan, and toss them with the 3 tablespoons vinegar and remaining 2 tablespoons olive oil. Set the pan aside. (Leave the oven on.)

To prepare the crostini, brush both sides of each bread slice with the olive oil, sprinkle with the parsley, and season with salt and pepper. Arrange the slices on a cookie sheet, place it in the oven, and bake until lightly toasted, about 7 minutes. Remove the crostini from the oven, spread about 2 tablespoons of the cooked greens on each one, and top each with 1 tablespoon of the goat cheese. Season with salt and pepper. Keep the crostini on the cookie sheet and warm them up right before serving them by placing them in a 350° oven until the cheese is warmed but not melted (about 7 minutes).

FOR SERVING:

1 head **frisée**

2 tablespoons minced **chives**

2 tablespoons minced **whole scallions**

Kosher salt

Freshly ground **black pepper**

Wash the frisée and snip the green tips off the leaves, leaving behind only the white and yellow part of the head. Cut the core off and tear the remaining leaves into medium pieces. Put the frisée in a salad bowl and reserve.

Reheat the beets over medium-high heat until warmed through, about 5 minutes. Add the warm beets to the frisée, sprinkle with the chives and scallions, and toss. Season the salad with salt and pepper to taste, and transfer it to a serving platter. Remove the crostini from the oven and arrange them around the beets. Serve immediately.

Heirloom Tomato Salad with Micro-greens, Burrata, and Balsamic-Basil Dressing

We grew up on Jersey tomatoes and we love them, don't get us wrong. But when we first tried California heirloom tomatoes, we were immediate converts. Their colors are vivid—we get everything from yellow to orange, pink, and even green—and during the summer their flavor is out of control. Plus, we're near a lot of local growers, which means we've got access to the freshest and tastiest of them all. For this recipe, we use Eric and Jasmine's microgreens and burrata, a fresh Italian cheese made from mozzarella and cream.

INGREDIENTS

12 ounces (about 3 balls) **burrata**

2 tablespoons **pine nuts**

1/4 cup **balsamic vinegar**

4 fresh **basil leaves**

1 tablespoon **Dijon mustard**

3/4 cup **rice bran oil** or **canola oil**

Kosher salt

Freshly ground **black pepper**

6 assorted **heirloom tomatoes**

2 cups (4 ounces) **microgreens**

1/4 cup **basil oil** (see page 235)

Serves 4

About 30 minutes before serving time, pull the burrata from the refrigerator and set it aside to come to room temperature.

Meanwhile, adjust the oven rack to the middle position and preheat the oven to 350°F.

Place the pine nuts on a cookie sheet and toast them in the oven until lightly browned, about 7 minutes. Let the nuts cool completely.

To make the dressing, put the vinegar, basil, mustard, and pine nuts in a blender and purée until smooth. With the blender running, add the rice bran oil or canola oil in a slow, steady stream, blending until the dressing is thick and emulsified. Season with 1 teaspoon salt and 1/4 teaspoon pepper, and set it aside.

Cut the burrata balls in half and season them generously with salt and pepper.

Cut the tomatoes into 1/4-inch-thick slices and arrange them on a serving platter. Season them generously with salt and pepper, and drizzle with some of the balsamic-basil dressing. In a mixing bowl, toss the greens with 1 tablespoon of the dressing; arrange them on top of the tomatoes. Place the burrata halves on top of the greens, soft center up, and finish with a drizzle of basil oil.

Grilled Prime Rib Steak with Red Wine Sauce

Grilled meat is very American, and grilling over a wood fire is very Big Sur Bakery—it's one of our favorite ways to prepare food. We consider ourselves to be a meat-and-potatoes restaurant because steak and potatoes never go out of style, and a good steak can satisfy the soul. Since fat means flavor, our prime rib steak has a silken outside layer of it and a marbling of fat throughout the meat. Our steaks come from the rib or the loin section and are always dry-aged. Be sure to buy your meat from a reputable source and go for the dry aging—it makes a real difference in the flavor.

INGREDIENTS

FOR THE RED WINE SAUCE:

1 tablespoon **unsalted butter**

1 tablespoon **rice bran oil** or **canola oil**

1 **shallot,** sliced

1 tablespoon **all-purpose flour**

1 cup **red wine,** preferably the kind you'll be drinking with dinner

2 cups **beef broth** (see page 60)

Kosher salt

Freshly ground **black pepper**

FOR THE STEAKS:

4 **boneless steaks** cut from prime rib, about 10 ounces each

2 tablespoons **black peppercorns**

1/4 cup minced **flat-leaf parsley**

Kosher salt

Serves 4

Make the red wine sauce first: Melt the butter in a small saucepan over medium-high heat. Add the oil and shallots and sauté until they're caramelized, about 7 minutes. Add the flour, mix it with the shallots and butter, and cook for 2 minutes. Then deglaze the pan with 1/4 cup of the red wine, scraping any brown bits from the bottom with a wooden spoon. Pour in the rest of the wine and whisk to help dissolve the flour. Add the beef broth, and season lightly with salt and pepper. Bring to a simmer and reduce, skimming the surface with a spoon or a ladle every once in a while to remove the foam that forms on the top, until the sauce is thick enough to coat the back of a spoon, about 30 minutes. Strain the sauce through a fine-mesh sieve into a bowl, and discard the shallots. Return the sauce to the pan. Check the seasoning, and add more salt and pepper if necessary. Keep warm over very low heat until ready to serve.

Remove the steaks from the refrigerator, arrange them on a plate, and allow them to come to room temperature, 15 to 30 minutes.

Meanwhile, preheat your grill, burning the wood down until you have a red-hot coal base. (See page 244 for preparing a wood-fired grill.)

Crack the peppercorns by placing them on a flat surface, like a cutting board, and pressing them with the flat bottom of a heavy pan until they split into pieces.

Season the steaks on both sides with the cracked pepper, the parsley, and salt to taste. Place them on the grill and leave them alone, giving the outside ample time to caramelize. When you can see that the meat has distinct grill marks, flip the steaks over and cook to your desired doneness—we recommend rare to medium-rare.

Remove the steaks from the grill, and let the meat rest for 3 minutes. Then serve, with the red wine sauce on the side.

Grilled Mackerel

Wayne went fishing for rockfish but instead hit on a school of mackerel, which he offered to us—so we got about twenty pounds of the most dazzling fish. With fish this fresh, simple is best: Phil fillets and debones them, brushes on some oil, and puts them on the grill. Finish it off with a squeeze of lemon juice or maybe a drizzle of great olive oil and balsamic vinegar. Grilled fresh mackerel pairs particularly well with sliced heirloom tomatoes and shaved fennel.

INGREDIENTS

4 fresh **mackerels,** filleted, with skin on and pin bones removed

1/4 cup **rice bran oil** or **canola oil**

6 tablespoons **chopped flat-leaf parsley**

Kosher salt

Freshly ground **black pepper**

2 **lemons,** preferably Meyer lemons, cut into wedges

Serves 4

Preheat the grill 30 minutes in advance, burning the wood down until you have a red-hot coal base. You don't want flames touching your fish. (See page 244 for preparing a wood-fired grill.)

Brush the mackerel fillets with the oil and sprinkle the parsley over them. Season them generously with salt and pepper. Grill them, skin side down, until flesh is opaque, 2 to 3 minutes. (Since mackerel skin is very thin and delicate, try not to move the fish until the skin begins to crisp up and get some color.)

Serve the grilled mackerel warm or at room temperature, accompanied by lemon wedges.

Apple Upside-Down Cake

For this recipe, we decided not to resort to the overused combination of apples and cinnamon and opted instead for nutmeg and vanilla to enhance the apple flavors. The cake, covered in caramel-soaked apples, goes particularly well with unsweetened whipped cream or vanilla ice cream.

INGREDIENTS

FOR THE APPLE BUTTER:

1 **vanilla bean**

6 **apples** (golden delicious, honey crisp, or Granny Smith), peeled, cored, and cut into 1/2-inch cubes

Juice of 1 **lemon wedge**

1/4 cup **apple juice**

2 teaspoons **freshly grated nutmeg**

1/4 cup **sugar**

FOR THE CARAMEL APPLES:

1/4 cup **unsalted butter**, softened

1 1/4 cups **sugar**

5 **apples**, peeled, cored, and each cut into 8 wedges

FOR THE CAKE:

1/2 cup **unsalted butter**, softened

1 cup (packed) **light** or **dark brown sugar**

1/2 teaspoon **kosher salt**

2 teaspoons **baking powder**

1 teaspoon **freshly grated nutmeg**

1 **egg**, beaten

1 3/4 cups **all-purpose flour**

Serves 8 to 10

Begin with the apple butter: Split the vanilla bean lengthwise with a paring knife, scrape out the pulp with the back of the knife, and put the pulp and the pod in a medium saucepan. Add the apples, a few drops of lemon juice, and the apple juice, nutmeg, and sugar. Cover and cook over medium heat until the apples are steamed and soft, 7 to 10 minutes. Smash the apples with the back of a wooden spoon until they form a sauce. Cook over low heat, stirring frequently to allow the excess moisture to evaporate, for another 10 to 15 minutes. The apple butter is ready when it becomes thicker and smoother and has a rich tan color. Let the apple butter cool to room temperature. Remove the vanilla pod.

Adjust the oven rack to the middle position and preheat the oven to 350°F.

To make the caramel apples, cream the butter and sugar in an electric mixer fitted with the paddle attachment for 1 to 2 minutes. Transfer the mixture to a 10-inch cast-iron skillet and cook over medium heat until it caramelizes to a deep golden brown, about 7 to 10 minutes. Carefully add the apple wedges, transfer the skillet to the oven, and bake for about 15 minutes, until the apples are tender but still retain their shape. Remove from the oven and let them cool completely in the skillet. (Leave the oven on.)

While the apples are cooling down, prepare the cake batter: Cream the butter, brown sugar, salt, baking powder, and nutmeg in an electric mixer fitted with the paddle attachment. Add the egg and 1 cup of the apple butter, and mix to combine. Add the flour and mix until just incorporated—be careful not to overmix the batter or the cake will be tough. Pour the cake batter directly over the caramel apples in the cast-iron skillet, and bake for 35 to 45 minutes. The cake is ready when a skewer inserted in the center comes out clean. Remove from the oven and let it cool slightly.

Using a pair of kitchen towels or oven mitts, invert the cake: Place a plate that's larger than the skillet over the top of the cake. Holding the skillet on the bottom, assertively flip the skillet and plate over together, inverting the cake onto the plate. Slowly lift off the skillet. If any apples stick to the skillet, remove them with a spatula and put them back on the cake. Let the cake sit for at least 20 minutes before cutting and serving it.

October

Phil
and Michelle

By the time they opened the Bakery, Phil and Michelle had already been together for years. They grew up in neighboring towns in New Jersey—their grandparents actually raised their parents on the same boulevard in Newark—and when Phil was nineteen and Michelle was seventeen, they met at a party in Phil's hometown of Metuchen. Phil, who was in college studying architecture, had just been in a major car accident and was taking time off to recover from multiple skull fractures. Michelle was still in high school. She likes to say that Phil spent the whole party ignoring her—but when he found out that she drove a 1967 Ford Mustang, he started to pay attention. She let him take it for a drive and, well, they've been together ever since.

When we got married on October 1, 2005, no one was surprised—after all, we'd been dating for over a decade. Originally we didn't think we were going to have our wedding in Big Sur, but then one day at the Bakery, a friend of ours offered to let us have the ceremony on her property. Her place is beautiful, with a terraced lawn right on the edge of a cliff overlooking the Pacific, but at first we didn't think we could take her up on it—she and her husband have a deal where one person isn't allowed to offer their property unless they've cleared it with the other person first. And besides, why would someone volunteer to host a hundred-person wedding at their private home?

But then a couple of days later her husband came into the Bakery and pulled us aside. "If you don't have your wedding at our house because you don't want to, that's fine," he said. "But if you don't have your wedding at our house because you think you'd be imposing on us, then I'll never eat at your restaurant again."

He left us no choice. We had the wedding on their property, and it couldn't have been a more beautiful spot: a three-tiered lawn, a gorgeous home, lavender and wildflowers, and a panoramic view of the ocean. We got married right on the edge of the cliff and then went up to the second tier where long banquet tables were set up on the lawn. Chuckie, who was then our sous-chef, led a drum procession (that's what happens when you get married in Big Sur), and we celebrated our wedding as the sun set over the Pacific.

When people ask us what it's like to run a restaurant as a couple, they're usually pretty surprised at our answer: we love it. We spent a lot of the past ten years working on different schedules or at different restaurants, and we usually didn't have much time off together. Even in Los Angeles when we were both working at Campanile, we were apart—the bakery and the kitchen were separated by the dining room floor, and with the chef (Phil) working

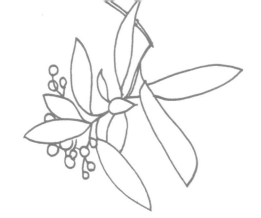

nights and the baker (Michelle) working days, we basically never saw each other. We used to joke that that was how we made our relationship work, especially in the early years.

But these days, we're always together. The Bakery is our life. Even when we go on vacation, we're constantly brainstorming about things we want to do when we get back.

The thing that makes it work is probably the fact that cooking and baking have very separate responsibilities and require different skills. Michelle enjoys the schedule and repetition of baking: if you're going to make five hundred cookies, you know exactly what you need to do before you even start. Phil, on the other hand, doesn't have that kind of attention span. He needs to be doing fifty things at once, finds unpredictability thrilling, and hates being around chocolate or anything sticky.

Even though we spend a huge amount of time together, we rarely fight. That's probably because we know each other so well that it's easy to figure out when one of us needs some time alone. Phil will play music and go to the beach, and Michelle will read or take walks with friends—we manage to be very independent despite the fact that our work and home lives are so intertwined. And we're especially lucky because our house consists of two parts: one section has a bedroom and band room, where Phil hangs out, and down a little hill is our living room and kitchen (which we never use), where Michelle goes to read and relax. Eventually we'd like to have a place where you don't have to go outside to get to the living room, but this is okay for now.

The best moments in the Bakery for us as a couple are the times when we get to work on food together, Phil doing the savory part, Michelle working on the dough or crust. We also love being alone in the kitchen together, but that hardly ever happens anymore. It's one of the best parts about Thanksgiving: a day in the kitchen together, working pretty much alone, on dishes that highlight what we each do best.

The other thing we tell people when they ask how we manage our relationship as spouses and business partners is that running a restaurant takes so much work that if you want to be married at the same time, you need to have a spouse who's as into the project as you are. Looking at things that way, our situation makes sense. We're married to the Bakery and we're married to each other. As long as we keep in mind which of those relationships is ultimately more important, it's an arrangement that works.

PROFILE: PHILIP / CHIEF

Pr: No. 8

Name: Philip Wojtowicz   Occupation: chef

How does your day start? It doesn't really start or stop— there's just a couple hours of sleep—

Date of Birth: August 22, 1974.   Signature: Philip Wojtowicz

How does it end?
With a couple glasses of wine. Actually the end of the day is the most stressful part because I have to see what we've used and what we have and figure out what to order.

Favorite time in the kitchen:
Probably between eight and nine in the morning. I roll out of bed, come straight to the Bakery, and have my first cup of coffee. If it's going to be a busy day, I'll start the soup. That wakes me up.

Best part about the Bakery:
I love the freedom—we get to do what we want our way. I feel like we're doing a good, honest thing. And the fact that we're in the middle of nowhere makes it more fun.

Would you ever have imagined yourself in Big Sur?
No. We were in Los Angeles following the same path that most young people who dedicate their lives to the cooking field follow. We broke away from that to come here.

Hard parts:
Most of our staff has minimal to no restaurant experience, so there's a huge curve in training. Also we don't have housing for our employees, which I hate. For a lot of the people who work here, this is a second job.

Favorite dishes to cook:
Lately I love cooking seared scallops, the smell of scallops, everything about them. But I love everything. I love perfect mashed potatoes. I love risotto. I love the roasted chicken— we've been serving it for six years and finally a week ago it's become what I'd consider a signature dish. That's the true test of an American chef: their chicken.

How do you keep learning?
I pull from everywhere. Farmers and purveyors contact me and colleagues ask questions. I'm always reading cookbooks—especially food history and chef biographies, things like that.

What is playing in the kitchen right now?
At least sometime during the day, the Clash will be played. Generally the Ramones fit in, too. But I like to let people play their own music, too.

Dream for the Bakery:
For this place to become a destination restaurant where people are coming specifically for the food—they're not necessarily just passing by.

Mentors? Heroes?
I don't really have a culinary hero, but I did have the luxury of working with a lot of great chefs: Joe Miller, Peter Roelant, Josiah Citrin, Mark Peel. They were all small independent restaurant owners running their own ships. The restaurants were like throwbacks to Europe even though they were highly Americanized.

Why California?
I think I should have been born here. I remember on the East Coast at like, three or four o'clock in the afternoon when the sun was overhead and heading west, I was always drawn to follow it. The California lifestyle was calling me.

PROFILE: MICHELLE / BAKER

Name: *Michelle Wojtowicz*   **Occupation:** *Baker*

Why Baking: *I love the idea of baking bread*
I'm a sucker for anything that's wholesome and simple.

Date of Birth: *October 4, 1976*   **Signature:** *Michelle Wojtowicz*

Pr: No. 9

What's the first thing you baked?
An apple pie for my grandfather. I saw a picture in a cookbook and then tried to make my apple pie look like it. When it came out I was disappointed. It seemed very challenging to be able to bake.

What was your first kitchen?
I worked in a restaurant called the Metuchen Inn in New Jersey—a fine dining restaurant in an old house.

Moment you realized you wanted to have a career in food:
The restaurant was newly opened and the chef was giving a lesson to the servers about how to explain his dishes. He spoke very eloquently about every ingredient. At that point I didn't even know you could have that level of understanding about food, and I thought, I want to know as much as this guy knows. I was seventeen.

Favorite things to bake:
I love making a really nice pie. I think it's one of the hardest things to do, no matter how many times you do it.

How much time do you spend at home?
The Bakery is like our home. We eat our meals here, we drink our coffee here, we have the majority of our interactions with friends here.

Describe your house's kitchen:
We don't even have an oven. We recently bought a camping stove with a propane tank attached, but we've never used it. The only two appliances we use to cook are an electric teapot and a popcorn maker. We do have a fridge but I don't even know why we keep it on sometimes.

Could you ever leave Big Sur?
Originally, Phil wanted to move here but I didn't. Then about two years into it he wanted to go, and I wouldn't. I'm just so proud of what we do here and feel so involved in the community. It'd be really hard for me to leave.

Favorite types of customers:
The ones who think they've pulled up to a roadside greasy spoon and then have an experience they never expected. A lot of people feel like it's a special place that they've personally discovered—they'll go home and say, I found this great place in Big Sur right behind a gas station.

What's your goal?
I'm not trying to reinvent the wheel, or create things people have never had before. I'm more the type of person who just wants to eat the best vanilla ice cream I've ever had, and bake a pie that I imagine rivals my great-grandmother's.

Yam and Sweet Potato Pie

Regular sharp cheddar works well in this pie, but we particularly love it with Cypress Grove Chevre's goat's-milk cheddar (see Resources)—it has a nice flavor that contrasts well with the sweetness of the potatoes and the yams. You can serve this straight out of the oven, but it looks even better if you cool it overnight, cut it into squares, and serve it with long-cooked greens, stewed leeks, or grilled fennel.

INGREDIENTS

1 tablespoon **rice bran oil** or **canola oil**

4 **egg yolks**

1 cup **heavy cream**

1 tablespoon **kosher salt**

¼ teaspoon freshly ground **black pepper**

2 medium **sweet potatoes,** peeled and sliced lengthwise into 1/8-inch-thick pieces

6 ounces **cheddar,** grated

2 medium **yams,** peeled and sliced lengthwise into 1/8-inch-thick pieces

Serves 6 to 8

Adjust the oven rack to the middle position and preheat the oven to 350°F.

Brush a 9 by 13-inch ceramic baking dish with the oil.

Whisk the egg yolks and cream together in a bowl. Season with the salt and pepper. Add the sliced sweet potatoes and toss them in the mixture. Form a layer of sliced sweet potatoes in the baking dish, overlapping them slightly so that the bottom is completely covered. Sprinkle the grated cheddar on top. Toss the sliced yams in the remaining cream mixture, and layer them on top of the cheese, just as you did with the sweet potatoes. Cover the baking dish with aluminum foil and bake for 1 hour, or until the yams and sweet potatoes are soft all the way through. Then remove the foil and bake for another 15 minutes.

Remove the dish from the oven and let it sit for at least 15 minutes before serving. (Or refrigerate it overnight. The next day, slice the pie into squares, reheat it in a 350°F oven, and serve.)

Stuffed Acorn Squash with Apples, Leeks, Mushrooms, and Walnuts

This recipe takes a bit of prep time, but once all the components are prepared, it's really easy to put together—and the filling's so satisfying that we think the effort's worth it. (It's also a good vegetarian entree.) The size of acorn squash makes them great vessels for a combination of fruit, nuts, and vegetables. Cut them in half, remove the seeds, and you have a perfect edible bowl. Finish with a drizzle of sage brown butter.

INGREDIENTS

FOR THE STUFFED ACORN SQUASH:

1/3 cup **walnut halves**

2 small **acorn squash**

5 tablespoons **unsalted butter**

1/4 cup **light brown sugar**

1/2 teaspoon **ground cinnamon**

Kosher salt

Freshly ground **black pepper**

1 medium **apple**, peeled, cored, and cubed

2 tablespoons **rice bran oil** or **canola oil**

3 cups **white button mushrooms**, quartered

2 tablespoons **dry white wine**

1 cup **stewed leeks** (opposite)

1 tablespoon minced **flat-leaf parsley**

1 tablespoon minced **chives**

1 whole **scallion**, trimmed and thinly sliced

1 small **shallot**, minced

FOR THE SAGE BROWN BUTTER:

6 tablespoons **unsalted butter**

2 fresh **sage leaves**, minced

Serves 4

Adjust the oven rack to the middle position and preheat the oven to 350°F.

Scatter the walnuts on a cookie sheet and toast them in the oven until they're golden through the center, 10 to 12 minutes. (To check if they're done, cut one open and inspect the color inside.) Set the walnuts aside. (Leave the oven on.)

Cut each squash in half through its equator and trim off just enough of the top and root ends so that the squash halves can sit flat. Scoop out and discard the seeds. Place the halves on a baking sheet, cavity side up. Melt 2 tablespoons of the butter, and brush it over the flesh of the squash halves. Combine the brown sugar and the cinnamon in a bowl, and sprinkle this mixture over the squash. Season with salt and pepper. Bake until the squash are soft, about 45 minutes.

While the squash are cooking, heat a sauté pan over high heat and add 2 tablespoons of the butter. Add the apples, season them very lightly with salt and pepper, and sauté until they are soft but still hold their shape, about 5 minutes. Set the apples aside.

Sauté the mushrooms next: Heat a large sauté pan over high heat, drizzle the oil into it, and add 1 tablespoon of the butter. Let the butter melt. Then add the mushrooms, season with salt and pepper, and sauté until they're soft, about 5 minutes. Deglaze the sauté pan with the white wine, scraping any brown bits from the bottom with a wooden spoon. Set the sauté pan aside.

Prepare the filling by combining the walnuts, apples, mushrooms, leeks, parsley, chives, scallions, and shallots in a medium bowl. Season the filling with salt and pepper to taste.

Remove the squash from the oven, and raise the oven temperature to 400°F.

Stuff each squash half with a heaping ½ cup of the filling, and roast in the oven for 15 to 20 minutes, until the filling is warmed through. Transfer the squash to a platter.

While the squash is roasting, make the sage brown butter. Melt the butter over medium-high heat, and cook until the butter separates and the white solids start to brown and smell nutty, about 7 minutes. Add the minced sage, and drizzle the warm brown butter over the stuffed squash. Serve immediately.

Stewed Leeks

Stewing leeks gives them a sweet onion flavor and a velvety texture. They're especially good with the yam and sweet potato pie (see page 146). They're also one of the building blocks for stuffed acorn squash (opposite). You can make them a day ahead. (The photograph on page 147 shows the leeks.)

INGREDIENTS

3 medium **leeks**

1 cup **unsalted butter**

1 cup **chicken stock** (see page 239)

Kosher salt

Freshly ground **black pepper**

Serves 4

Cut off the dark green end of the leeks, leaving behind the white bulb and the beginnings of the green stem. Slice the leeks into ¼-inch-thick coins. Thoroughly wash the leeks in a bowl of cold water, separating the rings to get out any residual dirt. Drain off the water and wash them again—no one likes gritty leeks.

Once they're clean, place the leeks in a saucepan and add the butter and stock. Season them lightly with salt and pepper, and cook over medium-low heat until they are tender, 10 to 12 minutes. Check the seasoning, and add more salt and pepper if necessary.

Roasted Chicken

Chicken has to be the most widely eaten bird in the world. That said, Phil believes that it's possible to rate the caliber of a chef by his chicken. Our roasted half chicken, served with garlic gravy, is one of our most popular dishes, and it stands up to the test. We buy fresh free-range organic chickens, and we do very little to them: debone the legs and thighs, brine them overnight, stuff them with herbs, garlic, and lemon, and finally roast them in the wood-fired oven.

INGREDIENTS

1 free-range **organic chicken,** 3 to 4 pounds

2 cups **kosher salt**

1/2 cup **light brown sugar**

2 **bay leaves**

5 **black peppercorns**

1 **lemon,** sliced into coins

1 **garlic clove,** sliced

1 tablespoon **flat-leaf parsley leaves**

2 tablespoons **olive oil**

3 **celery stalks**

Serves 2

Carefully debone the legs and thighs while leaving them attached to the chicken.

Fill a large pot with 5 quarts water and bring it to a boil over high heat. Turn off the heat. Add the salt, brown sugar, bay leaves, and peppercorns and stir until the salt and sugar are fully dissolved. Set the brine aside to cool completely.

Once the brine has cooled, put the chicken in the pot and set a heavy plate on top of it to keep it submerged. Cover the pot with plastic wrap, put it in the refrigerator, and let it sit for 8 to 12 hours.

Pull the chicken out of the brine, rinse it under cold running water, and pat it dry with paper towels. Discard the brine. Leave the chicken out until it comes to room temperature, about 15 minutes.

Adjust the oven rack to the middle position and preheat the oven to 425°F.

Using your fingers to separate the skin from the meat, slide a lemon slice, a few garlic slices, and 1 teaspoon of the parsley leaves under the skin of each breast. Put the remaining lemon slices, garlic slices, and parsley leaves in the chicken cavity. Close the cavity by crossing the legs and securing them together with a wooden or metal skewer.

Brush the chicken with the olive oil. Cut each celery stalk in half crosswise. In a roasting pan, arrange the celery pieces in a line like ties on a railroad track (you're creating a base to prevent the chicken from sticking to the pan). Lay the chicken right on top of the celery. Roast the chicken for 20 minutes, until the skin starts to develop a tan color. Then reduce the oven temperature to 350°F and roast for another 50 to 60 minutes, until its internal temperature is 165°F. (Use a meat thermometer to take the temperature, inserting it between the breast and the thigh and making sure it isn't touching the bone.) Allow the chicken to rest for 10 minutes before carving.

To split the chicken in half, separate the breasts by making a long cut along the spine with a sharp knife to reveal the bone. Carefully carve each breast off the carcass and cut the joint that keeps the wing bone attached, while keeping the breast connected to the leg and thigh. Transfer to a serving platter or two separate plates, and serve immediately.

Quail Stuffed with Chanterelles and Foie Gras, with Polenta and Jus

Quail is a chef's bird: one bird is the perfect size for an appetizer, and two make an entree. If the idea of dealing with a whole quail seems intimidating, you can buy your quail semi-boneless (in fact, many grocery stores sell quail only this way).

INGREDIENTS

FOR THE JUS:

1 tablespoon **rice bran oil** or **canola oil**

1 tablespoon **unsalted butter**

1 **shallot**, sliced

1 cup **dry red wine**

1 tablespoon **all-purpose flour**

1 **star anise pod**

2 cups **beef broth** (see page 60)

Kosher salt

Freshly ground **black pepper**

FOR THE POLENTA:

4 cups **whole milk**

2 **garlic cloves**

2 **thyme sprigs**

1 cup **coarsely ground polenta**

3 cups **chicken stock** (see page 239)

Kosher salt

Freshly ground **black pepper**

1/4 cup **grated Parmesan**

Serves 4 as an appetizer

Start with the jus: Heat a medium saucepan over medium heat, and drizzle the oil into it. Add the butter and wait until it melts. Then add the shallots and sauté until they're well caramelized, 7 to 10 minutes. Deglaze the pan with 1/4 cup of the red wine, scraping any brown bits from the bottom with a wooden spoon. Whisk in the flour, and add the remaining wine and the star anise. Reduce over medium-low heat for about 5 minutes, until the liquid has thickened. Then add the beef broth, season with salt and pepper, and cook for 20 minutes, until the sauce is thick enough to coat the back of a spoon. Make sure not to let the sauce boil, and skim the surface with a spoon or a ladle every once in a while to remove the foam that forms. Strain the sauce through a fine-mesh sieve into a bowl. Check the seasoning, and add more salt and pepper if necessary. Return the strained sauce to the saucepan and set it aside.

Prepare the polenta: Combine the milk, garlic, and thyme sprigs in a medium saucepan and heat until the milk just begins to boil. Remove the garlic and thyme with a slotted spoon and discard them. Pour the polenta into the milk and stir until smooth. Reduce the heat to medium-low and add 1 cup of the stock. Cook the polenta slowly, stirring it frequently and gradually adding the remaining 2 cups stock, for 45 minutes to 1 hour. Remove the pan from the heat and season the polenta with salt and pepper. Set it aside. (Do not use the Parmesan yet.)

Clean the chanterelles using a dry pastry brush to gently dust off all the dirt; then cut them into uniform small pieces. Heat a large sauté pan over medium-high heat and drizzle the oil into it. Add the butter and wait until it starts to brown. Then add the mushrooms, tossing them quickly with a wooden spoon to coat them with the oil and butter. Cook the mushrooms until they start to shrink and release their liquid, about 3 minutes. Stir in the shallots, preserved garlic, parsley, and thyme. Deglaze the pan with the white wine, scraping any brown bits from the bottom with a wooden spoon. Continue to cook until the liquid has evaporated, about 2 minutes. Season the chanterelles with salt and pepper to taste, and set them aside to cool.

FOR THE CHANTERELLES:

8 ounces **fresh chanterelles**

1 tablespoon **rice bran oil**
or **canola oil**

1 tablespoon **unsalted butter**

1/2 **shallot,** minced

1 1/2 teaspoons **preserved garlic**
(see page 234)

1 1/2 teaspoons minced
flat-leaf parsley

Leaves from 2 **thyme sprigs**

1 tablespoon **dry white wine**

Kosher salt

Freshly ground **black pepper**

FOR THE QUAIL:

3 tablespoons **rice bran oil**
or **canola oil**

1/2 small **yellow onion,**
finely chopped

1/2 small **carrot,** finely chopped

1/2 **celery stalk,** finely chopped

4 ounces **foie gras,**
cut into 4 chunks

Kosher salt

Freshly ground **black pepper**

4 **quail,** semi-boneless

Four 4-inch **bamboo skewers**

To make the stuffing for the quail, heat a sauté pan over medium-high heat and drizzle 1 tablespoon of the oil into it. Add the onions, carrots, and celery, and sauté until the vegetables are soft, about 5 minutes. Transfer the vegetables to a plate and let them cool.

Season the foie gras pieces generously with salt and pepper, and place one piece in the cavity of each quail. Combine the cooked vegetables and the chanterelles, and divide the mixture evenly among the quail, stuffing it around the foie gras. Season the skin of the quail generously with salt and pepper. Cross the legs to close the cavity, and secure with a skewer.

Adjust the oven rack to the middle position and preheat the oven to 350°F.

Heat a large cast-iron skillet over high heat, and drizzle the remaining 2 tablespoons oil into it. Place the birds, breast side down, in the pan (you might need to work in batches). Cook the quail until the skin is golden, about 3 minutes. Flip the birds over and cook for 2 to 3 minutes, until the other side is golden as well. Cook the quail on both remaining sides for 1 minute apiece. Once their skins have been seared, place the quail on a baking sheet, and roast in the oven for 4 to 5 minutes. When they are done, the skin will be a nice golden brown all around and the meat will be pink.

While the quail is roasting, reheat the jus in the saucepan over medium-low heat. Taste the polenta, and add more salt and pepper if needed. Stir the Parmesan into the polenta.

Polenta will retain heat for a long time. If the polenta has cooled too much, reheat it slightly over medium heat, stirring until warm.

To serve, spoon the polenta onto a platter, arrange the quail on top, and drizzle the jus over the birds and around the polenta.

Quince Paste

We get our quince from the ranch we live on. There are two trees, and once our landlords have taken their fill for jams and fruit leather, we get the leftovers. (The trees are so productive that we easily have enough quince to last through the fall.)

Quince looks like a bumpy yellow cross between an apple and a pear. Inside, its seeds resemble an apple's, but don't be fooled: the flesh is extremely astringent and can't be eaten raw. But once you start to cook a quince, something magical happens. The flesh transforms from white to light pink to a beautiful translucent red and gives off a unique floral, fruity scent.

Quince paste is often paired with hard, salty cheeses like Manchego, but at the Bakery we use it more in desserts like stollen or panforte. You can also fold it into rice pudding or just cut it into small pieces, toss it in sugar, and serve it as dessert on its own.

INGREDIENTS

1 tablespoon **rice bran oil** or **canola oil**

1 **vanilla bean**

1 cup **dry white wine**

1 cup **orange juice**

1 **cinnamon stick**

6 **quinces**, peeled, cored, and quartered

Sugar

Makes eighty 1-inch squares

Line an 8 by 10-inch baking sheet with parchment paper. Brush the paper with the oil.

Split the vanilla bean lengthwise with a paring knife, scrape out the pulp with the back of the knife, and put the pulp and the pod into a large pot. Add 1 cup water and the wine, orange juice, and cinnamon stick. Add the quince and cook over high heat until tender, about 15 minutes.

Remove and discard the vanilla bean and the cinnamon stick. Purée the quince, with the cooking liquid, in a food processor or blender. Weigh the resulting purée and put it back in the pot. Add an equal amount of sugar to the quince purée in a one-to-one ratio—as in 1 pound sugar for every 1 pound purée.

Cook the quince purée over medium-low heat, stirring constantly with a wooden spoon, until the paste is very thick and the quince has turned from a light pink to a translucent burnt orange, 45 minutes to 1 hour. (Be careful—the mixture will bubble and spurt like a volcano and can leave nasty burns. We recommend wearing a long-sleeved shirt and an oven mitt.) Spread the paste onto the prepared baking sheet and refrigerate it until the paste is firm, about 2 hours.

Once the paste has set, invert the pan over a cutting board lined with plastic wrap and lift off the parchment. Cut the paste into 1-inch squares or into your desired shapes. Store the paste in an airtight container in the refrigerator; it'll keep for months.

Pumpkin Bread

Baked daily all fall, this is one of our favorite seasonal breads. We serve it on our bread plate and use it to make French toast for brunch—and since the bread itself is actually shaped like a pumpkin, it's a nice gift and looks great on display. If your spices have been sitting on the shelf for a while, buy fresh whole spices and grind them right before using them—it'll make a difference. Michelle uses organic canned pumpkin instead of fresh for this recipe, since fresh pumpkins tend to have different moisture levels that can affect the end result. She strains the pumpkin purée overnight to get rid of extra moisture. The result is a much more concentrated pumpkin flavor.

INGREDIENTS

1 pound canned **pumpkin purée**

10 whole **allspice berries**

4 whole **cloves**

1 teaspoon **ground cinnamon**

1 teaspoon **freshly grated nutmeg**

2 teaspoons **ground ginger**

2 teaspoons **active dry yeast**

4 3/4 cups **bread flour,** plus extra for dusting

1 tablespoon plus 1 teaspoon **powdered milk**

1 **egg**

1/2 cup plus 3 tablespoons (packed) **light** or **dark brown sugar**

1 tablespoon **fine sea salt**

1/4 cup **unsalted butter,** softened

Makes 2 loaves

Start the night before: Put the pumpkin purée in a sheet of cheesecloth. Bundle it up and tie it. Put a rack inside a large pan, suspend the bundle over the rack, and let it drain in the refrigerator overnight to release the excess moisture, leaving behind only the dense pulp.

The next day, remove the pan from the refrigerator. Discard the liquid collected in the bottom, and reserve the pulp in the cheesecloth.

Grind the allspice and cloves in a spice grinder, and combine with the cinnamon, nutmeg, and ginger.

Pour 1 cup plus 2 tablespoons lukewarm water into a bowl, and rain the yeast over it. Stir, and set it aside to activate for 5 minutes.

In an electric mixer fitted with the dough hook attachment, combine the yeast mixture with 3 cups of the flour and the powdered milk, egg, brown sugar, sea salt, and pumpkin purée on very low speed. Over a 1-minute period, add the spice mixture and the remaining 1 3/4 cups flour, a scoop at a time. Add the butter and mix until combined. Turn the speed up to medium and mix for 2 minutes. Stop the mixer, scrape down the sides of the bowl with a rubber spatula (the dough should be sticky), and then mix on high speed for 5 minutes. The dough will become shiny, somewhat firm, and less sticky. Transfer the dough to a bowl that's large enough for the dough to double in size. Place the bowl in a large plastic bag, tie it loosely, and set it aside in a warm place in the kitchen until the dough has doubled in size, 1 to 1 1/2 hours.

Turn the dough onto a floured surface and divide it in half. Pinch off a nugget of dough about the size of a walnut from each of these halves; these will be used as the stems of the pumpkins. At this point you should have two large pieces of dough and two walnut-size pieces. Flatten each of the dough pieces with the palm of your hand and roll them into loose balls. Cover with a plastic bag and let them rest for 10 to 15 minutes.

Reshape the dough pieces into tight balls. Line two medium bowls with a linen napkin and dust them generously with flour. Put one of the large dough balls in each bowl. Top each large ball with a small dough ball. Loosely cover each bowl with plastic wrap, giving it room to expand, and let the dough rise in a warm place in the kitchen until doubled in size, 1 to 1 1/2 hours.

Meanwhile, adjust the oven rack to the middle position and put a baking stone on it. Place a cast-iron skillet on the bottom rack of the oven and fill it 2 inches deep with water (to increase the level of moisture inside the oven). Preheat the oven to 450°F.

Gently turn one of the pumpkin breads into your hands. Put the bread on a floured pizza peel (a flat wooden or metal shovel with a long handle) with the stem side up. With a razor blade or a sharp paring knife, make 1/4-inch-deep cuts into the bread, from the stem to the bottom, to create the ribs of the pumpkin. Immediately slide the bread directly onto the baking stone. Reduce the oven temperature to 375°F and bake for 35 to 45 minutes, until golden brown.

While the first pumpkin bread is baking, place the second one in a cooler spot to prevent it from over-proofing.

The bread is done when a thermometer inserted in the middle reads 200°F. Transfer it to a wire rack and let it cool for at least 1 hour before cutting.

Repeat the process for baking the second pumpkin.

November

Thanksgiving

Thanksgiving always seems to be the purest expression of what we do at the Bakery. It isn't about making a buck—it's about creating an amazing meal, gathering friends and family around large tables next to a glowing fire, and taking time to appreciate all that we have. It's about reliving memories and creating new ones, inundating our senses with the smells and tastes of turkey and stuffing and pumpkin pie. A perfect Thanksgiving comforts; it brings people together. It forces you to slow down, even if only because you've eaten too much to move.

At the Bakery, we create that Thanksgiving. We give the day off to as many of our staff as possible and do the cooking ourselves, working in near silence as we prepare the evening's feast. We've both spent plenty of holidays cooking in restaurant kitchens, but at the Bakery, the restaurant kitchen is our own, and in its stillness we find a quiet rhythm to our work. Phil brines the turkeys and chops the vegetables; Michelle turns out desserts, cranberry sauce, and loaves of savory bread, shaped like a pumpkin, that she bakes in our wood-fired oven. In some ways, Thanksgiving is simpler than other days at the Bakery: everyone eats the same meal, so our menu is straightforward. We try to make food that reminds people of their own family Thanksgivings—comforting and familiar—but we also want to serve them the best Thanksgiving dinner they've ever had.

On Thanksgiving we make the Bakery itself look more like a home than a restaurant—albeit a home with table service and no cleanup duties. Erik builds a pyramid of retro-style canned vegetables on the mantel and dangles frozen turkey dinner boxes from the ceiling as a reminder of what is *not* being served that night. A fire crackles, and as we cook in the kitchen, Erik and Mike pile pumpkins in corners and scatter golden sycamore leaves, gathered from a nearby creek bed, across the tables and the floor.

Throughout the day the Bakery fills with smells of vanilla, nutmeg, and ginger as Michelle pours fillings into pie crusts—delicious concoctions of pumpkin and sweet potato accented with cinnamon and clove and spiked with white pepper. And then there are her Parker House rolls: delicate and light, baked close together in the pan so that they need to be pulled apart at

the table. They take a lot of work—Michelle makes them only on Thanksgiving—but they're worth it, twice-brushed with butter and perfect for sopping up Phil's garlic gravy. Michelle used to hang a sign at the Bakery so that people could order the rolls for their own tables, but she got so many requests that now it's only by word of mouth. Yet somehow, every year the list grows.

Sometimes it's hard for us to appreciate our lives at the Bakery, when the road goes out or business is dead and we forget why the hell we decided to open a restaurant in Big Sur. But it's times like Thanksgiving, when we're surrounded by friends brought together over tables of our food, that remind us of how lucky we are. We choose our ingredients. We design our own menus. We've created a community at the restaurant that, in times like this, feels like family. For us, Thanksgiving in the Bakery is what it's all about.

As any true fan of Thanksgiving knows, the meal hasn't been a success unless it puts everyone into a coma afterward. Thank God, then, for the food. Starting at 3:30, heaping platters of Phil's creations emerge from the kitchen and are set down family-style at tables full of hungry guests.

We don't sit down to eat until 8:30, after everyone else has been served. There are usually a dozen or so people left by this point—our servers, our staff, and Big Sur locals who consider the restaurant a second home. We pull the tables together, Mike pours hearty glasses of wine, and then, finally, we get to enjoy what Phil's been working on all day: butternut squash soup, stuffed turkey legs, long-cooked greens with onion and garlic, herbed mashed potatoes. Just when it seems impossible to keep eating, out come Michelle's desserts: pumpkin and pecan pies, pear and quince crisp, apple confit, bread pudding. Thanksgiving is about tradition, not experimentation, so we limit our menu to food that people might see on their tables at home—only better.

As the evening wears on, we pass plates and make toasts. The fire burns down. Other friends, finished with their family Thanksgivings at home, drop by to say hello, share a glass of wine, and snag a slice of pie.

And then, finally, it's over, the last guest staggering out the door, a bag of leftovers in hand. Michelle sets aside turkey to use for sandwiches the next day, and Phil grabs the mangled carcasses for soup. Satisfied and stuffed, we stumble home to collapse, exhausted, into bed. Winter has officially begun.

PROFILE: ERIK / "THE EYE"

Name: Erik "the Eye" Semska   **Occupation:** Freelance bohemian.

Job at the Bakery: Cruising, color, design, and arrangement. In that order.

Age: I feel twenty-three. Michelle says I have the enthusiasm of a nine-year-old.

Though, at my age you just don't say.   **Signature:** Erik J Semska

Pr: No.10

Former jobs:
Growing plants for a nursery, freelance display work, a job in a mail-order warehouse for the Boston Museum of Fine Arts, where we shipped jigsaw puzzle reproductions of Chinese dragon bowls across America.

Former homes:
Clearwater, Florida. Boston, Brooklyn Heights, San Francisco.

Why Big Sur?
I moved down for a design job on a 560-acre ranch with no electricity in the mountains of Big Sur, living in a tiny hand-built redwood cabin from the '40s. When I got there it was a garbage-strewn, dope-growing, rat-infested squatter-house-slash-dumping-ground. I spent the next year painting every inch of it and decorating it with found objects. In the process, I fell in love with Big Sur, met the Bakery clan, and decided to stay and help them fix up their place.

How did you find the Bakery?
Coming from the Northeast makes you a complete snot about coffee, food, and pastries. I was working in this totally isolated cabin and needed human contact, so one day I came down here and I saw this funky little place that had just opened, and they had incredible bread and pastries and this great latte. I thought, Oh my God, this can be my Sunday routine. I'll get the *New York Times*, go down to the Bakery, and get really good coffee.

What was the Bakery like before you got there?
It was off to a good start; there was enough to keep me interested, but it was painted with a color that the eye did not approve of. It was the coffee from their bald genie barista and the fried egg sandwich that kept me here.

What are some of your artistic influences in Big Sur?
I love gathering natural flotsam and jetsam that have been pounded by the waves. I love driftwood, pieces of glass and rocks that have been made smooth by the ocean. As for color, I love the look of a 1950s color palette, the sort of shades found in paint-by-numbers. Sea glass and sea pottery find their place in my work—basically, if it's rusted and bent, I can't help picking it up.

What's hanging from the ceiling now?
An autumn display. It's modeled after the old-fashioned method of drying fruits, where people would hang them from wires in a drying room in the attic. I used real persimmons and pomegranates.

Describe the dynamics at the Bakery:
We're like a family. A big, dysfunctional family.

What is your relationship with Michelle?
Think father/daughter. Then see dysfunctional family comment above.

Butternut Squash Soup

Peter Roelant was one of the first chefs Phil worked for in Los Angeles. Swiss-born and trained in Europe by the famous Frédy Girardet, Peter was a follower of the culinary movement known as nouvelle cuisine, which strives for clean flavors and less fat. Our soups are inspired by that same philosophy.

Silky smooth and easy to make, this is a great starter for Thanksgiving dinner, or for any chilly evening. Puréed soups like this are a staple at the Big Sur Bakery, and they all share the same base: a mixture of vegetables such as carrots, onions, celery, serrano chile, garlic, and potatoes that are sweated until soft or browned at high temperature. (For the butternut squash soup, we caramelize the vegetables to add depth to their flavor.) Then we add an equal amount of whatever the primary vegetable is and purée everything together. For our puréed cauliflower soup, we omit the carrots and stick to a neutrally colored vegetable like fennel to keep the soup light.

INGREDIENTS

2 large **butternut squash**, about 5 pounds total

1/4 cup **rice bran oil** or **canola oil**

3 medium **yellow onions**, roughly chopped

3 **celery stalks**, roughly chopped

2 large **carrots**, roughly chopped

8 **garlic cloves**

1 small **serrano chile**

2 large **russet potatoes**, peeled and cubed

Kosher salt

1 1/2 quarts **chicken stock** (see page 239), plus extra if needed

Freshly ground **black pepper**

5 tablespoons **crème fraîche**

Serves 10

Peel the squash with a vegetable peeler. Cut them in half with a sharp knife, scoop out the seeds with a spoon, and cut the flesh into 2-inch pieces. Reserve.

Heat a large pot over medium-high heat, and drizzle the oil into it. Add the onions and sauté until lightly browned, about 5 minutes. Add the celery, carrots, garlic, and chile, and sauté until the vegetables begin to caramelize, 10 to 12 minutes.

Add the squash and cook for 10 minutes. Then add the potatoes, season with 2 tablespoons salt, and cover with the stock. Let the soup simmer over medium heat for 40 to 45 minutes, until the vegetables are very soft. Then purée the soup in a blender or food processor until smooth.

Return the puréed soup to the pot and check the consistency: the soup should be smooth and thick, but not as thick as baby food. If it is too thick, thin it out with additional chicken stock. If it's too thin, let the soup reduce over medium-low heat until it thickens to the desired consistency. Check the seasoning, and add pepper and more salt if necessary. Keep warm over very low heat until ready to serve.

Pour the soup into a tureen or into individual soup bowls. Garnish each portion with a dollop of crème fraîche, and serve.

Roasted Turkey Breast

Have you ever noticed how at Thanksgiving people often gravitate toward the moist turkey legs and leave the poor, dried-out breast sitting forlornly on the platter? Not so at the Bakery. We roast our turkey in two different stages to ensure that both the legs and the breast remain moist. The secret to the breast is brining it: leaving it to soak overnight keeps it moist and allows the flavors of the salt and pepper to penetrate the flesh thoroughly so that all the meat has flavor instead of just the skin. As for the legs, they've got their own recipe: deboned, butterflied, and stuffed with long-cooked greens (see opposite).

Come November, supermarkets are stocked to the ears with frozen turkeys. We believe in doing some research and finding a reputable and skilled butcher so you're able to purchase your organic, free-range turkey broken up in parts. To serve ten guests we recommend ordering 1 combined breast, 2 wings, 6 legs (deboned and butterflied), and 2 thighs on the bone. Those who are cooking for smaller groups of people can focus on just preparing the roasted turkey breast and skip the stuffed turkey legs . . . or vice versa. And you'll have plenty of parts for turkey stock.

INGREDIENTS

FOR THE BRINE:

2 cups **kosher salt**

1/2 cup (not packed) **light brown sugar**

2 **bay leaves**

5 **black peppercorns**

FOR THE TURKEY BREAST:

1 free-range **turkey breast**

2 **yellow onions**

2 tablespoons **unsalted butter, melted**

Kosher salt

Freshly ground **black pepper**

Serves 10

The day before Thanksgiving, fill a large pot with 5 quarts water and bring it to a boil over high heat. Turn off the heat. Add the salt, brown sugar, bay leaves, and peppercorns and stir until the salt and sugar are fully dissolved. Set the brine aside to cool completely.

Once the brine has cooled, put the turkey breast in it, placing a heavy plate on top to keep it submerged. Cover the pot with plastic wrap and let it sit for 24 hours in the refrigerator.

The next day, pull the breast out of the brine, rinse it under cold running water, and pat it dry with paper towels. Discard the brine. Leave the breast uncovered in the refrigerator until you're ready to roast it.

Adjust the oven rack to the middle position and preheat the oven to 425°F.

Slice both onions into four 1-inch-thick rings and lay them in a roasting pan (to use them as props under the turkey breast). Lay the breast right on top of the onions, and brush it with the melted butter. Season the skin with salt and pepper—but do so lightly, since the bird will already be salty from the brine.

Roast the turkey breast for 30 minutes. Then turn the oven temperature down to 375°F and continue to cook the turkey until its internal temperature is 165°F. (Use a meat thermometer to take the turkey's temperature, inserting it slightly off-center and not touching the bone.) This will take approximately 1 hour (10 to 12 minutes per pound).

Remove the roasting pan from the oven and allow the breast to rest for 20 minutes before carving it. (While roasting at high heat, the liquid in the meat will have traveled toward its surface. This cooling time allows the juice to be absorbed back into the meat, and helps ensure that it will stay moist.) Carve into 1/4-inch-thick slices at the table, and serve.

Turkey Legs Stuffed with Long-Cooked Greens

We use long-cooked greens to stuff our turkey legs—the onion and garlic add a great flavor to the meat—but you can also serve them on their own. Our greens recipe pays homage to Southern cooking; it's a simple comfort food with only a few ingredients and no fancy knife skills required. We use big onion slices, whole garlic cloves, hot red pepper flakes for heat, and sturdy greens like escarole, chard, beet greens, collards, or frisée. Mix and match your own, grab a glass of wine, and let them cook. This recipe isn't about being in a rush.

INGREDIENTS

FOR THE LONG-COOKED GREENS:

3 pounds **assorted greens,** such as beet greens, escarole, chard, collards, and/or frisée

1/4 cup **olive oil**

10 small **yellow onions,** cut into 1/4-inch-thick slices

10 **garlic cloves**

1 teaspoon **hot red pepper flakes**

1/4 cup **red wine vinegar**

2 tablespoons **kosher salt,** plus extra if needed

FOR THE STUFFED TURKEY LEGS:

6 **turkey legs,** deboned and butterflied

Kosher salt

Freshly ground **black pepper**

3 tablespoons **rice bran oil** or **canola oil**

3 cups **turkey stock** (see pages 169) or **chicken stock** (see pages 239)

Serves 10

Prepare the long-cooked greens first: Wash the greens, but don't run them through a salad spinner. Leaving them slightly wet will help add moisture while they're cooking.

Heat a large pot over low heat. Add the olive oil, onions, garlic, and red pepper flakes, and cover with a lid. Cook for 12 minutes, until the onions are translucent. Pour in the red wine vinegar, toss in the damp greens, and sprinkle with the salt.

Cook the greens over very low heat, covered, stirring them occasionally, for 45 minutes to 1 hour. You're not in a rush—the slow cooking allows the greens' complex flavors to develop. The greens are finished when they're tender to the bite and have a deep dark green color. Check the seasoning and add more salt if needed. Transfer the greens to a dish and let them cool.

Adjust the oven rack to the middle position and preheat the oven to 350°F.

Spread the turkey legs on a flat surface and put 1/2 cup of the long-cooked greens in the center of each leg. Roll each leg up and tie it with butcher's twine. Season the skin lightly with salt and pepper. Save the remaining greens to serve as a side dish.

Heat a large cast-iron skillet over high heat and drizzle the oil into it. Put the legs in the pan and sear the skin until golden, about 5 minutes. Flip them over and sear the other side as well, about 5 minutes. Place the legs in a roasting pan, and add the stock. Braise in the oven for about 1 hour, until the meat is tender and cooked through.

Remove the legs from the roasting pan and let them sit for 10 minutes. Then slice the legs into medallions and serve, accompanied by the remaining long-cooked greens.

Big Sur Bakery Mushroom Stuffing

This is the best stuffing, hands down. What's more, it's so easy that Phil's sister Christine has time to make it each year for Thanksgiving, even with three kids under the age of five. So no more excuses about not making your stuffing from scratch!

INGREDIENTS

2 loaves **Pullman bread**
(or dense white sandwich bread)

9 tablespoons **rice bran oil**
or **canola oil**

5 tablespoons **unsalted butter**

3 cups **white button mushrooms,**
sliced

Kosher salt

Freshly ground **black pepper**

6 tablespoons **dry white wine**

3 cups **shiitake mushrooms,** sliced

3 cups **cremini mushrooms,** sliced

1 **yellow onion,** chopped

2 **carrots,** chopped

3 **celery stalks,** chopped

10 **fresh sage leaves,** julienned

2 tablespoons **fresh thyme leaves**

6 tablespoons minced
flat-leaf parsley

5 to 6 cups **turkey stock** or
chicken stock (see pages 239)

Serves 10

The night before Thanksgiving, cut the crust off the loaves of bread and cut them into large cubes; you should end up with about 16 cups cubed bread. Spread the cubes out on a long, deep sheet pan, or two smaller ones, and leave it out, uncovered, for the bread to dry overnight.

The next day, adjust the oven rack to the middle position and preheat the oven to 350°F.

Heat a large sauté pan over high heat, and add 2 tablespoons of the oil and 1 tablespoon of the butter. Add the white button mushrooms, season with salt and pepper, and sauté until they're soft and slightly brown, 5 to 7 minutes. Deglaze the pan with 2 tablespoons of the white wine, scraping any brown bits from the bottom with a wooden spoon. Set the mushrooms aside. Repeat the process with the shiitake and cremini mushrooms, using 2 tablespoons oil and 1 tablespoon butter for each batch, and deglazing the pan each time.

Once all the mushrooms are sautéed, wipe the sauté pan clean with paper towels, put it back on the stove, and drizzle the remaining 3 tablespoons oil into it. Add the onions, carrots, and celery and sweat over medium-low heat until they're soft, about 7 minutes. Transfer the cooked vegetables to a large bowl. Add the mushrooms and the cubed bread, and toss.

Sprinkle the sage, thyme, and parsley over the stuffing. Add just enough stock to moisten the bread—you don't want it to be soggy. Season the mixture with 1 tablespoon plus 1 teaspoon salt and 1/2 teaspoon pepper. Press the stuffing into a baking pan. Dot it with the remaining 2 tablespoons butter, and cover the pan with aluminum foil. Bake for 45 minutes. Then uncover the pan and bake until the stuffing is crusty on top, about 20 minutes.

Garlic Gravy

We think gravy is the most important part of any Thanksgiving celebration. Thickened with puréed vegetables and garlic rather than flour, this gravy adds incredible flavor to the turkey. We blanch the garlic three times to remove its pungency and tenderize it. The strong base adds great depth of flavor and color. This gravy can be made a day in advance, which not only will lighten your load on Thanksgiving day but will actually improve its flavor.

INGREDIENTS

25 **garlic cloves**

3 tablespoons **rice bran oil** or **canola oil**

2 medium **yellow onions,** roughly chopped

3 **carrots,** roughly chopped

3 **celery stalks,** roughly chopped

6 cups **turkey stock (recipe follows)** or **chicken stock (see page 239)**

Kosher salt

Freshly ground **black pepper**

Makes about 2 quarts

To triple-blanch the garlic, place the cloves in a saucepan and add enough water to cover. Bring the water to a boil over high heat, and then strain the garlic. Put the garlic cloves back in the saucepan, cover with cold water, bring to a boil again, and strain. Repeat the process one more time. Reserve the blanched garlic.

Heat a large saucepan over medium-high heat, and drizzle the oil into it. Add the onions and brown them lightly, 7 minutes. Add the carrots and celery and cook until they have softened, about 7 minutes. Add the garlic and cook for 7 more minutes. Add the stock, 1 tablespoon salt, and 1/8 teaspoon pepper. Simmer for 30 to 35 minutes.

Purée the gravy in a blender or food processor, and strain it through a fine-mesh sieve into a bowl. Check the seasoning, and add more salt and pepper if necessary.

Turkey Stock

INGREDIENTS

2 **turkey thighs on the bone**

2 **turkey wings**

1 **yellow onion,** halved

1 **carrot,** roughly chopped

2 **celery stalks,** roughly chopped

1 **bay leaf**

1 **flat-leaf parsley stem**

1 **thyme sprig**

1 **garlic clove**

5 **black peppercorns**

Makes 6 quarts

Put all the ingredients in a large pot, add 8 quarts water, and bring to a boil over high heat. Reduce the heat to medium-low and let the stock simmer, uncovered, for 2 hours, skimming the surface with a spoon or a ladle every once in a while to remove the foam that forms.

Strain the stock into containers, and discard the solid ingredients.

Field Greens Salad with Pecans, Croutons, and Ranch Dressing

We make our own field greens salad mix according to the time of year. In November, we mix frisée (also called curly endive), radicchio, Belgian endive, hydroponic mâche (also known as lamb's lettuce), and the tender light green leaves of "living" butter lettuce. We toss the salad with a tart ranch dressing made with mayonnaise thinned out with buttermilk and vinegar. You have to make the mayonnaise from scratch, but trust us—it's well worth it. Don't even think about using mayo from a jar; the dressing just won't be the same. Ranch dressing develops a better flavor after sitting for several hours.

INGREDIENTS

FOR THE RANCH DRESSING:

1/2 cup **buttermilk**

2 tablespoons **crème fraîche**

2 tablespoons **champagne vinegar**

1/2 cup **homemade mayonnaise** (see page 236)

1 small **shallot**, minced

1 whole **scallion**, trimmed and thinly sliced

1 tablespoon minced **flat-leaf parsley**

1 tablespoon minced **chives**

Kosher salt

Freshly ground **black pepper**

FOR THE SALAD MIX:

2 heads **frisée**

1 head **butter lettuce**

1 head **radicchio**

2 heads **Belgian endive**

2 handfuls **mâche**

FOR THE PECANS:

3/4 cup **pecan halves**

2 teaspoons **rice bran oil** or **canola oil**

Kosher salt

Serves 10

For the dressing, combine the buttermilk, crème fraîche, and vinegar in a spouted measuring cup. Put the mayonnaise in a bowl, and slowly pour in the buttermilk mixture while whisking vigorously. Add the shallots, scallions, parsley, and chives, and season with salt and pepper to taste. Let the dressing sit in the refrigerator for at least 30 minutes and up to 4 hours.

Wash the frisée and trim the green tips off the leaves, leaving behind only the white and yellow part of the head. Cut the core off, tear the remaining leaves into medium pieces, and put them in a large mixing bowl. Wash the butter lettuce. Pull the leaves off the butter lettuce and the heads of radicchio and discard the cores. Tear the leaves into random pieces and add to the frisée. Carefully pull the leaves off the Belgian endive, cut them into strips, and add the strips to the other lettuces. Add the mâche, gently toss the greens together, and keep refrigerated until ready to serve.

Adjust the oven rack to the middle position and preheat the oven to 350°F.

Place the pecans in a bowl. Drizzle them with the oil and season them lightly with salt. Scatter the pecans on a cookie sheet and toast in the oven until they're golden through the center, about 10 minutes. (To check if they're done, cut one open and inspect the color inside.) Let them cool completely. (Leave the oven on.)

FOR THE CROUTONS:

2 cups 1-inch bread cubes cut from **sourdough** or **country bread** (crust removed)

2 tablespoons **unsalted butter,** melted

Kosher salt

Toss the bread cubes with the melted butter in a bowl, and season lightly with salt. Place the cubes on a cookie sheet and bake for 12 to 15 minutes, until the croutons are golden brown on the outside but still soft on the inside. Let them cool completely.

Right before serving, dress the field greens gently with about 1 cup of the ranch dressing, and season with salt and pepper to taste. Transfer the salad to a serving bowl, and sprinkle with the pecans and the croutons.

Herbed Mashed Potatoes

On a chilly fall evening, what's better than mashed potatoes? We like ours chunky, flavored with our favorite herbs.

INGREDIENTS

8 medium **russet potatoes,** peeled

Kosher salt

6 **garlic cloves**

3/4 cup **heavy cream**

6 tablespoons **unsalted butter**

1/4 cup minced **chives**

1/3 cup minced **flat-leaf parsley**

3 whole **scallions,** trimmed and thinly sliced

1 **shallot,** minced

Freshly ground **black pepper**

Serves 10

Put the potatoes in a large colander, place the colander in the kitchen sink, and rinse the potatoes under cold running water to wash off some of the starch. Transfer the potatoes to a large pot and fill it with water. Add 1 tablespoon salt and the garlic cloves. Cook over medium-high heat until you can easily pierce the potatoes with a paring knife, 30 to 40 minutes, depending on the size of the potatoes. Strain the potatoes and garlic in a colander.

Heat the cream and butter together in a small saucepan. Put the potatoes and garlic in a large mixing bowl, and mash them with a potato masher or the back of a wooden spoon until they're somewhat smooth but still chunky. Pour in the cream mixture and combine. Add the chives, parsley, scallions, and shallots. Season with salt and pepper to taste.

Parker House Rolls

Parker House rolls were invented at the Parker House, a hotel in Boston that also claims to be the birthplace of the Boston cream pie. They're American cuisine at its best, and Thanksgiving is an ideal time to highlight these buttery rolls.

Parker House rolls are our staff's absolute favorite, soft and perfect for dipping in gravy. While we are preparing Thanksgiving dinner, we like to make ourselves little sandwiches from these. The next day, we use the leftover rolls to make bread pudding.

INGREDIENTS

2 1/4 cups **whole milk**

3 tablespoons **active dry yeast**

6 3/4 cups **all-purpose flour,** plus extra for dusting

1/4 cup plus 1 tablespoon **sugar**

1 tablespoon plus 1 teaspoon **kosher salt**

2 **eggs**

1/4 cup **unsalted butter,** softened

1 cup **unsalted butter,** melted, for coating the bowl and brushing

Makes 24 rolls

Put the milk in a small saucepan and warm it over very low heat until lukewarm. Remove the pan from the heat. Rain the yeast over the milk, stir, and set it aside to activate for 5 minutes.

In an electric mixer fitted with the dough hook attachment, combine the yeast mixture with 3 cups of the flour on low speed. Over a 1-minute period, add the remaining 3 3/4 cups flour and the sugar, salt, eggs, and softened butter. Increase the speed to medium and mix for 3 minutes. Stop the mixer and scrape down the sides of the bowl with a rubber spatula. Turn the speed up to high and mix for 5 minutes. Transfer the dough to a buttered mixing bowl that is large enough to let the dough double in size. Cover it loosely with plastic wrap and set it aside in a warm area for 45 minutes to 1 hour, until the dough has doubled.

Turn the dough out onto a lightly floured surface, cut it into 2-ounce pieces (about the size of walnuts), and arrange them in equal rows on the work surface. Cover them with a kitchen towel so they won't dry out. Starting with the first piece that you cut, shape the dough pieces into balls and set them back in their rows, a few inches apart from one another. Let them rest, covered, for 10 to 15 minutes.

Meanwhile, line a baking sheet with parchment paper, and brush the parchment lightly with melted butter.

Working with 3 dough balls at a time, flip the balls over and use a rolling pin to stretch each one into an elongated oval. Brush them with the melted butter, and fold them to form a half-moon. Place the folded rolls on the prepared baking sheet so that they are close together, almost touching, in 4 rows of 6 rolls each. Brush the tops of the rolls with melted butter, and place the entire baking sheet inside a large plastic bag. Tie the bag loosely and let the rolls rise in a warm place in the kitchen until they double in size and are touching, 30 to 45 minutes.

While the rolls are rising, adjust the oven rack to the middle position and preheat the oven to 375°F.

Remove the baking sheet from the bag and bake the rolls for 25 to 35 minutes, until they're evenly golden brown. Remove the baking sheet from the oven and while the rolls are still warm, brush them again with melted butter. Let them rest for a few minutes, and serve warm.

Cranberry Sauce

It's really easy to make homemade cranberry sauce—we like to make large amounts and store it in the refrigerator to have around during the colder months. The tartness of cranberries makes them a good complement for red meat or turkey, but this cranberry sauce can brighten many other simple winter dishes, too, savory or sweet.

INGREDIENTS

3 cups fresh **cranberries**

3/4 cup (packed) **light** or **dark brown sugar,** plus extra if needed

1 cup **apple juice**

1 teaspoon **freshly grated nutmeg**

Makes about 3 cups

Combine all the ingredients in a medium saucepan and cook over medium heat, stirring constantly, until all the berries are soft and the sauce has the consistency of jam, about 15 minutes. Check its sweetness; if the sauce is too tart, add a little more brown sugar. Serve warm or cold. It'll keep for about a week in the fridge.

Pumpkin Pie

Sure, it's easy to go to the store and buy canned pumpkin—we're certainly not above using it in a pinch, and it works perfectly in our pumpkin bread—but the best way to make a pumpkin pie is to roast a pumpkin yourself. Michelle likes sugar pie pumpkins, which are smaller than typical carving pumpkins and have a great consistency for baking. Since they contain more moisture than canned pumpkin, she adds a sweet potato to the recipe to make sure the filling's not too watery.

INGREDIENTS

FOR THE PIE DOUGH:

3 1/4 cups **all-purpose flour**

1/2 cup cold **unsalted butter,** cut into cubes

3/4 cup cold **lard**

1 1/4 teaspoons **kosher salt**

2/3 cup **ice water**

1 **egg,** beaten

FOR THE ROASTED PUMPKIN:

1 **sugar pie pumpkin,** 2 to 3 pounds

2 **cinnamon sticks**

1 thumb-size piece **fresh ginger,** peeled and cut into 1/4-inch pieces

1/4 cup **unsalted butter,** softened

1/2 cup (packed) **light brown sugar**

Pinch of **kosher salt**

Pinch of freshly ground **white pepper**

1 medium **sweet potato**

Makes one 9-inch pumpkin pie, plus one extra piece of pie dough

Make the dough: place the flour, butter, lard, and salt in a bowl and chill in the freezer for 30 minutes.

Remove the bowl from the freezer, and use a pastry cutter to break up the butter and lard into dime-size pieces. Make a well in the center and pour in the ice water and the egg. Mix with your hands until the dough comes together, but don't worry about getting it too smooth; bits of butter should still be visible. Cut the dough in half and flatten each half into a disk. Wrap each one in plastic wrap and refrigerate them for at least 30 minutes or as long as 3 days.

While the dough is chilling, start cooking the pumpkin: adjust the oven rack to the middle position and preheat the oven to 375°F.

Using a sharp knife, cut the pumpkin into eighths. Remove the seeds and membranes with a large spoon, and discard them. Place the pumpkin pieces in a large baking pan, and add the cinnamon sticks, ginger, and dots of butter. Sprinkle with the brown sugar, salt, and white pepper. Add 1 cup water and cover the pan with aluminum foil.

Put the baking pan in the oven. Wrap the sweet potato in aluminum foil and place it directly on the oven rack right next to the baking pan. Bake for 45 minutes, or until the pumpkin and sweet potato can be easily pierced with a paring knife. Remove from the oven and let cool for a few minutes.

When the pumpkin is cool enough to handle, scrape the flesh off the skin. Peel the sweet potato. Purée the pumpkin with the sweet potato in a food processor until smooth. Set aside to cool completely. (Leave the oven on.)

Reduce the oven temperature to 325°F.

While the purée is cooling, roll one piece of the pie dough out on a lightly floured surface to form a round about 12 inches in diameter. (Reserve the other piece for another use.) Pick it up by rolling the dough onto the rolling pin, and lay it into a 9-inch pie pan. Gently press the dough over the bottom of the pan and up the sides, leaving a lip around the edge. Trim the excess dough just to the border of the pie pan, and crimp the edges (or seal the pie by pressing the edges with a fork).

FOR THE PIE SHELL AND FILLING:

Nonstick cooking spray

3 large **whole eggs**

1 large **egg yolk**

1 1/2 cups **heavy cream**

1/3 cup (packed) **light brown sugar**

1/2 cup **maple syrup**

1 teaspoon **ground cinnamon**

1/2 teaspoon **ground ginger**

1/8 teaspoon **ground cloves**

1/8 teaspoon **freshly grated nutmeg**

Pinch of freshly ground
white pepper

1 teaspoon **kosher salt**

FOR SERVING:

Whipped cream

Refrigerate for at least 30 minutes.

Take the pie shell out of the refrigerator, coat it lightly with nonstick cooking spray, line it with two or three coffee filters, and fill the shell with dried beans (to prevent the crust from puffing). Bake the shell for 20 to 25 minutes, or until golden. Remove it from the oven and let it cool completely. Remove the beans and coffee filters and discard them.

Reduce the oven temperature to 300°F.

To prepare the pie filling, combine the pumpkin purée, eggs, egg yolk, heavy cream, brown sugar, and maple syrup in a mixing bowl. Whisk in the cinnamon, ginger, cloves, nutmeg, white pepper, and salt.

Pour the filling into the cooled pie shell, and bake until the filling has set but still jiggles in the center, approximately 1 hour. Remove the pie from the oven and allow it to cool. Slice, and serve the pie with fresh whipped cream.

December

Christmas Eve

At home, we're not Christmas people. We don't put up a tree or hang stockings. We avoid shopping unless we must. But at the Bakery, we make up for it tenfold. Inspired by our Catholic guilt (not to mention our access to the catches out of Monterey Bay), we host a yearly Fishermen's Feast on the night before Christmas—a meat-free, multi-course meal featuring the freshest seafood Phil can get his hands on. To add to the Christmas spirit, we build gingerbread houses and decorate the restaurant with local bay and holly. Sometimes we even have a friend play Christmas carols on a cello, which makes the restaurant feel like it's straight out of a storybook, with handmade garlands hanging from the rafters and the room full of friends and customers enjoying our feast.

Early on Christmas Eve, Erik and Michelle drive out to Pfeiffer Ridge and prune bay trees, stuffing the Jeep full of fragrant cuttings. Back at the Bakery, we make cocoa and take orders from Erik for the next two hours, climbing up ladders, hanging ropes from the ceiling, and carefully attaching our bay and berries as Phil preps food in the kitchen. Then, right before the guests arrive, we light the candles—and the festivities begin.

While the guest lists are often the same, our Christmas feast has a totally different atmosphere than Thanksgiving. On Thanksgiving we serve huge portions family-style, at long tables set up to make people feel like they're at home. For the Fishermen's Feast, we do a prix-fixe menu served in small courses. This year, we started with wood-roasted oysters that Phil steamed in the shell until they were just slightly warm and incredibly plump. Each person had just one—enough to whet their appetite for a thick shrimp bisque flavored with the shells and paired with sweet, meaty Dungeness crab. After a seared tuna salad came the choice of roasted wild striped bass or salmon trout wrapped in prosciutto. And just before everyone was filled to capacity we presented dessert: candy-cane bonbons and mont blancs—meringues topped with rum chestnut purée, eggnog ice cream, whipped cream, chocolate sauce, and shaved chocolate. Anyone who still had room finished things up with a thin slice of stollen.

Putting together a meal like that wipes us out, so we take Christmas Day off. We go to a beautiful cabin in the woods and invite friends to bring potluck. There, still recovering from the excesses of the night before, the only food we make is our morning coffee.

Winter Debt

For much of America, December is a season of giving and receiving, a month of holidays and parties and ample opportunities to drop cash on those you love. For businesses in Big Sur, though, December is about going broke.

Or, if not actually going broke, incurring what we around here like to call "winter debt." It's a time—stretching roughly from Thanksgiving until Memorial Day—when business slows and every employee starts to look like a dollar sign walking out the door. The nadir hits between Thanksgiving and Christmas, when business is so stagnant that we actually close for a few weeks. In reality, we don't have a choice: staying open would cost us money. But we like to think that we're just treating ourselves and our staff to a much-needed break after the busy season, and pretend that we are successful restaurateurs who actually can afford things like "vacation."

When it comes to shutting down, we're not alone. Traditionally, many businesses in Big Sur have closed for months in winter (our version of hibernation), reopening only when spring brings back the tourists. Luckily, we only have to shut down for a few weeks, not months, and we use the break to take stock of how bad our winter debt is going to be. It's a time when Mike remembers what a seasoned Big Sur restaurateur told him when the Bakery first opened: "You need to charge a lot more than you're comfortable with, or I guarantee you'll be out of money come winter." Every year when business slows to a trickle, Mike is haunted by those words.

Our winter debt depends on a couple of things: how busy the summer was, whether we've had to buy new equipment—this year we got a new refrigerator—and, of course, our relationship with our purveyors' accounting departments. (Let's put it this way: we're not above using pastries as bribes.) Marilyn handles the bookkeeping, but we call Mike in to deal with the purveyors and any negotiating that needs to happen. He has an uncanny ability to convince people that it's in their best interest to help us.

Winter is also a great time to second-guess what we're doing here. Why did we open a restaurant so far away from people, linked to the outside world by a single, easily closable road? The most frustrating times are when potential customers hear about bad weather or a road closure that's nowhere near us, but which they assume must affect Big Sur—rumors about problems with Highway 1 can slow down business for weeks. Those are the nights when we'll reduce our staff to just five or six people and *still* be left standing around, keeping each other entertained when the customers just don't show.

But then again, we've survived eight off-seasons so far—and damn, do we eat well in the winter. It's hard not to freak out when business is slow, but we've learned to reframe the winter as a chance to put together new menus, spend time together, and get things organized for the coming season. We do our best not to get too worried about business, and luckily for our stress levels, every year there seems to be more.

Big Sur Bakery
peach jam
peaches, sugar, lemon juic
bigsurbakery.co

PROFILE: MARILYN / BEAN COUNTER

Name: Marilyn F. Epp   **Occupation:** Bookkeeper, finance juggler

Languages: Arabic and one can't exist on the border

without some Spanish

Date of Birth: December 13, 1981   **Signature:** MFEpp

Pr: No. 11

Places you have lived:
Southern California, Wyoming, but mostly Texas, which is very different from the Big Sur experience. I never thought I'd miss El Paso, but the Big South can sometimes drive a person to strange things.

Previous jobs:
I worked in a retirement community for a while—which was probably a good prep for working in customer service. I held the typical odds-and-ends jobs, and was in the Air Force. I was an Airman First Class and Basic Arabic Linguist.

Languages:
Arabic, and one can't exist on the border without some Spanish.

Personal heroes:
My dad, for instilling a sense of duty. And my Grams, for instilling a desire for grace and tact in all things.

Life goals:
To serve my country and give back to society. Raise my children to be decent, introspective human beings. Make my small sphere of existence a better place.

Why did Mike decide to hire you?
After shocking Mike with a typewritten résumé and substantiating my honesty with top secret security clearance from the Air Force, it ultimately came down to being a Sagittarius.

Hardest part of your job:
It's been a steep learning curve. Stretching the money from summer to last through the desolate winter is a trial every year.

Biggest loss in Big Sur:
Six weeks after my son was born, the house my boyfriend and I were renting burned to the ground with all our possessions in it.

Soul mate?
My beau, Eric, of course. But let's not kid ourselves—I love Michelle Wojtowicz like no other. There is probably no one I can be as frank and openly pessimistic with and who understands me so completely. Eric calls her my "intellectual lover."

What do you do with your time outside of the Bakery?
Despite doing my best never to try, much less enjoy, yoga, it happened. One day you're going about your business, referring to people who do yoga as trendy assholes, and the next thing you know, you're in the middle of a sun salutation and hating yourself for loving every moment of it.

Seared Ahi Tuna with Mixed Baby Lettuces and Seafood Dressing

We designed this salad for the Fishermen's Feast on Christmas Eve, but its flavors and textures make it great for any time you want a salad with some bite. The chief lettuce for us is baby frisée, mixed with radicchio and mizuna, a spicy Japanese mustard green. For something crispy we add the bright hearts of romaine lettuce.

INGREDIENTS

FOR THE SEAFOOD DRESSING:

1 cup **lobster stock** (see page 190)

1/4 cup **golden (or white) balsamic vinegar**

1 tablespoon **tomato paste**

1 tablespoon **fresh tarragon leaves**

1 cup **rice bran oil** or **canola oil**

Kosher salt

Freshly ground **black pepper**

FOR THE SEARED AHI:

1 tablespoon **black peppercorns**

One 10-ounce piece **ahi tuna loin**

Kosher salt

1 tablespoon **rice bran oil** or **canola oil**

FOR THE SALAD MIX:

1 head **frisée**

1 head **radicchio**

1 **romaine heart**

1 handful **mizuna**

1 **shallot,** minced

2 whole **scallions,** trimmed and thinly sliced

1 tablespoon minced **flat-leaf parsley**

1 tablespoon minced **chives**

2 tablespoons **fresh tarragon leaves**

Kosher salt

Freshly ground **black pepper**

Serves 4

Start with the dressing: Place the lobster stock in a small saucepan and reduce it over high heat until you're left with 2 tablespoons, about 10 minutes. Put the reduced stock, vinegar, tomato paste, and tarragon into a blender. With the blender running, add the oil in a slow, steady stream. Blend until the dressing is thick and emulsified. Season the dressing with salt and pepper to taste. Refrigerate until ready to use.

To make the seared ahi, first crack the peppercorns by placing them on a flat surface, like a cutting board, and pressing them with the flat bottom of a heavy pan until they split into pieces. Season the tuna generously with salt and with the cracked pepper. Heat a cast-iron skillet over high heat and drizzle the oil into it. Put the tuna in the hot pan and sear on all four sides for a few seconds, until nicely browned. (Searing should take less than a minute on each side—you're trying to quickly brown the outside while keeping the interior rare.) Place the tuna on a plate and cool it in the refrigerator.

Wash the frisée and snip off the green tips of the leaves, leaving behind only the white and yellow part of the head. Cut the core off, tear the remaining leaves into medium pieces, and put them in a large mixing bowl. Pull the leaves off the head of radicchio and discard the core. Wash the leaves, then tear them into random pieces and add them to the frisée. Pull the leaves off the romaine heart, wash them, break them into random pieces, and add to the other lettuces. Add the mizuna, shallots, scallions, and herbs, and gently toss the greens together.

Dress the salad mix with about 1/2 cup of the seafood dressing—just enough to lightly coat the greens. Season with salt and pepper to taste, and arrange the greens on a platter. Cut the tuna into 1/4-inch-thick slices, lay them on top of the greens, and drizzle with the remaining seafood dressing. Serve immediately.

Roasted Striped Bass

Wild striped bass is an Atlantic line-caught fish that weighs ten to fifteen pounds. Its flesh is white, and once it has been scaled, the skin can be made crisp fairly easily. (Of course, it helps to have a 700°F wood-burning oven.) We consider striped bass a very approachable fish because it's widely available and mild in flavor. And we also appreciate the fact that this dish can be made from start to finish in less than twenty minutes.

INGREDIENTS

4 **striped bass fillets,** about 6 ounces each, skin on

1/4 cup **rice bran oil** or **canola oil**

Kosher salt

Freshly ground **black pepper**

2 **lemons,** sliced into thin coins

8 **thyme sprigs**

Serves 4

Preheat the broiler.

Score a 1 to 2-inch X on the skin of each fillet with a sharp knife. Brush both sides of the fillets with the oil, and season them generously with salt and pepper. Put the lemon slices and thyme sprigs in a roasting pan (to use as props under the striped bass). Lay the fillets, skin side up, on top of the lemon and thyme. Broil the fish for 12 to 15 minutes, until its skin becomes crispy but not black. When it's cooked, the flesh will be flaky and mostly opaque (the center can still be a little translucent, though—you don't want to overcook it). Remove the pan from the oven and let the fish rest for 3 minutes.

Gently transfer the fish fillets to a platter, and serve.

Salmon Trout Wrapped in Prosciutto

Salmon trout is a pink-fleshed fish, abundant in the lakes and rivers of Idaho, that feeds on krill. After the fish is cleaned, you can stuff the cavity with almost anything. Salmon trout combines the best of both worlds: the beautiful coral color of salmon and the subtle taste of trout. If you have difficulty finding salmon trout, you can use rainbow or brown trout instead.

Trout is a fairly delicate fish, so wrapping it in prosciutto helps to keep it moist. Plus, the crispy prosciutto adds a rich flavor and delicious texture.

INGREDIENTS

Kosher salt

1 pound **baby spinach**

2 tablespoons minced **flat-leaf parsley**

2 tablespoons minced **chives**

2 whole **scallions**, trimmed and thinly sliced

1 small **shallot**, minced

4 whole **salmon trout**, scaled, heads and tails removed

Freshly ground **black pepper**

16 thin **prosciutto slices**

4 tablespoons **rice bran oil** or **canola oil**

2 tablespoons **unsalted butter**

1 recipe **Meyer lemon dressing** (see page 237)

Serves 4

Adjust the oven rack to the middle position and preheat the oven to 375°F.

Fill a medium bowl halfway with water and put about a dozen ice cubes in it. Set it aside.

Bring 4 quarts water to a boil in a large pot. Add 1 tablespoon salt and blanch the spinach in the boiling water until it's bright green, about 40 seconds. Immediately strain it, place it in the ice water, and let it cool for 2 minutes (the ice water will stop the spinach from overcooking and help it retain its color). Squeeze the spinach dry with a kitchen towel.

Combine the parsley, chives, scallions, and shallots in a small bowl. Open each fish like a book, season the cavity generously with salt and pepper, and sprinkle with the herb mixture. Stuff the trout with the blanched spinach, and close the fish back up.

To create a prosciutto wrapper for each trout, take 4 slices prosciutto and arrange them into a large rectangle, with the edges overlapping by 1/2 inch to help keep the pieces together. You should end up with what looks like a rectangular patchwork quilt of ham. Take one of the stuffed fish and wrap it in the prosciutto as if you were rolling it tightly in a piece of newspaper. When you're finished, the fish should be entirely wrapped in prosciutto. Smooth down the loose ends of prosciutto with your fingers to seal it. Repeat this process with each fish.

Heat a cast-iron skillet over medium-high heat, drizzle 2 tablespoons of the oil into it, and add 1 tablespoon of the butter. Put 2 fish in the skillet and cook until the prosciutto is crisp, about 4 minutes. Flip the fish over and cook until the prosciutto on the other side is crisp as well, another 4 minutes. Transfer the trout to a baking sheet lined with aluminum foil. Wipe the skillet clean with paper towels and repeat with the remaining fish, using the remaining 2 tablespoons oil and 1 tablespoon butter.

When all the fish are ready, place the baking sheet in the oven and bake for 8 to 10 minutes, until the flesh of the trout has turned opaque. Let them rest for 2 minutes. Then carefully transfer the baked trout to a cutting board, and using a sharp knife, halve each fish crosswise so that your guests can appreciate the trout's pinkish color and its spinach center. Arrange the trout on a platter, drizzle with the Meyer lemon dressing, and serve.

Grilled Oysters with Champagne Mignonette

Our philosophy on oysters is that they should be sucked down, not eaten with tiny forks. And while we love raw oysters, we also like spicing things up a bit. So when Phil heard that Native Americans used to cook oysters over a fire, we decided to try sticking them in the wood-fired oven. It turns out that the heat plumps the oysters up and makes them easier to shuck, and serving them this way sometimes wins over people who are squeamish about eating them raw. Here we've adapted our recipe for a wood-fired grill. The trick is to cook the oysters only until they warm up and steam slightly in their shells. You don't want them to open on the grill because if they do, you'll lose the tasty juice called "oyster liquor."

At the Bakery, we serve our oysters in lucky sevens, but if you prefer to eat your oysters in groups of a different number, don't let us stop you. "Mignonnette" is French for "peppercorn," and a mignonette sauce consists of cracked black pepper, vinegar, and minced shallots. In this recipe, we add a splash of champagne for fizz. When it comes to oysters, we like medium-size ones like Oysterville Select out of Washington, Fanny Bay from British Columbia, or the smaller Kumamoto from Point Reyes.

INGREDIENTS

1/2 teaspoon **black peppercorns**

1/4 cup **champagne vinegar**

1/4 cup **champagne**

2 teaspoons minced **shallot**

1 teaspoon minced **flat-leaf parsley**

28 medium **oysters**

Serves 4

Preheat the grill 30 minutes in advance, burning the wood down until you have a red-hot coal base. (See page 244 for preparing a wood-fired grill.)

While the grill is heating, crack the peppercorns by placing them on a flat surface, like a cutting board, and pressing them with the flat bottom of a heavy pan until they split into pieces. Combine the peppercorns, champagne vinegar, champagne, shallots, and parsley in a bowl. That's your mignonette.

Once the grill is hot, place the oysters directly on the grate with the flat shell up. Grill the oysters until the shell starts to dry out and look calcified—on an open flame, they will warm through in less than 3 minutes. Remove them from the grill and let them cool slightly.

Line a platter with a linen napkin (this will prevent the oyster shells from sliding).

If you've never shucked an oyster before, don't despair: it'll take a couple of broken shells to get the hang of it. Cover one hand with a towel, and hold an oyster, flat shell up, in that hand. Rest your hand on a flat surface. With the other hand, insert an oyster knife in the connecting muscle between the flat shell and the cup, and turn the knife to separate the shells. Discard the flat shell. Use the knife to loosen the oyster from the cup, being careful not to drip any of the oyster liquor. As you shuck them, arrange the oysters, in their shells, on the napkin-lined platter. Drizzle each oyster with some of the mignonette, making sure to get shallots and crushed peppercorns on all of the oysters. Serve immediately.

Variation

Substitute the Meyer lemon dressing (see page 237) for the mignonette, and garnish the oysters with finely minced chives.

Shrimp Bisque with Basil Toast

A bisque is traditionally a shellfish soup that's thickened with pulverized shells. We make ours with white shrimp that's sustainably farm-raised in the Gulf of Mexico. We like to use lobster stock instead of fish stock, just to keep things in the shellfish family. The homemade lobster stock makes the bisque richer without having to add any heavy cream.

INGREDIENTS

FOR THE LOBSTER STOCK:

2 tablespoons **rice bran oil** or **canola oil**

1 **yellow onion,** roughly chopped

1 **carrot,** roughly chopped

1 **celery stalk,** roughly chopped

Shell from 1 **lobster** (reserve the meat for another use)

1/2 cup **tomato sauce** (see page 238)

1/4 cup **dry white wine**

1 small **bay leaf**

1 tablespoon **fresh oregano leaves**

FOR THE BISQUE:

3 pounds **shrimp**

3 tablespoons **rice bran oil** or **canola oil**

2 medium **yellow onions,** roughly chopped

2 **celery stalks,** roughly chopped

2 large **carrots,** roughly chopped

1 small **fennel bulb,** roughly chopped

Serves 6

Start with the lobster stock: Heat a large pot over medium-high heat and drizzle the oil into it. Add the onions, carrots, and celery and sauté until they're lightly browned, about 6 minutes. Then add the lobster shell and cook for 10 minutes. Add the tomato sauce and cook for 2 minutes more. Deglaze the pan with the white wine, scraping any brown bits from the bottom with a wooden spoon. Add 3 quarts water, the bay leaf, and the oregano. Simmer, uncovered, over medium-low heat for 1 hour. Strain the stock through a fine-mesh sieve into a bowl, and discard the solids. Reserve.

To make the bisque, peel and devein the shrimp, making sure to save the shells. Heat a large pot over medium-high heat and drizzle the oil into it. Add the onions, celery, carrots, fennel, mushrooms, and garlic, and sauté until they're caramelized, about 10 minutes. Add the reserved shrimp shells and continue to cook for about 2 minutes, until the shells turn pink. Add the tomato sauce and cook for another minute. Deglaze the pan with the cognac, scraping any brown bits from the bottom with a wooden spoon. Pour in the lobster stock and simmer, uncovered, for 1 hour.

Strain the liquid from the solids, reserving both. Place the solids (including the shrimp shells) in a blender and add just enough of the liquid to cover them. Begin to purée, adding more liquid as needed until the purée is very smooth. Then strain the purée into a bowl. (Don't use a fine-mesh sieve—you want a thick bisque, and using a strainer that's too fine will strain off the body of the soup.) Put the bisque back in the pot on the heat, season with salt and pepper, and add the shrimp. Poach the shrimp in the hot liquid until they are just pink and tender, about 5 minutes. Keep the bisque warm over very, very low heat until ready to serve.

Adjust the oven rack to the middle position and preheat the oven to 375°F.

To make the basil toasts, fill a medium bowl halfway with water, and put about a dozen ice cubes in it. Set it aside.

3 **white button mushrooms,** sliced

3 **cremini mushrooms,** sliced

6 **garlic cloves,** crushed

1/4 cup **tomato sauce** (see page 238)

1/4 cup **cognac**

Kosher salt

Freshly ground **black pepper**

FOR THE BASIL TOASTS:

Kosher salt

1 cup (packed) **fresh basil leaves**

1/2 cup **flat-leaf parsley leaves**

1 tablespoon **fresh tarragon leaves**

1/2 cup **rice bran oil** or **canola oil**

Freshly ground **black pepper**

6 slices **sourdough bread,** cut 1/2-inch thick

FOR SERVING:

1/4 cup **basil oil** (see page 235)

Bring 4 quarts water to a boil in a large pot. Add 1 tablespoon salt, and blanch the basil, parsley, and tarragon in the boiling water for 10 to 20 seconds, until they're bright green. Immediately strain the herbs through a colander and place the colander in the ice water to cool for 2 minutes (the ice water will stop them from overcooking and help them retain their color). Drain, and squeeze the herbs dry with a kitchen towel. Combine the herbs and the oil in a blender or food processor, and pulse for a few seconds until smooth. Season the mixture with salt and pepper. Brush both sides of the bread slices heavily with the herb purée, and lay them on a cookie sheet. Bake the toasts until the bread is crisp, 7 to 10 minutes.

To serve, transfer the warm bisque to a tureen or individual bowls. Garnish with the basil oil, and serve the basil toasts on the side.

Beluga Lentils with Marinated Beets and Parsley Sauce

Beluga lentils, the smallest of the lentil family, are shiny black pearls with a remarkable resemblance to beluga caviar. They are stunning when combined with brightly colored beets and a green parsley sauce. We came up with this dish for our yearly Fishermen's Feast, where we cook a series of courses for a large number of guests. Once the lentils and the beets are ready, this dish can be put together in seconds. Try serving it as an accompaniment to roasted fish.

INGREDIENTS

FOR THE MARINATED BEETS:

20 assorted **baby beets**

Kosher salt

Freshly ground **black pepper**

4 tablespoons **olive oil**

1 tablespoon **red wine vinegar**

FOR THE LENTILS:

1 cup dried **beluga lentils**

2 tablespoons **rice bran oil** or **canola oil**

1/2 small **yellow onion, chopped**

1/2 **carrot, chopped**

1 small **celery stalk, chopped**

3 **garlic cloves, sliced**

4 cups **chicken stock** (see page 239)

1 **bay leaf**

1 small **serrano chile**

2 **thyme sprigs**

Kosher salt

Freshly ground **black pepper**

FOR THE PARSLEY SAUCE:

Kosher salt

1 cup (lightly packed) **flat-leaf parsley leaves**

Freshly ground **black pepper**

Serves 4

Adjust the oven rack to the middle position and preheat the oven to 350°F.

Wash the beets, making sure not to puncture their skin. Arrange the beets in a single layer in a roasting pan, season them with salt and pepper, and drizzle with 2 tablespoons of the olive oil and about 1/2 cup water. Cover the pan with aluminum foil and roast the beets until they are fork-tender, 35 to 45 minutes depending on their size. When they're done, carefully remove them from the roasting pan while they're still warm and use a kitchen towel to rub the skin off the beets. (Choose a towel you don't care about, though, since it'll get stained.) Cut the beets in half, put them in a bowl, and toss them with the remaining 2 tablespoons olive oil and the vinegar. Let them marinate at room temperature for 30 minutes.

Put the beluga lentils in a strainer and rinse them under cold running water. Heat a medium saucepan over medium heat and drizzle the oil into it. Add the onions, carrots, and celery and sauté until lightly browned, about 5 minutes. Add the garlic and cook for 2 minutes more, until the garlic is tender. Add the chicken stock, lentils, bay leaf, serrano chile, and thyme sprigs. Cook uncovered, until the lentils are tender, about 30 minutes. Discard the serrano chile, thyme sprigs, and bay leaf. Season the lentils with salt and pepper to taste. Keep them warm over very low heat until ready to serve.

Now you're ready to make the parsley sauce: Fill a medium bowl halfway with water, and put about a dozen ice cubes in it. Set it aside.

Bring 2 quarts water to a boil in a medium saucepan. Add 2 tablespoons salt, and blanch the parsley in the boiling water for 10 to 20 seconds, until it turns bright green. Immediately strain the parsley through a colander, and place the colander in the ice water to cool for a minute (the ice water will stop the blanching process and help the parsley retain its color). Drain, and squeeze the parsley dry with a kitchen towel. Combine the parsley and 1/2 cup water in a blender, and purée until the sauce has the consistency of pesto. Season with salt and pepper to taste.

When ready to serve, spoon the warm beluga lentils onto a platter, arrange the marinated beets on top, and drizzle the parsley sauce over them.

Mont Blanc

When Steven Jaeger and Alice Post built the Bakery's building back in the 1930s, they named it Loma Vista—"mountain view"—honoring the view of Mount Manuel from the restaurant's front patio. We're lucky enough to be able to see it from our front yard at home, too, and we never get tired of watching the sun set on the mountain, or the fog drape its slopes. In the winter, its peak sometimes even gets snow.

When Michelle rediscovered a dessert called Mont Blanc, named after the famous Swiss mountain, she decided to reproduce it to celebrate all the mountains that surround us. It uses meringues topped with eggnog ice cream, chestnut purée, whipped cream, chocolate sauce, and chocolate shavings to create a dessert that evokes a snow-capped mountain. It's also a tasty way to introduce friends to the flavor of chestnut.

INGREDIENTS

FOR THE MERINGUES:

4 **egg whites**

1/2 cup **granulated sugar**

3/4 cup **powdered sugar**

FOR THE EGGNOG ICE CREAM:

2 cups **heavy cream**

2 cups **whole milk**

2 teaspoons **freshly grated nutmeg**

1/4 cup **honey**

3/4 cup **sugar**

1 **vanilla bean**

12 **egg yolks**

1/4 to 1/2 cup **dark rum**

Serves 8

Adjust two oven racks to the middle positions, and preheat the oven to 250°F.

Line two cookie sheets with parchment paper, and set them aside.

Start by making the meringues: In an electric mixer fitted with the wire whisk attachment, whisk the egg whites at medium speed until frothy. With the machine running, slowly add the granulated sugar in small batches. Continue whisking until the meringue is thick and shiny. Sift the powdered sugar over the whites, and fold it in with a rubber spatula.

Spoon 8 little mounds of meringue onto one of the prepared cookie sheets, keeping them about an inch apart. On the second cookie sheet, divide the remaining meringue into 8 large dollops. Make a deep well in each of the large meringues with the back of a spoon. Put both cookie sheets in the oven. Bake for 30 minutes, and remove the small meringues from the oven. Continue to bake the large meringues for 30 minutes more (1 hour total), or until they pull away easily from the parchment paper and sound hollow when tapped. Turn the oven off and leave the large meringues in the oven for another 30 minutes, until they dry completely. The meringues should be white. Set the meringues aside in a plastic or Tupperware container.

Next, make the ice cream: Combine the cream, milk, nutmeg, honey, and half the sugar in a medium nonreactive saucepan. Split the vanilla bean lengthwise with a paring knife, scrape out the pulp with the back of the knife, and add the pulp and the pod to the saucepan. Bring the mixture to a boil, remove it from the heat, and let the mixture steep for 30 minutes.

Meanwhile, whisk the egg yolks with the remaining sugar in a large bowl until smooth.

FOR THE CHESTNUT PURÉE:

One 8-ounce jar **chestnut purée**

1/4 cup **dark rum,** or more to taste

1/4 cup **powdered sugar**

FOR SERVING:

1 cup **heavy cream**

2 tablespoons **crème fraîche**

1 cup **chocolate sauce** (double the recipe on page 67)

Dark chocolate shavings

Bring the cream mixture back to a boil and temper the hot liquid into the yolks by adding it a ladle at a time while whisking vigorously. Strain the liquid through a fine-mesh sieve into a bowl. Discard the vanilla bean. Return the strained liquid to the saucepan and cook over very low heat, stirring constantly with a wooden spoon, until it is thick enough to coat the back of the spoon. Add the rum to taste, and refrigerate until it's cold. Freeze the mixture in an ice cream maker according to the manufacturer's directions.

To make the chestnut purée, combine the jarred chestnut purée, rum, and powdered sugar in an electric mixer fitted with the paddle attachment, and mix until well combined. Add 1 or 2 more tablespoons rum if desired.

When you're ready to serve the Mont Blancs, whip the cream with the crème fraîche in a bowl until it forms soft peaks.

To assemble the desserts, pour a bit of the chocolate sauce in individual bowls, put the large meringues in, and place 2 scoops of eggnog ice cream on each one. Top the ice cream with a small meringue. Spoon a dollop of chestnut purée on each small meringue, top with a spoonful of whipped cream, and garnish with the chocolate shavings.

Dresden Stollen

Michelle's dad always refers to her as the Grinch because she never puts up a Christmas tree and because, ever since she started working in the restaurant business, she hasn't been able to join her family for their traditional Italian Christmas celebration on the East Coast. So Michelle developed her own traditions to try to force the Christmas spirit upon herself, and discovered that nothing makes her happier than making stollen, a German Christmas bread that is supposed to resemble the baby Jesus in a blanket.

Stuffed with rum raisins, candied fruit, and almond paste and dipped in butter and sugar, stollen takes a lot of work. Michelle makes the quince paste in the fall, and then right before the Bakery's annual winter closing (the week after Thanksgiving), she pours rum over the raisins and/ or currants so that they can soak for a month. She makes a big batch of vanilla sugar and orders all her spices fresh. And then, as soon as she gets back from "vacation," she starts candying kumquats and Buddha hand (a large, oddly shaped citrus fruit), clarifying huge amounts of butter, and grinding the spices.

If you don't want to make the ingredients from scratch, you can use any store-bought candied fruit and zests, or use the candied zest recipe on page 239 to prepare coins of kumquats or chunks of Buddha hand. If you're looking for a distraction from holiday chaos—or for that matter, for an unusual homemade gift—stollen might make for a great new family tradition.

INGREDIENTS

FOR THE CURRANTS:

2 cups **currants, golden raisins, or raisins**

3 cups **dark rum**

FOR THE SPONGE:

3/4 cup plus 2 tablespoons **milk,** heated to lukewarm

1 cup **bread flour**

1 tablespoon **instant yeast**

Unsalted butter, softened, for coating the bowl

Serves 8

At least one day ahead (or as much as a month ahead), combine the currants and the rum in a bowl, and set it aside.

On baking day, start with the sponge: In an electric mixer fitted with the dough hook attachment, combine the lukewarm milk, bread flour, and yeast. Beat on low speed until a dough is formed, 3 to 5 minutes. Transfer the dough to a buttered bowl that is big enough for the sponge to double in size. Cover it with plastic wrap, place it in a warm part of the kitchen, and let it rise until it doubles in size, 30 to 60 minutes.

Meanwhile, start the stollen mixture: In the electric mixer fitted with the dough hook attachment, cream the butter, all the spices, sugar, and salt together until light and fluffy. Split the vanilla bean lengthwise with a paring knife, scrape out the pulp with the back of the knife, and add the pulp to the butter mixture. Add the egg yolks and almond extract, and mix to combine.

Preheat the oven to 350°F.

Drain the currants, reserving the rum. Drain the candied fruit from the syrup (if homemade). Scatter the almonds on a cookie sheet and toast them in the oven

FOR THE STOLLEN:

1 1/4 cups **unsalted butter,** softened, plus extra for coating the bowl

1/4 teaspoon **ground cardamom**

1/4 teaspoon **ground cloves**

1/4 teaspoon **ground allspice**

2 teaspoons **ground cinnamom**

1/2 teaspoon **freshly grated nutmeg**

1/2 cup **sugar**

1 teaspoon **kosher salt**

1 **vanilla bean**

2 **egg yolks,** beaten

2 teaspoons **almond extract**

1 1/4 cups **candied fruits** or **candied zest** (preferably homemade)

1/2 cup **unblanched almonds**

3 cups **bread flour,** plus extra for dusting

10 ounces **almond paste** (or marzipan)

24 **quince paste squares** (see page 154)

FOR FINISHING:

1 cup **unsalted butter,** melted

1 cup **granulated sugar**

1 1/2 cups **powdered sugar**

until very light brown, about 10 minutes. Cut an almond in half to check the color. Let them cool completely, and then roughly chop them. Toss the currants, candied fruit, and toasted almonds together in a bowl, and reserve.

In the electric mixer fitted with the paddle attachment, combine the sponge, the bread flour, and the butter mixture. Mix on medium speed until the dough is shiny and pulls away from the sides of the bowl, 15 to 20 minutes.

Turn the dough out onto a lightly floured surface. Flatten it slightly and then roll it out to form a 1/2-inch-thick rectangle. Add two thirds of the currant mixture, and fold the dough over it. Add the remaining currant mixture and roll the dough into a ball, making sure to keep a smooth skin of dough around the currant mixture so that none leaks out. Place the dough in a buttered bowl that is large enough to let it double in size, and cover it with plastic wrap. Let it rise in a warm part of the kitchen until it has doubled, 1 to 1 1/2 hours.

Transfer the dough to a floured surface and cut it into 4 pieces. Shape each piece into a football, keeping the smooth skin on top and tucking the cut edges underneath so that the currant mixture stays inside. Let the loaves rest for 7 minutes, covered with plastic wrap. Then, working with one piece of dough at a time, flip it over on your work surface. Punch it to get rid of any air bubbles, and fold the dough onto itself, almost as if you're rolling it up, to form a tight football shape. Repeat with the other 3 pieces of dough. Let them rest on the table, loosely covered with a plastic bag, for 15 minutes.

While they're resting, cut the almond paste into 4 pieces and roll them to form 4 logs, each about 6 inches long.

Take one loaf and flip it over onto a floured surface. Using a rolling pin, roll the center of the loaf until it's 1/2-inch thick, creating a cradle about 4 inches wide while keeping the edges thick. Dot 6 quince paste squares in each loaf. Place a log of almond paste in the center and fold one half of the dough over it. Using the side of your hand, form a crease between the log and the two thick pieces of dough. Doing so should pull the top layer back slightly, leaving you with a loaf of bread that, if cut crosswise, would have three lobes. (The end result is supposed to look like a baby wrapped in a blanket—but if your shape isn't perfect, don't sweat it.) Repeat with the remaining loaves, quince paste, and almond paste. Put the shaped loaves on two baking sheets lined with parchment paper, apart from each other so they can rise until doubled in size. Place the baking sheets in large plastic bags, and leave them in a warm part of the kitchen for 1 to 1 1/2 hours, until the dough has almost doubled and is spongy to the touch.

Adjust the oven rack to the middle position and preheat the oven to 375°F.

Bake the stollen for 35 to 45 minutes, until they are a deep golden brown. Remove them from the oven and let them cool for 15 minutes. Once the loaves are cool enough to handle, brush them generously with the reserved rum and the melted butter. Sprinkle with the granulated sugar, and dust with the powdered sugar. Eat right away or store at room temperature wrapped in plastic wrap.

January

Chanterelles

Wayne is our chanterelle source at the Bakery. He learned how to find them when his son Rowan and Rowan's cousin got interested in selling chanterelles to local restaurants as a way to earn pocket money. It's since become a yearly routine: once the winter rains have set in, Wayne and the boys head out to forage.

No one has figured out a way to domesticate chanterelles, so the only way to get them is in the wild. Luckily, Wayne and the boys have noticed some patterns. Chanterelles seem to like to grow near redwoods, bay trees, oak trees, and poison oak—which makes Rowan's habit of foraging barefoot seem like an especially daring move.

Despite their bright yellow color, chanterelles can be hard to find. They're often concealed by dead leaves, and it takes time to train your eye to spot them peeking out from beneath the brown. But once you find one, chances are there'll be more, thanks to their mycelia, the threadlike network under the soil from which the mushrooms sprout. Wayne and the boys try not to disrupt the mycelia when they harvest the chanterelles, instead cutting them cleanly at their base. And with a little practice, they've gotten good at finding them—by the end of their second year of foraging, they'd discovered seventeen different patches.

Every year we buy some of their chanterelles and use them in eggs and on toast, in soup, in quinoa, and on pizzas. For the boys, chanterelle foraging is the Big Sur version of suburban kids' paper routes or lawn-mowing jobs.

Bartering

Thanks to Big Sur's plentiful orchards and gardens, neighbors often stop by the Bakery with bags of limes, lemons, grapefruits, oranges, and even tomatoes and avocados. Sometimes we buy the produce; other times, we barter. When the trees are really in full swing, people occasionally just give their fruit away.

Wayne helps us get chanterelles, but he's also an informal source of fresh meat. Unfortunately for our customers, there are stricter regulations around meat than around produce, so we usually have to eat his catches ourselves—with certain exceptions, like fresh rockfish or mackerel he harvests right off the coast.

But he doesn't just bring us food from the sea. Wayne spent much of his childhood living off the land, learning to hunt everything from deer to quail, wild pigeons, turkeys, and gray squirrels. He takes well-deserved pride in knowing that if something calamitous happened and we didn't have access to our normal store-bought supplies, he could support a small community of people by hunting and foraging. He has passed along his knowledge to his two sons, Noel and Rowan—right now, he's teaching Rowan how to use a bow and arrow.

Since Highway 1 has yet to crumble entirely into the ocean, so far we haven't had to rely on Wayne for our survival. Instead, we just get to enjoy the food. Wayne likes bringing his catches to us because he's as impressed by Phil's cooking as Phil is by Wayne's hunting, so the two of them have developed a great symbiotic relationship: Wayne supplies the materials, and Phil turns them into dinner. The rest of us are lucky if we're around to taste the result.

PROFILE: WAYNE / HUNTER AND FORAGER

Pr: No. 12

Name: Wayne D. Hyland

Role at the Bakery: I supply half a cord of wood a week for the oven. And I bring in interesting types of meat.

Date of Birth: Sept. 28, 1949 **Signature:** Wayne D Hyland

Past jobs:
I owned a gas station in Monterey in the early 1970s. I was an electrician and a carpenter and an engineer. I've been a commercial fisherman for at least thirty years. I built an abalone boat. In my wild days, I sailed boats from north of Norway to the Arctic Circle and back down to England.

Current job:
In addition to fishing, I oversee one end of a property called Rancho Rico. I'm in charge of all the infrastructure. I thought I was in charge of the renters' happiness, too, but I found that was beyond my ability.

Favorite job:
I love ocean fishing. I feel like out of all the things I do, providing food for other people—large groups—is what I do best.

What attracted you to the Bakery?
I like people who are workers, who have a strong work ethic in their lives. I'd known Gilly for years, and I met Phil and Michelle the first day they were here. Their dedication fires me up and makes me want to help in any way I can.

Family background?
My grandfather was one-hundred-percent Miwok— California Indian. My father was half British.

Why teach your sons to be outdoorsmen?
So they'll grow up to be stewards of the land. I want them to understand how the natural world works—and where the food is.

Do you ever hunt for sport?
I killed a lot of birds with a BB gun when I was little. Then one time my friend and I were killing sparrows and his dad goes, "You know, you don't really have to kill those little birds." And for the first time we thought about what we were doing and realized we were just being mean. After that I changed. I only kill for food.

What are some of the most dangerous creatures you've seen in the ocean?
I've seen numerous great whites. I've been charged by a blue whale twice. I had a rogue killer whale come and circle me once—I sailed away when I got the feeling that I was bait.

What happened to your original house?
It slipped down the hill toward the ocean in a landslide in 1997. I kept living in it for about nine months, but then it started to slide again. I tried to convince Rowan's mom that we should anchor it on cables so we could slide along on its way to the sea. But she disagreed.

Why do you like California?
It's always changing, always moving. I don't like tradition, where things in your family remain the same for two hundred years. I'd rather have turmoil and disruption. It makes you more accepting of the possibility that things might change for the better, instead of just staying stagnant.

Steamed Mussels with White Wine and Sourdough Toast

Mussels are actually incredibly easy to cook. Our favorite mussels for this recipe are small varieties like the black mussels from Prince Edward Island—their size won't scare people who might not like the idea of a whole mouthful of shellfish. (But if you're the sort of person who finds that appealing, by all means, buy yourself some big ones like the New Zealand green lips.) Toasted or grilled bread is a classic accompaniment. We suggest dipping morsels of bread in the liquid that the mussels cooked in.

To clean the mussels, scrub the buildup on the shells with an abrasive sponge or pot scrubber. Remove the beards by pulling them assertively down and then up.

INGREDIENTS

FOR THE SOURDOUGH TOASTS:

2 tablespoons **unsalted butter**

4 slices **sourdough baguette,** cut 3/4 inch thick on a sharp diagonal

FOR THE MUSSELS:

2 pounds **fresh black mussels,** scrubbed and debearded

2 tablespoons **rice bran oil** or **canola oil**

1 teaspoon **kosher salt**

1/4 teaspoon freshly ground **black pepper**

1/4 cup minced **flat-leaf parsley**

1/4 cup minced **chives**

4 whole **scallions,** trimmed and thinly sliced

1/4 cup **minced shallots**

1 cup **dry white wine**

1 tablespoon **unsalted butter**

Serves 4

Adjust the oven rack to the top position and preheat the oven to 350°F.

First, prepare the toasts: Melt the butter in a small saucepan. Brush both sides of the bread slices with the melted butter, place them on a cookie sheet, and toast them in the oven until golden brown, about 10 minutes. Set the toasts aside.

Heat a large sauté pan over high heat. While it is heating, toss the mussels in a large bowl with the oil, salt, pepper, parsley, chives, scallions, and shallots. Pour the mixture into the hot pan; then remove the pan from the heat for a moment and add the white wine. Immediately cover the pan with a lid. Cook over high heat until the mussels start to open, which should happen within 2 to 3 minutes. As the mussels open, remove them with a pair of tongs and put them in a serving bowl. Discard any unopened mussels.

Add the butter to the cooking liquid and reduce the liquid until large bubbles start to form, 3 to 5 minutes. Pour the liquid over the mussels, and serve with the sourdough toasts on the side.

Seared Scallops with Cauliflower Purée and Tangerine Reduction

Scallops are Phil's favorite shellfish, and he loves pairing their sweet briny taste and meaty texture with this cauliflower purée and a tangerine reduction. Seek out scallops that are labeled "sustainable," "diver," or "day-boat"—diver scallops have been harvested by hand, which is more ecologically sound. If you can buy the scallops still live in their shells, even better. You're looking for plump scallops that smell ocean-fresh.

INGREDIENTS

FOR THE TANGERINE REDUCTION:

1 cup **tangerine juice** (from 6 to 8 tangerines)

FOR THE CAULIFLOWER PURÉE:

1 small **head cauliflower**

Kosher salt

1 tablespoon **champagne vinegar** or any **white vinegar**

1/4 cup **chicken stock** (see page 239)

1/2 cup **heavy cream**

Freshly ground **black pepper**

FOR THE SEARED SCALLOPS:

8 large **day-boat scallops**

Kosher salt

Freshly ground **black pepper**

2 tablespoons **rice bran oil** or **canola oil**

1 tablespoon **unsalted butter**

Serves 4

Place the tangerine juice in a small saucepan and reduce it over medium-high heat until it is syrupy, 10 minutes. You should be left with about 2 tablespoons. Set it aside.

Cut the cauliflower into florets, making sure they are similar in size. Fill a medium pot with water and bring it to a boil. Add 1 tablespoon salt, the vinegar, and the cauliflower, bring back to a boil, and cook until the cauliflower is very tender, about 12 minutes. Drain the cauliflower.

Combine the chicken stock and heavy cream in a small saucepan, and warm the mixture over medium heat. Put the cooked cauliflower and the warm cream mixture in a blender or food processor, and purée until smooth. Season with salt and pepper to taste. Transfer the purée to a small saucepan and keep it warm over very low heat.

Season the scallops with salt and pepper. Heat a large cast-iron skillet over high heat and drizzle the oil into it. Add the butter and let it melt. Place the scallops, flat side down, in the skillet. Don't move the scallops! It takes only about 3 minutes to quickly sear the scallops and create a caramelized exterior, and moving them will prevent this from happening. When the scallops have a rich brown color, flip them over and cook for another 3 minutes.

To serve, spoon the cauliflower purée onto a platter. Put the scallops right on top (always put the purée on the plate first—if you pour it over the scallops, you'll ruin the caramelized surface), and finish with a drizzle of the tangerine reduction, warmed a little if needed.

Chanterelle Pizza

What we love about this pizza is that it proves that vegetarian dishes can be filling and satisfying. Our chanterelles come from patches hidden all over the local mountains, and their robust flavor is best paired with stronger cheeses like Fontina.

INGREDIENTS

FOR THE CHANTERELLES:

1 pound **fresh chanterelles**

2 tablespoons **rice bran oil** or **canola oil**

2 tablespoons **unsalted butter**

1 small **shallot,** minced

1 tablespoon **preserved garlic** (see page 234)

1 tablespoon minced **flat-leaf parsley**

1 tablespoon **fresh thyme leaves**

2 tablespoons **dry white wine**

FOR THE PIZZA:

Bread flour, for dusting

1/2 recipe **pizza dough** (see page 235), shaped into 2 balls and refrigerated at least overnight

1/4 cup **preserved garlic** (see page 234)

1/2 cup grated **Parmesan**

1 1/2 cups grated **Fontina**

1 tablespoon minced **flat-leaf parsley**

1 tablespoon minced **chives**

2 whole **scallions,** trimmed and thinly sliced

1 **shallot,** minced

Kosher salt

Freshly ground **black pepper**

Makes two 12-inch pizzas

One hour before you plan to start baking, adjust the oven rack to the middle position and place a baking stone on it. Preheat the oven to 450°F.

Clean the chanterelles, using a dry pastry brush to gently dust off all the dirt, and then cut them into uniform small pieces. Heat a large sauté pan over medium-high heat and drizzle the oil into it. Add the butter and wait until it starts to brown. Then add the chanterelles, tossing them quickly with a wooden spoon to coat them with the oil and butter. Cook the chanterelles until they start to shrink and release their liquid, about 3 minutes. Stir in the shallots, preserved garlic, parsley, and thyme. Deglaze the pan with the white wine, scraping any brown bits from the bottom with a wooden spoon. Continue to cook until the liquid has evaporated. Transfer the mixture to a plate, and set it aside to cool.

Generously dust the surface of a pizza peel (a flat wooden or metal shovel with a long handle) with bread flour. Lightly flour a work surface.

Working with one ball of pizza dough, dip your hands and the dough in the bread flour to make them less sticky, and pat the dough down into a disk shape with the tips of your fingers. Once the disk is large enough, drape the dough over your fists and carefully start stretching and expanding the dough from underneath to form a round that is 10 to 12 inches in diameter. (If you're feeling lucky, try tossing the dough over your head in a circular motion to stretch the dough.)

Place the dough on the prepared peel. Spread half the preserved garlic evenly over the surface of the dough, leaving a 1/2-inch border uncovered. Sprinkle with half of the Parmesan, Fontina, chanterelles, parsley, chives, scallions, and shallots. Season with salt and pepper to taste.

Before you put the pizza in the oven, do the "stick test": shake the peel slightly to make sure the pizza is not sticking (if it is, carefully lift the section that is sticking and sprinkle a bit more flour underneath). Then slide the pizza directly onto the baking stone and bake it for 8 to 12 minutes, checking on it after 5 minutes and rotating it if necessary to ensure that it's baking evenly. When the crust is golden and the cheese is bubbly, use the peel to remove the pizza from the oven and place it on a cutting board. Let it cool for 2 minutes. Then slice and serve immediately.

Prepare your second pizza the same way.

Cauliflower with Pine Nuts and Dried Cranberries

This is one of our most popular vegetable sides at the restaurant. In order to maximize flavor, it's important to caramelize the flat side of the cauliflower floret when you sauté it and to take the time to reduce the sauce slightly after adding the butter.

INGREDIENTS

1/4 cup **pine nuts**

1 head **cauliflower**

Kosher salt

1 tablespoon **champagne vinegar**

3 tablespoons **unsalted butter**

1/4 cup **chicken stock** (see page 239)

1/4 cup **unsweetened dried cranberries**

1 whole **scallion,** trimmed and thinly sliced

1 tablespoon minced **shallots**

1 tablespoon minced **chives**

1 tablespoon minced **flat-leaf parsley**

Freshly ground **black pepper**

Serves 4

Adjust the oven rack to the middle position and preheat the oven to 350°F.

Place the pine nuts on a cookie sheet and toast them in the oven until very light brown, 8 to 10 minutes. Let them cool completely.

Cut the cauliflower into florets, making sure they are similar in size. Fill a medium pot with water and bring it to a boil. Add 1 tablespoon salt, the vinegar, and the cauliflower and cook until the cauliflower is fork-tender, about 12 minutes. Strain the cauliflower in a colander.

Heat a large sauté pan over medium-high heat and add 1 tablespoon of the butter. Add the cauliflower and brown it lightly, 3 minutes. Deglaze the pan with the chicken stock, scraping any brown bits from the bottom of the pan with a wooden spoon. Add the toasted pine nuts and the cranberries, scallions, shallots, chives, parsley, and the remaining 2 tablespoons butter. Cook until the liquid reduces and forms a little bit of a sauce, 2 minutes. Season with salt and pepper to taste, and serve.

Braised Venison Osso Buco

We had wanted to put a venison dish on our menu for a while, but we wanted to find an alternative to venison steak. Our purveyor suggested we try osso buco, and it turned out to be a wonderful idea.

Osso buco means "bone with a hole," and that's exactly what this piece of meat is: a shinbone surrounded by meat, plus a bone filled with marrow. This dish hails from Milan and is traditionally prepared with lamb shanks and white wine.

INGREDIENTS

FOR THE OSSO BUCO:

Kosher salt

2 cups **light brown sugar**

2 **bay leaves**

5 **black peppercorns**

4 pieces **venison osso buco**

Freshly ground **black pepper**

2 tablespoons **rice bran oil** or **canola oil**

FOR THE BRAISING LIQUID:

2 tablespoons **rice bran oil** or **canola oil**

1 medium **yellow onion,** roughly chopped

1 **carrot,** roughly chopped

1 **celery stalk,** roughly chopped

4 **garlic cloves**

1 cup **port wine**

4 **flat-leaf parsley sprigs**

2 **thyme sprigs**

2 **bay leaves**

2 cups **beef broth** (see page 60)

Serves 4

Fill a large pot with 5 quarts water and bring it to a boil over high heat. Turn off the heat. Add 2 cups salt, the brown sugar, bay leaves, and peppercorns and stir until the salt and sugar are fully dissolved. Set the brine aside to cool completely.

Put the venison in the cooled brine, placing a heavy plate on top to keep it submerged. Cover the pot with plastic wrap and let it sit for 4 hours in the refrigerator.

Pull the meat out of the brine, rinse it under cold running water, and pat it dry with paper towels. Discard the brine. Season the osso buco pieces lightly with salt and pepper. (The meat is already brined, so don't go too crazy with the salt—the additional seasoning just helps the meat caramelize as it sears.) Heat a large cast-iron pan over high heat and drizzle the oil into it. Arrange the osso buco in the pan without overcrowding, and sear the meat until all sides are nicely caramelized, 5 minutes on each side.

Meanwhile, adjust the oven rack to the middle position and preheat the oven to 300°F.

Prepare the braising liquid: Heat a large sauté pan over medium-high heat and drizzle the oil into it. Add the onions and cook until they're slightly browned, about 10 minutes. Add the carrots and celery and cook for another 6 minutes, until softened. Add the garlic and cook for another 5 minutes. Deglaze the pan with the port wine, scraping any brown bits from the bottom with a wooden spoon, and continue to cook till the liquid has reduced to about 1/3 cup, 10 minutes.

Arrange some of the vegetables in a roasting pan, and place the seared osso buco on top. Add the rest of the vegetables with the port reduction, along with the parsley, thyme, and bay leaves. Pour in the beef broth, and cover the pan with aluminum foil. Braise in the oven for 3 hours, until the meat is practically falling off the bone and is so tender that it can be easily pulled apart.

CONTINUED >>

1 tablespoon **rice bran oil**
or **canola oil**

1/2 **yellow onion,** chopped

1 small **carrot,** chopped

1 small **celery stalk,** chopped

Kosher salt

Freshly ground **black pepper**

Allow the venison to cool in its braising liquid until it reaches room temperature, about an hour, then remove the meat from the bones and set them aside. Strain the braising liquid through a fine-mesh sieve into a bowl, and discard the solids.

Heat a medium saucepan over medium heat and drizzle the 1 tablespoon oil into it. Add the onions, carrots, and celery, and sweat until the vegetables are soft, about 7 minutes. Add the strained braising liquid and reduce by half over medium-high heat, skimming the surface with a spoon or a ladle every once in a while to remove the foam that forms on top, 10 to 15 minutes. Check the seasoning, and add salt and pepper if necessary. Reheat the osso buco and the bones in the simmering liquid until the meat is warm all the way through, about 10 minutes. Transfer the osso buco, the braising liquid, and the bones to a large bowl, and serve. The marrow is delicious.

Marmalade Tart

This free-form tart is one of Michelle's favorites—she loves the combination of citrus, marmalade, and buttery dough. At the Bakery we make our own marmalade from local Meyer lemons, but you can also use a high-quality store-bought marmalade such as June Taylor's. (The fewer the ingredients in the marmalade, the better—for ours, we use just lemons and sugar.) The more variety in color and size of the citrus slices, the prettier the tart—so even though the recipe calls for just two citrus fruits, feel free to use slices from a larger assortment (oranges, blood oranges, Cara Cara oranges, and grapefruit are all good options) and serve the leftover citrus on the side as a garnish. This tart is so beautiful that you can leave it as a centerpiece on your table. It's great served with butterscotch ice cream or a dollop of whipped cream.

INGREDIENTS

FOR THE ALMONDS:

3/4 cup **unblanched almonds**

FOR THE TART DOUGH:

1 1/2 cups cold **unsalted butter,** cut into small cubes

3 cups **all-purpose flour,** plus extra for dusting

1/2 cup **sugar**

Grated zest of 1 **orange**

1 teaspoon **kosher salt**

1 tablespoon plus 1 1/2 teaspoons **orange juice**

Makes one 10 by 14-inch tart

Adjust the oven rack to the middle position and preheat the oven to 350°F.

Scatter the almonds on a cookie sheet and toast them in the oven until they're golden through the center, about 10 minutes. (To check if they're done, cut one open and inspect the color inside.) Remove them from the oven and let them cool completely. Then finely chop the almonds and set them aside. (Leave the oven on.)

To make the tart dough, combine the butter cubes with the flour, sugar, orange zest, and salt in a bowl, and chill it in the freezer for 30 minutes.

Using an electric mixer fitted with the paddle attachment, work the chilled mixture until it's very crumbly. Then add the orange juice and continue to mix until the dough comes together. Turn the dough onto a lightly floured work surface and knead until it is smooth, about 2 minutes. Flatten the dough into a disk, wrap it in plastic wrap, and chill it in the refrigerator for at least 30 minutes or as long as a week.

While the dough is chilling, make the almond cream: In an electric mixer fitted with the paddle attachment, cream the butter, powdered sugar, almond extract, orange zest, and salt until the mixture is light and fluffy. Add the beaten egg a little bit at a time, mixing until incorporated. Then add the flour and mix well. Use a rubber spatula to fold in the chopped almonds—the cream itself should be smooth, but the almonds will make it look like chunky peanut butter. Reserve the almond cream at room temperature until ready to use.

Increase the oven temperature to 375°F. Line a cookie sheet with parchment paper or lightly coat it with nonstick cooking spray.

CONTINUED >>

FOR THE ALMOND CREAM:

6 tablespoons **unsalted butter, softened**

1/2 cup plus 1 tablespoon **powdered sugar**

1 1/2 teaspoons **almond extract**

Grated zest of 1 small **orange**

1/2 teaspoon **kosher salt**

1 **egg,** beaten

3 tablespoons **all-purpose flour**

FOR ASSEMBLING THE TART:

Nonstick **cooking spray**

1 cup high-quality **citrus marmalade (orange or lemon)**

2 **citrus fruits**

1 **egg,** beaten

2 tablespoons **sugar**

1 tablespoon **cold unsalted butter**

Remove the dough from the refrigerator and roll it out over a generously floured countertop until it's 1/4 inch thick. Cut out a 12 by 16-inch rectangle with a paring knife. Gather the excess dough into a ball, flatten it into a disk, wrap it in plastic wrap, and keep in the refrigerator for another use. Carefully transfer the dough rectangle to the prepared cookie sheet. Spread the marmalade evenly over the dough, leaving a 1-inch border all the way around the tart. Spread the almond cream over the marmalade. Fold the edges of the dough over to create a crust—this will keep the marmalade from seeping out. Place the tart in the refrigerator for 30 minutes.

While the tart is chilling, prepare the citrus: Cut off both ends of the fruit with a sharp knife. Place the citrus on a cutting board, one cut end down, and following the curve of the fruit, shave off the rind from top to bottom with the knife, revealing the flesh of the citrus and leaving absolutely no pith. Place the citrus on its side and cut it crosswise into 1/4-inch-thick rounds, carefully removing seeds as you come across them.

Remove the tart from the refrigerator and arrange the citrus rounds over the almond cream, placing them close together but without letting them overlap. Brush the edges of the tart with the beaten egg. Sprinkle the sugar over the entire tart, going a bit heavier on the dough edges. Dot the citrus rounds with the butter (to prevent them from burning). Bake for 40 to 45 minutes, until the almond cream and the crust are a deep golden brown. Remove the tart from the oven and let it cool on the sheet for at least 15 minutes.

Serve warm or at room temperature. Make sure to save a slice to eat with your coffee the next morning.

February

Our Inspiration

From a business perspective, February in Big Sur sucks. Tourism slows to a trickle, it's the rainy season, and this year we even got hail. It's the time of year when it's easy to ask ourselves why we gave up our jobs and paychecks in Los Angeles and moved north to a place where even the electricity isn't guaranteed. But whenever we start thinking this way, we know what we have to do: go see Terry and Rachel.

Ever since we got to Big Sur, Terry has kept us under his wing. He provided us with conversation, stories, emotional counseling, and, of course, Hide bread, as we took the first steps toward starting the Bakery.

He also helped mold our philosophy. For Terry, life is all about experience. He has managed to carve out a life for himself doing exactly what he wants to do—and has stayed remarkably happy in the process. That's part of what attracted his girlfriend, Rachel, a talented artist in her own right who designs and makes beautiful beaded jewelry. Like Terry, she has built a life around her art. She used to run a shop near the Bakery that she opened with Terry's help, but about a year and a half ago she sold it so that she could devote all her time to designing jewelry. Today, ten years since they started to date, she and Terry live at the top of a narrow dirt road in a converted greenhouse with a view of the Pacific Ocean, supporting themselves by doing what they love.

Together, Terry and Rachel are a major inspiration in our life at the Bakery. They're living proof that you can support yourself with your art, whether it's sandal-making or beading, baking or cooking. At the same time, they're a constant reminder that life shouldn't *just* be about work, no matter how much you enjoy what you're doing. You have to make time for other things.

Most of all, they've taught us that it's important not to let daily frustrations get in the way of the bigger picture. And every time February comes around, we keep in mind one of Terry's favorite sayings: "If you're unhappy in Big Sur, you're looking at it wrong."

PROFILE: TERRY / SANDALMAKER   RACHEL / BEADER

Pr: No. 13

Names: _Terry Prince_   _Rachel Moody_

Terry's Nickname: _"Hide"_

Terry's Hometown: _London_   **Rachel's Hometown:** _Pacific Grove_

Signatures: _"Hide"   Rachel R Moody_

Story of your house:
It was built by Jack Curtis, a writer who wrote screenplays for *Bonanza* and *Rawhide*. It used to be his writing studio and a greenhouse.

How long have you lived in Big Sur?
Rachel's been here for fifteen years, Terry for thirty.

Rachel's nickname for Terry:
Commen-terry, because he has something to say about everything, but there's nothing common about him.

Rachel's oddest Big Sur job:
Llama walking. We were trying to train them as pack animals.

Terry's hidden talent:
He has a degree in psychology and is working on his second book.

Terry's signature foods:
Hide bread, toasted with butter, and rocket fuel (black tea with honey and half-and-half, brewed strong).

What are Hide sandals?
Handmade leather sandals, custom-crafted to fit your feet. Terry's been making them for years.

Ordering instructions for Terry's sandals:
Stand on sheet of paper. Outline foot. Trace between big toe and the next one. Scribe inside of arch. Repeat for opposite foot. (Also, if you pay first, they'll get made faster.)

Where does Terry find business?
It finds him.

Philosophy toward work:
Work smart, not hard. What's the point of living here if you're not getting to enjoy this place?

Hide Bread

Terry "Hide" Prince is known up and down the California coast for three things: his hand-crafted leather sandals, his homemade Hide bread, and his uncanny ability to look at the bright side of life. Terry has been making this bread for over twenty-five years, basing the recipe on his knowledge of nutrition and his love for toast. The result is an unfussy, simple loaf that's somewhere between an Irish soda bread and a grain-filled English muffin. Terry packs patties of Hide bread with him when he goes camping, and has even been known to carry one in his pocket, pre-toasted and buttered, as a snack.

When we first moved to Big Sur, we were fascinated by Terry's habit of feeding his friends with a constant supply of these little breads. He would toast them up, make us the best cup of tea we'd ever had, and inspire us with stories of his adventures. These quickly became our favorite bread to snack on, and Terry's patties powered us through our long days of work as we started the Bakery. A few months later, we drew inspiration from his recipe and created the nine-grain whole-wheat baguette that we serve on our daily bread plate.

Terry buys his flour and seeds in bulk and creates his own bread mix, which he stores in a five-gallon bucket. Every morning, he scoops out a portion of the mix and combines it with water, milk, buttermilk, or beer. The bread patties keep for several days, but when they get too hard to munch on, Terry butters them and gives them to his dog. No Hide bread is ever wasted.

Terry's recipe uses a nutritious blend of oat bran, flax, sesame, quinoa, amaranth, and seaweed. Rather than adding salt, Terry gathers kelp from the beach in Big Sur, dries it, pulverizes it in a coffee grinder, and adds it to the bread. If you don't have access to fresh kelp, you can replace it with dulse flakes, available at most health food stores. Another alternative is to add brown sugar, honey, chocolate chips, and a little butter to the mix and turn it into cookies. The idea is to take the recipe and adapt it to your tastes and nutritional desires.

INGREDIENTS

5 cups **all-purpose flour,**
plus extra for dusting

1/2 cup **flax seeds**

1/2 cup **sesame seeds**

2 cups **oat bran**

1/4 cup **sunflower seeds**

1/2 cup **amaranth, quinoa,
millet, or poppy seeds,** or
a combination of any of these

2 tablespoons **dulse flakes,**
or 1/2 teaspoon **kosher salt**

1 teaspoon **baking soda**

1/4 cup plus 2 tablespoons **beer**

2 1/2 cups **buttermilk, half-and-half,
milk, or water**

Unsalted butter, softened,
for serving

Makes about fifteen 4-inch patties

Adjust the oven rack to the middle position and preheat the oven to 375°F. Line a baking sheet with parchment paper, if desired.

Place all the dry ingredients in a bowl, stir them together, and make a well in the center. Add the beer and the buttermilk. Mix with the handle of a wooden spoon until a thick, wet batter forms. Sprinkle a layer of flour over the top. Turn the batter onto a lightly floured surface and roll it into a loose log about 2 inches in diameter. Cut it into 1 1/2-inch-thick slices and pat them down with your hands to form patties. Place the patties on the baking sheet and bake them for 45 minutes, until golden brown. Let them cool completely.

To serve, slice each patty in half, toast it well, and smear with butter. (Seriously, make sure to toast it. Hide bread is similar to an English muffin in that if you don't toast it, it'll taste raw.)

Mâche Salad with Citrus, Avocado, Almonds, and Grapefruit Dressing

Mâche, also known as lamb's lettuce, is a very small green with a fine texture, subtle nutty flavor, and delicate leaves. This salad is one of Michelle's favorites because it screams "California."

INGREDIENTS

FOR THE ALMONDS:

1/4 cup **unblanched almonds**

1 teaspoon **rice bran oil** or **canola oil**

Kosher salt

Freshly ground **black pepper**

FOR THE GRAPEFRUIT DRESSING:

Juice of 1 **ruby red grapefruit**

2 tablespoons **golden (or white) balsamic vinegar**

1 teaspoon **Dijon mustard**

Juice of 1/2 **lemon**

1/2 cup **rice bran oil** or **canola oil**

Kosher salt

Freshly ground **black pepper**

FOR THE SALAD:

1 **blood orange**

1 **ruby red grapefruit**

1 **Cara Cara orange**
(or a navel orange if
Cara Cara aren't available)

1 **avocado**

8 cups **mâche rosettes**

1 tablespoon minced **flat-leaf parsley**

1 tablespoon minced **chives**

1 whole **scallion**, trimmed and thinly sliced

1 small **shallot**, minced

Serves 4

Adjust the oven rack to the middle position and preheat the oven to 350°F.

Scatter the almonds on a cookie sheet. Drizzle with the oil, season with salt and pepper, and toast in the oven until they're golden brown through the center, about 10 minutes. (To check if they're done, cut one open and inspect the color on the inside.) Let the almonds cool, and then roughly chop them.

To make the dressing, put the grapefruit juice in a small saucepan. Reduce the juice over high heat until syrupy, 7 to 10 minutes—you should be left with about 1 tablespoon. Whisk the reduced grapefruit juice, vinegar, mustard, and lemon juice together in a medium bowl until well combined. Add the oil in a slow, steady stream, whisking until the dressing is thick and emulsified—it should come together pretty quickly. Check the seasoning, and add salt and pepper to taste.

Prepare the citrus next: Cut off both ends of the fruit with a sharp knife. Place the citrus on a cutting board, one cut end down, and following the curve of the fruit, cut off the rind from top to bottom, revealing the flesh of the citrus and leaving absolutely no pith. Then remove the segments by carefully cutting each one out of its membrane sheath.

Cut the avocado in half with a knife. Remove the pit, and scoop each half from the skin with a large spoon in one swoop. Cut each half into quarters, and season them with salt and pepper.

Gently toss the mâche in a bowl with the parsley, chives, scallions, and shallots. Add the citrus segments and add just enough dressing to lightly coat the mâche and the fruit, about 1/4 cup. Season with salt and pepper to taste. Arrange the salad on a platter, and garnish with the avocado quarters.

Chicken Soup

Chicken soup is no joke. Its healing properties have been recorded since ancient times . . . or at least since before Campbell's hit the supermarkets. Whenever we feel under the weather, we treat ourselves to this soup, which incorporates elements from a bunch of different recipes in this book. You can tailor the soup to your taste by adding or subtracting different vegetables or by adding barley, noodles, or rice. (Cook the starches separately and add them right before serving.)

INGREDIENTS

1 **roasted chicken**
(see page 151)

1 cup **fingerling potato confit**
(see page 234)

2 tablespoons **rice bran oil**
or **canola oil**

1 small **yellow onion,**
finely chopped

1 **carrot,** finely chopped

2 **celery stalks,** finely chopped

1 cup **cooked chanterelles**
(see page 206)

1 cup **long-cooked greens**
(see page 167)

3 quarts **chicken stock**
(see page 239)

Kosher salt

Freshly ground **black pepper**

3 tablespoons minced
flat-leaf parsley

3 tablespoons minced **chives**

3 whole **scallions,** trimmed
and thinly sliced

1/4 cup **grated Parmesan**

8 **basil toasts**
(see page 190)

Serves 8, with plenty of leftovers

Pick the meat off the roasted chicken and discard the skin and bones. Cut the confit potatoes into 1/4-inch coins, and set them aside.

Heat a large pot over medium-low heat and drizzle the oil into it. Add the onions, carrots, and celery, and sweat until the onions are translucent and the other vegetables are slightly softened, about 5 minutes. Add the fingerling potatoes, chicken, chanterelles, and long-cooked greens. Cover with the chicken stock, and season with salt and pepper to taste. Simmer for 5 to 10 minutes, until all the flavors begin to meld together. Right before serving, stir in the parsley, chives, and scallions.

Transfer the soup to a serving tureen or individual soup bowls. Serve sprinkled with the grated Parmesan and accompanied by the basil toasts.

Spicy Fresh Calamari

When we first moved to Big Sur, fishermen friends used to drop off five-gallon buckets of fresh squid from Monterey Bay as a gift to Phil. This was a mixed blessing: we love squid, but man, cleaning them takes time. Once they're cleaned, though, they can cook up in minutes, and we think it's worth the effort. This recipe yields the tenderest of calamari.

INGREDIENTS

3 pounds **fresh squid**, or 2 pounds **cleaned squid** (not frozen!)

1 cup **tomato sauce** (see page 238)

1/4 cup **chicken stock** (see page 239)

Hot red pepper flakes

Kosher salt

4 tablespoons **rice bran oil** or **canola oil**

2 tablespoons **unsalted butter**

2 tablespoons minced **flat-leaf parsley**

Serves 4

Cut each squid in half, right above the tentacles and below the eyes. (Don't use a wooden cutting board—or any other material that will stain—just in case you break the ink sacs.) Working with the tentacle halves, squeeze out the beaks (they look like hard, dark pearls) and set aside the tentacles. For the other halves, use the flat side of a knife to scrape off the external skin and wings, leaving behind just the white tubes of flesh. Then slice open each tube and scrape its interior to remove the entrails, making sure not to miss the clear piece of cartilage inside. You should be left with clean rectangles of white flesh. Score what used to be the outside of the squid with tightly spaced diagonal lines (these lines will help make the squid curl when you cook it). Next, cut the rectangles into quarters.

Put the tomato sauce and chicken stock in a small saucepan and keep warm over medium-low heat. Season the squid with 1/4 teaspoon red pepper flakes and 1 teaspoon salt. Heat a large sauté pan over high heat, and drizzle 2 tablespoons of the oil into it. Add half of the squid. Within 7 seconds the bodies will start to curl; quickly add 1/2 cup of the tomato sauce mixture. Stir to combine, and cook for 30 seconds more—keeping in mind that overcooked squid will have a rubbery texture. Remove the pan from the heat and add 1 tablespoon of the butter. Check the seasoning, and add more salt and red pepper flakes if necessary. Transfer to a serving bowl.

Wipe the sauté pan clean with paper towels, add the remaining 2 tablespoons oil, and prepare the remaining squid the same way.

Garnish with the minced parsley, and serve immediately.

Roasted Duck Breast with Ginger Sauce

Ducks have a much thicker layer of fat under the skin than store-bought chickens, which makes many people think of duck as an inherently greasy bird. But it doesn't have to be. The secret is to take the time to render the fat slowly and to remove it from the pan as it melts. The result is delicious crispy skin and red, rich flesh that's not too greasy at all.

Our favorite ducks come from one of our locals, Mary Trotter. She's the only woman in her hunting club, and at least once a year she stops by the restaurant with some fresh ducks for Phil to cook. It's a great arrangement: she loves the fact that Phil will cook them specifically to her taste (she likes her meat blood-rare), and Phil is psyched because he gets to keep one for himself.

Our sauces in the restaurant never include flour, but since most people at home have access to canned or packaged beef broth rather than gelatinous veal stock made from scratch, we added a small amount of flour to help thicken your sauce.

INGREDIENTS

2 tablespoons **rice bran oil** or **canola oil**

1 tablespoon **unsalted butter**

2 **garlic cloves**, minced

2 whole **scallions**, trimmed and thinly sliced

1 thumb-size piece **fresh ginger**, peeled and roughly chopped

1 **shallot**, minced

3 **black peppercorns**

1 tablespoon **light brown sugar**

1 cup **dry white wine**

1 tablespoon **all-purpose flour**

2 cups **beef broth** (see page 60)

Kosher salt

Freshly ground **black pepper**

4 **duck breasts**, about 6 ounces each

Serves 4

Adjust the oven rack to the middle position and preheat the oven to 450°F.

Heat a small saucepan over medium heat and drizzle the oil into it. Add the butter and wait until it melts. Then add the garlic, scallions, ginger, shallots, and peppercorns, and sweat for about 5 minutes. Add the brown sugar and stir until it starts to caramelize, about 3 minutes. Deglaze the pan with 1/4 cup of the white wine, scraping any brown bits from the bottom with a wooden spoon. Add the remaining 3/4 cup wine and reduce until almost all the liquid has evaporated, about 5 minutes. Add the flour and stir to form a paste. Add the beef broth and reduce until the sauce is thick enough to coat the back of a spoon, about 10 minutes.

Strain the sauce and discard the solid ingredients. Return the strained sauce to the pan, season with salt and pepper, and keep warm over very low heat until ready to serve.

Using a sharp knife, score the skin of each duck breast with three diagonal slashes. Be careful not to cut all the way through the fat—you don't want to expose the red flesh. Season the skin generously with salt and pepper. Heat a cast-iron skillet that is large enough to hold the 4 duck breasts without overcrowding over high heat. Place the breasts, skin side down, in the skillet and immediately lower the heat to medium so the fat doesn't burn. It shouldn't take long before the fat starts to render out; use a spoon to transfer the melted fat to a heat-resistant container as the duck cooks. The skin should be browned in 6 to 8 minutes.

Once the skin is browned, place the skillet in the oven. Roast the duck to your desired doneness. Medium-rare is the best; this should take 5 to 7 minutes in the oven. Remove the skillet from the oven, transfer the duck breasts to a plate, and allow them to rest for 3 minutes.

Serve whole or sliced into 1/2-inch-thick pieces cut diagonally against the grain. The ginger sauce can be spooned directly onto the plate or served in a separate dish for guests to help themselves.

Butter Lettuce with Fennel, Herbs, Meyer Lemon Dressing, and Shaved Pecorino

The Meyer lemon tree is a native of China whose fruit is more orange-like, sweeter, and less acidic than normal lemons, and in Big Sur pretty much everyone seems to have one. Since all the trees start to bear fruit at the same time, we get hit with waves of locals all talking about their lemons—and wondering what to do with them. So this one is for the people. We like to add crunchy thin slices of fennel to complement the soft, silky texture of the butter lettuce. People have different preferences when it comes to the licorice flavor of fennel, so feel free to use as much or as little of the bulb as you like.

INGREDIENTS

1/2 **fennel bulb**

2 heads **butter lettuce**

1/4 cup fresh **tarragon leaves**

2 tablespoons minced **shallots**

2 tablespoons minced **chives**

2 tablespoons minced **flat-leaf parsley**

1/2 cup **Meyer lemon dressing** (see page 237)

Kosher salt

Freshly ground **black pepper**

2 ounces **Pecorino,** thinly shaved with a vegetable peeler (about 1/2 cup)

12 to 16 pieces **candied Meyer lemon zest** (see page 239)

Serves 4

Using a mandoline, carefully slice the fennel into paper-thin shavings. Tear the butter lettuce leaves from the cores, and put them in a large mixing bowl. Add the tarragon, shallots, chives, parsley, and fennel, and toss. Gently dress the salad with just enough Meyer lemon dressing to coat the leaves. Season with salt and pepper to taste.

Transfer the salad to a platter, top it with the shaved Pecorino, and garnish it with the candied lemon zest. Serve immediately.

Pearl Barley with Kale and Butternut Squash

People who haven't eaten barley don't know what they're missing. Hearty and spongy, when it's cooked right, barley pops in your mouth. It's an annual cereal grain and a member of the grass family—and a staple cereal of ancient Egypt, where it was used to make bread and beer. You can also use barley in soups and stews and even as a coffee substitute. We like serving it with spicy kale and sweet squash as a hearty side dish, or even as a vegetarian meal.

INGREDIENTS

FOR THE BARLEY:

1 cup **pearl barley**

4 tablespoons **rice bran oil** or **canola oil**

Kosher salt

Freshly ground **black pepper**

1/2 medium **yellow onion,** finely chopped

1 small **carrot,** finely chopped

1 **celery stalk,** finely chopped

1 small **serrano chile,** minced

2 **garlic cloves**

1 **bay leaf**

1 **flat-leaf parsley stem**

2 cups **Irish-style stout** (such as Guinness)

2 cups **chicken stock** (see page 239)

1 cup **beef broth** (see page 60)

FOR THE SQUASH:

1 small **butternut squash,** peeled, halved, and seeded

2 tablespoons **olive oil**

Kosher salt

Freshly ground **black pepper**

FOR THE KALE:

3 bunches **kale**

1/2 cup **olive oil**

Serves 4

Adjust the oven rack to the middle position and preheat the oven to 350°F.

In a small bowl, mix the barley with 2 tablespoons of the oil, 1 teaspoon salt, and 1/4 teaspoon pepper. Scatter the mixture on a baking sheet and toast in the oven until the barley is golden—really golden—about 20 minutes. Set the barley aside but leave the oven on.

Heat a large pot over medium-high heat and drizzle the remaining 2 tablespoons oil into it. Add the onions, carrots, celery, serrano chile, garlic, bay leaf, and parsley stem. Cook until the vegetables are caramelized, about 10 minutes. Add the toasted barley and sauté for 2 minutes. Deglaze the pot with the beer, scraping any brown bits from the bottom with a wooden spoon, and reduce until almost dry, about 10 minutes. Add the chicken stock and beef broth, and simmer for 40 minutes. If the barley seems to be drying out before it's tender, add extra water and continue to simmer until it's done. Check the seasoning, and add more salt and pepper if necessary. Remove the bay leaf and parsley stem.

While the barley is cooking, dice the squash into 1-inch cubes. Toss them in a bowl with the oil, and season with salt and pepper. Transfer the squash to a baking sheet and roast in the oven until fork-tender, 20 to 25 minutes.

Trim the kale off the ribs and tear it into medium pieces. Rinse thoroughly under cold running water and leave somewhat wet (the residual water helps the kale when it's cooking). Heat a large pot over medium heat and add the olive oil. Add the onions, garlic, and red pepper flakes, and sweat until the vegetables are softened, about 10 minutes. Add the kale and cook, covered, over low heat, for 10 minutes, until the kale is tender but still has some bite.

1/2 medium **yellow onion**, sliced

5 **garlic cloves**

1 teaspoon **hot red pepper flakes**

FOR SERVING:

2 tablespoons **unsalted butter**

1 tablespoon minced
flat-leaf parsley

1 whole **scallion**, trimmed and
thinly sliced

Kosher salt

Freshly ground **black pepper**

Right before serving, heat a large sauté pan over medium heat and add the butter. Add the parsley and scallions, then the barley, kale, and squash. Check the seasoning, and add more salt and pepper if necessary. Transfer to a platter and serve.

Grapefruit Pudding

This dessert could have been a disaster for Michelle. When she was a student at the Culinary Institute of America, she had to prepare this pudding for a banquet where it would be evaluated by a team of chefs. She didn't have time to chill the dessert before showing it for review and was sweating as she waited to hear their verdict. Luckily, they loved the dessert, especially served warm!

INGREDIENTS

Nonstick **cooking spray**

3 cups **ruby red grapefruit juice**

1 cup **sugar**

1/3 cup **all-purpose flour**

1/2 teaspoon **kosher salt**

1 cup **whole-milk yogurt**

1/2 cup **crème fraîche**

Grated zest of 2 **grapefruits**

4 **eggs**, separated

Powdered sugar, for sprinkling

Serves 6 to 8

Adjust the oven rack to the middle position and preheat the oven to 350°F.

Coat a 10-inch round baking dish lightly with nonstick cooking spray. Set it aside.

Pour the grapefruit juice into a stainless-steel pot and let it simmer over medium heat until it has reduced to 1/2 cup, 15 to 20 minutes. Set it aside until it has cooled completely.

Combine the sugar, flour, and salt in a bowl and make a well in the center. In a separate bowl, whisk together the reduced grapefruit juice, yogurt, crème fraîche, grapefruit zest, and the egg yolks. Pour the grapefruit mixture into the well and whisk to combine.

In an electric mixer fitted with the wire whisk attachment, whisk the egg whites until soft peaks form. Gently fold the whites into the grapefruit mixture.

Pour the mixture into the prepared baking dish and bake for 20 to 25 minutes, until the top is golden and the pudding is set but still jiggles in the center. Let it sit for 5 minutes before serving. Sprinkle with powdered sugar, and serve while still warm.

Epilogue

When we first decided to keep a journal of a year in our lives in Big Sur, we thought it'd be a nice record for us to look back on. We didn't imagine that the process itself would substantially affect our lives. As it turned out, not only did we strengthen our relationships with the friends we featured and learn new things about the people with whom we interact each day (Jim won a "Man Against Horse" race? Justin had his tires slashed by vegans?), but we ourselves have changed as well. Mike adopted a hive of bees that Jack is helping him learn to care for. Eric and Jasmine somehow found time between caring for their newborn and writing their own book on microgreens to help Phil and Michelle plant a garden. Marilyn gave birth to a baby girl. Justin achieved his goal of finding an affordable place to be a butcher and own a home (unfortunately for us, it's in Pittsburgh—but there's always overnight delivery). As for Phil and Michelle, we've expanded our own family to include Henry, our beautiful son.

And as proof that you really never can tell what will happen in Big Sur, just as the summer season was getting under way, a lightning storm started what became a massive forest fire near the Bakery. Mike's house burned down early in the fire and he once again found himself sleeping on the Bakery floor, comforted by waking to the smell of freshly baked bread. Yet, despite the destruction, there was still beauty in Big Sur—and a sense of community that only grew stronger as the fires spread. Michelle, Phil, and Wayne snuck away and caught fish for a feast for friends and family; a few nights earlier, we served a huge pizza dinner to the firemen to thank them for keeping us safe. We eventually had to evacuate until the firemen could control the blazes, but just two weeks later, we were back, open for business, and looking forward to the season ahead. Even in the worst of it, when we looked up at the charred hills and smelled the fire's smoke, we were reminded just what a fragile, special place this is—and how lucky we are to call it home.

Basics

Fingerling Potato Confit

Confit is a French term referring to a preservation method where food—usually meat like goose, duck, or pork—is slowly cooked in fat and preserved with the fat packed around it as a seal. In this recipe, potatoes are submerged in oil and cooked slowly over low heat, steaming in their own jackets. We add these to our Fresh Garbanzo-Bean Stew (page 120), but you can also eat them on their own—they don't actually absorb the oil they're cooked in.

INGREDIENTS

1 pound **Russian banana fingerling potatoes,** similar in size

1 **rosemary sprig**

3 **garlic cloves**

6 **black peppercorns**

1 tablepoon **kosher salt**

4 cups **rice bran oil** or **canola oil**

Makes 1 pound of potatoes

Place the potatoes, rosemary sprig, garlic, peppercorns, and salt in a medium saucepan. Cover the potatoes with the oil, and bring to a slow simmer over medium-low heat. Cook until the potatoes are just tender (check them with a toothpick), about 30 minutes. (Don't overcook them, or they'll be mushy.) Let the potatoes cool in the oil.

As with other types of confit, the potatoes will keep in the oil, refrigerated, for several days.

Preserved Garlic

Peeling the garlic might take a while, but once it's been preserved, it will keep for a long time in the refrigerator. It's so delicious, though, that you shouldn't expect it to last for long. Substitute this preserved garlic in any recipe that calls for raw garlic—it's particularly good in Caesar salads, or even just spread on toast.

INGREDIENTS

Cloves from 1 **garlic head**

3/4 teaspoon **kosher salt**

1/2 cup **rice bran oil, canola oil, peanut oil,** or **any vegetable oil** that's neutral in flavor

Makes 3/4 cup

Peel the garlic cloves and put them in a food processor. Add the salt and 1/4 cup of the oil, and process for 10 seconds. Scrape the sides of the bowl and process for another 10 seconds, until the garlic is chopped very fine. (If you like your garlic pieces bigger, that's fine, too—just make sure the pieces are somewhat uniform in size.)

Transfer the garlic to a small saucepan, cover with the remaining 1/4 cup oil, and cook slowly over very low heat for 20 to 25 minutes. The garlic is ready when its flavor changes from sharp to mild and its color turns from bone white to cream. Let the garlic cool in its cooking oil, and store (in the oil) in the refrigerator for up to several weeks.

Pizza Dough

This is our basic pizza dough recipe, which we created when we first started experimenting with the wood-fired oven during our first couple of months in Big Sur. We like to use this dough the day after it's made. And it's even better two days after.

INGREDIENTS

1/2 teaspoon **active dry yeast**

1 1/2 cups plus 2 tablespoons **bread flour**, plus extra for dusting

1 teaspoon **kosher salt**

Makes dough for two 12-inch pizzas

Place 3/4 cup lukewarm water in the bowl of an electric mixer. Rain in the yeast, stir, and set it aside to activate for 5 minutes.

Add the flour to the yeast mixture and sprinkle the salt on top. Fit the mixer with the dough hook attachment, and combine on slow speed for 1 minute, until all the ingredients start to come together. Increase the speed to medium and mix for 2 minutes. Then increase the speed to high and mix for 2 more minutes.

Immediately turn the dough out onto a lightly floured surface and divide it in half. Roll each half into a tight round. Place the balls on a floured baking sheet. Place the baking sheet in a large plastic bag and tie the bag loosely. Refrigerate overnight (or for 2 nights).

The next day, about 1 hour before baking the pizzas, pull the baking sheet out of the refrigerator and leave it in a warm area till you're ready to use the dough.

Follow the chosen pizza recipe.

Basil Oil

We use this flavorful oil to "green light" many of our entrees and salads as they come out of the kitchen.

INGREDIENTS

1 tablespoon **kosher salt**

3 big bunches **basil** (leaves and stems)

1 cup **rice bran oil** or **canola oil**

Makes 1 cup

Fill a bowl halfway with water and put about a dozen ice cubes in it. Set it aside.

Bring 4 quarts water to a boil in a large pot. Add the salt and blanch the basil in the boiling water until it's bright green, 20 to 30 seconds. Immediately strain the basil and place it in the ice water. Let it cool for 2 minutes (the ice water will stop the basil from overcooking and help it retain its color). Squeeze the basil dry in a kitchen towel.

Put the blanched basil (stems and all) in a blender, add the oil, and purée. Let the purée sit for 2 hours at room temperature.

Strain the purée through a fine-mesh sieve into a container. Reserve the basil oil at room temperature until ready to use. It will keep in the refrigerator for several weeks.

Homemade Mayonnaise

Making your own mayo is a truly satisfying experience, but watch out—once you try it this way, you'll never want to buy the jarred stuff again. There is a small chance that raw eggs may carry salmonella; if you're very young or old, pregnant, or have health concerns, please seek out pasteurized eggs.

INGREDIENTS

2 **egg yolks**

1/2 **lemon**

1 tablespoon **Dijon mustard**

1 1/2 cups **rice bran oil** or **canola oil**

1 teaspoon **kosher salt**

1/8 teaspoon freshly ground **black pepper**

Makes about 1 cup

To make the mayonnaise by hand, whisk the egg yolks with a few drops of lemon juice and the mustard in a nonreactive mixing bowl. Start to form a stable emulsion by adding a little of the oil, a few drops at a time, while whisking vigorously. Continue adding the oil in a thin stream—you want to do this slowly to ensure that the oil is fully emulsified into the yolks from the get-go. Once you've incorporated about 1 cup of the oil (the mixture should be very thick at this point), add 1 tablespoon water and a few more drops of lemon juice. Season with the salt and pepper, and then continue to slowly add the remaining 1/2 cup oil while whisking vigorously. Transfer the mayonnaise to a glass jar or plastic container and refrigerate until ready to use.

To make the mayonnaise in a food processor, put 1 tablespoon water, the egg yolks, a few drops of lemon juice, and the mustard in the processor. With the processor running, gradually add a few drops of the oil. Continue adding the oil in a thin stream—you want to do this slowly to ensure that the oil is fully emulsified into the yolks from the get-go. Once you've incorporated about 1 cup of the oil (the mixture should be very thick at this point), add another tablespoon of water and a few more drops of lemon juice. Season with the salt and pepper, and continue to slowly add the remaining 1/2 cup oil while the processor is still running on high speed. Transfer the mayonnaise to a glass jar or plastic container and refrigerate until ready to use.

The mayonnaise will keep for up to 3 days under refrigeration.

Variation

For a thinner mayonnaise, whisk in more water, a tablespoon at a time, until you achieve the desired consistency.

Meyer Lemon Dressing

We use this dressing all the time. It's great on oysters, grilled fish, chicken, and salads, or you can toss it with roasted or grilled veggies like asparagus and beets. The reduction of the orange juice concentrates the flavor and adds viscosity to the dressing. This dressing keeps for several days in the refrigerator.

INGREDIENTS

1/2 cup freshly squeezed **orange juice**

2 tablespoons golden (or white) **balsamic vinegar**

1 1/2 teaspoons **Dijon mustard**

3/4 teaspoon **kosher salt**

2 tablespoons freshly squeezed **Meyer lemon juice**

Grated zest of 1 **Meyer lemon**

3/4 cup **rice bran oil** or **canola oil**

Makes 1 cup

Pour the orange juice into a small saucepan and reduce it over medium-high heat until syrupy, 5 to 7 minutes—you should be left with about 1 tablespoon. Put the reduced orange juice, vinegar, mustard, salt, lemon juice, and lemon zest into a blender. With the blender running, add the oil in a slow, steady stream, blending until the dressing is thick and emulsified. Transfer the dressing to a plastic container or glass jar and refrigerate until ready to use.

Tomato Sauce

We both have Italian grandparents and grew up in households where homemade tomato sauce was such a staple that Phil's family, like many Italian households, referred to it as "gravy." Phil's mom made a good sauce, Michelle's father also makes a good sauce, and now we make our own version as well. It's not just for pizzas—we use it with sardines and in our bisque, and add spice to it for calamari and barbecue sauce. Its uses are unlimited—just adjust the consistency and add spice.

INGREDIENTS

3/4 cup **olive oil**

1 large **onion,** roughly chopped

2 medium **carrots,** roughly chopped

2 **celery stalks,** roughly chopped

1 small **fennel bulb,** roughly chopped

10 **garlic cloves**

1 **serrano chile,** stem removed

Six 16-ounce cans **whole organic tomatoes**

1 tablespoon **kosher salt,** plus more if needed

Makes a lot of sauce—you can never have too much!

Heat a large pot over medium-high heat and add the olive oil. Add the onions, carrots, celery, fennel, garlic, and chile, reduce the heat to medium-low, and cook slowly until the vegetables are caramelized, about 20 minutes.

Add the tomatoes (with their juice) and salt, and bring to a lazy simmer. Cook for at least 1 hour. The sauce's red color will deepen and darken as it cooks. Basically, you're cooking out the moisture and developing the flavor.

Transfer the mixture to a blender and purée until smooth. Check the seasoning, and add more salt if necessary. Let the sauce cool completely. Store it in a plastic or ceramic container in the refrigerator for up to 2 weeks.

Candied Meyer Lemon Zest

This candied zest is a great garnish for dishes that call for our Meyer lemon dressing, like the butter lettuce salad with fennel and Pecorino (see page 229). You can also sprinkle it on lemon desserts or use it to flavor any cookie dough.

INGREDIENTS

4 **Meyer lemons**

1 1/2 cups **sugar**

Makes about 1 cup

Peel off the outer yellow skin of the lemons with a vegetable peeler, trying to get as little pith as possible. Julienne this zest into long, thin strips and place them in a small saucepan. Add just enough cold water to cover them. Bring to a boil, then immediately remove the pan from the heat and strain off the water (you're blanching the zest to remove its bitterness).

Add the sugar and 1 1/2 cups fresh water to the zest and bring to a boil over high heat. Reduce the heat to low and simmer until the zest becomes translucent and can be cut easily with a fork, 20 to 25 minutes.

Transfer the zest and its syrup to a glass jar or plastic container, cover, and keep in a warm part of the kitchen until needed. If you keep it in its sugar syrup, it'll last for weeks.

Chicken Stock

INGREDIENTS

1 free-range **chicken,**
3 to 4 pounds

1 **yellow onion,** halved

1 **carrot,** roughly chopped

2 **celery stalks,** roughly chopped

1 **bay leaf**

1 **flat-leaf parsley stem**

1 **thyme sprig**

1 **garlic clove**

5 **black peppercorns**

Makes 6 quarts

Put the chicken in a large pot, and add 8 quarts water and all the other ingredients. Bring to a boil over high heat. Reduce the heat to medium-low and let the stock simmer for 2 hours, skimming the surface with a spoon every once in a while to remove the foam that forms on top.

Strain the stock into containers, and discard the solid ingredients. We like using ours fresh, but you can freeze it if necessary.

Equipment

We believe that the caliber of your equipment can affect the quality of your cooking. But there's no need to go crazy—outfitting your kitchen doesn't require breaking the bank.

Our essentials: a chef's knife, paring knife, sharpening stone, and cast-iron pan. If you're a serious dessert person, throw in an electric mixer and an ice cream maker.

CHEF'S KNIFE

As a chef, your most important tool is your knife. You want to find a knife that's efficient and safe, with a grip that feels comfortable and secure in your hand. Knife sets are tempting, but in reality, there's no need for anything too elaborate: a good chef's knife can be used for chopping, slicing, carving, and mincing. Standard chefs' knives are usually 8 to 10 inches long, but if you find that length difficult, opt for a shorter blade. You can get knives in a variety of materials, but we like stainless steel—it's affordable and easy to care for.

PARING KNIFE

Paring knives are smaller than chefs' knives, which means they can be used for more delicate tasks, like cutting segments off an orange or splitting a vanilla bean in half.

SHARPENING STONE

More important than the brand of your knife is the sharpness of its blade. What's the point of owning a high-quality knife if it's dull? Get in the habit of sharpening regularly—sharpening stones are affordable and easy to find. Slide the blade over the porous surface of the stone in one swift movement, pressing the blade lightly against the stone while keeping it at about a 20-degree angle. It takes practice, but most people get the hang of it. If you're not one of those people, you can always have your knives professionally sharpened—try the store where you bought them.

CAST-IRON PAN

Cast-iron pots and pans are versatile and durable, suitable for stovetop cooking and for oven-roasting. Cast-iron is also a very efficient heat conductor, which means that the temperature is even across the surface of the pan. After buying your cast-iron pan, wash it and "season" it by rubbing it with oil and heating it in a 350°F oven for 30 minutes. This will prevent food from sticking to it. To avoid rusting, wash the pan with water and wipe it dry immediately after each use (don't use soap or you'll wash off the seasoning). We own cast-iron cookware in all kinds of sizes, but we find that the 10- and 12-inch pans are the most useful.

ELECTRIC MIXER

We like stand-up electric mixers better than hand-held mixers. Depending on the brand, the difference in price can be astronomical, but think of it as a one-time investment. These days, the stand-up electric mixers designed for home cooks are durable and come equipped with wire whisk, paddle, and dough hook attachments. Some models are so multipurpose that you can even plug in a meat grinder.

ICE CREAM MAKER

It's possible to drop a lot of cash on a gelato spinner imported directly from Italy, but we recommend starting small and purchasing a basic home model that can hold at least 2 quarts of ice cream. It shouldn't cost you more than an electric blender or food processor.

Techniques

Choose your cooking technique based on your raw ingredients—different foods benefit from different methods. For example, large cuts of meat full of connective tissue need to be cooked slowly over a long period of time to break down their fiber and make them easier to chew, whereas ripe fresh berries are best simply macerated for a few minutes before serving. Delicate vegetables need nothing more than a quick sautéing or blanching to highlight and amplify their natural flavors, but root vegetables need to be thoroughly cooked before becoming edible. Each food has a specific need; your job as a cook is to learn to listen.

When we're designing a new dish and are deciding how to approach a particular ingredient, we think about its texture, flavor, density, fat content, and appearance. Then we ask ourselves questions. How can we make a roasted leg of lamb juicier? How can we add more body to the soup without saturating it with fat? How long should we infuse the cream with nuts and flowers so that it absorbs their perfume without becoming cloying? In other words, we try to pick a complementary cooking method for each food. Here are some of the basics.

BLANCHING

Blanching is a technique commonly used to precook vegetables and legumes. It involves submerging them briefly in salted boiling water and then "shocking" them in an ice-water bath to preserve their color and prevent them from overcooking. Blanching is also used to soften the bitterness of vegetables like rapini, and to make fruits like peaches easy to peel.

BRAISING

Braising uses both moist and dry heat to create tender, drop-off-the-bone meat—a perfect braise will almost melt in your mouth. It's a particularly good technique for tougher cuts, like veal shank, pork shoulder, chicken thighs, and duck legs. Typically, braising involves searing the meat until it's nicely caramelized on the outside, then covering it with liquid (the moist heat) and cooking it slowly in the oven (the dry heat) until the muscle fibers and the connective tissues break down. As the meat cooks, its collagens and gelatins dissolve into the cooking liquid, leaving you with a tasty sauce.

Braising is not restricted to meat. We like to braise vegetables like green garlic, artichokes, and even fennel in chicken stock, seasoning, and a little olive oil. They come out amazingly rich and sweet.

BLIND BAKING

This is a term widely used in the pastry kitchen. It refers to prebaking a tart or pie shell before adding the filling, to ensure that the crust will bake properly and not get soggy. To prevent the crust from puffing up as you blind-bake it, coat the shell lightly with nonstick cooking spray, line it with three coffee filters that are slightly overlapping, and fill it with dried beans or rice. Then bake the shell until golden. Remove the beans and coffee filters, and pour the pie filling of your choice into the prebaked shell.

BRINING

Brining, also known as pickling, is a common practice in our kitchen. We brine many of our proteins—like whole chicken, leg of lamb, pork shoulder, and turkey breast—prior to roasting or making a confit. Traditionally, brining is the first step in meat preservation, but for us, it's also an efficient way of enhancing the meat's flavor. Not only does it give large cuts time to absorb their seasonings, but it also tenderizes and moistens the meat and makes it more likely to brown while roasting in the oven.

All brines start with salt and water, but our brine solution also contains sugar (regardless of what else we add, the proportions of those three ingredients always stay the same). Depending on the kind of meat we're using, we may also include spices, herbs, or aromatic vegetables. The time required depends on the size and the density of the cut of meat—our recipes usually say to brine for about 12 hours. To ensure that the salt and sugar are fully dissolved, start with boiling water (this will also discourage bacteria growth), and make sure to cool the brine down completely before adding your meat. For safety's sake, start with cold meat, use a nonreactive container to hold the meat, and keep it in the refrigerator while it's brining. We also recommend setting a heavy plate on top of the meat to make sure that it stays submerged in the brine.

BROILING

Broiling is a vague term that usually refers to cooking food directly under or above the heat source. At the Bakery, we never use a broiler—first, because we don't have one, and second, because that's what the wood-fired oven is for. But most home cooks don't have 700°F wood-fired ovens, so if you're thinking of using a recipe that calls for one, we recommend using your broiler. Crank it up as high as it will go.

BROWNING VS. SWEATING

Browning means cooking on a hot pan with a small amount of fat to caramelize the exterior of the food (that is, turn it brown). We brown certain proteins before braising them, and we brown vegetables to deepen their flavor. When we pan-fry delicate foods such as fish, we brown the outside to enrich their taste and give them a crispy exterior while keeping the interior moist.

Sweating, on the other hand, means cooking in a pan with a small amount of fat until the food softens but doesn't brown, which requires using low heat. When working with delicate vegetables like leeks, we prefer sweating to browning—it preserves and accentuates the vegetables' subtle flavors that browning might destroy.

DEGLAZING

To *deglaze* means to add a small amount of liquid to a pan in which you just browned or sautéed something; its purpose is to dislodge any particles of flavor that might be sticking to the pan and sometimes to add a desirable new flavor. After adding a small amount of water, wine, or stock, use a wooden spoon to scrape up any stuck brown bits. Deglazing adds another dimension to the dish; it's so effective that we often deglaze a pan several times.

GRILLING

Grilling is Big Sur Bakery's favorite technique—the grill makes us feel like we're having a cookout every night and provides an adrenaline rush that comes from literally cooking with fire. We use our grill for everything from steaks to sardines, oysters, potatoes, vegetables, and squid—the list goes on and on. No other cooking method uses such direct exposure to fire, and the result is food with a flavorful blackened exterior and smoky undertones.

Using the grill can be challenging. The most important thing is to remember that you're cooking at a very high heat, which means that your food needs to be prepared in relatively small portions; larger items will burn before they're cooked all the way through.

HOW TO LIGHT AN OUTDOOR GRILL

We recommend using hardwood or hardwood lump charcoal for your grill (or barbecue). If you can find it, wood from oak, fig, or cherry trees is best. To light your grill, stack the wood or gather the charcoal in a pile in the center of the grill. (Once the food is on the grill, it's too late to burn more wood or add more charcoal, so be sure to start with enough fuel for what you're cooking.) To light, begin burning a small bundle of newspaper directly beside the wood or charcoal, and encourage the fire to spread by using a piece of stiff cardboard to fan air toward the center of the grill. Your goal is to create a red-hot coal base, not a bonfire. Once the grill is running hot, it'll give off intense heat, making it almost unbearable to stand right in front of it. If this isn't the case, wait. It usually takes about 30 minutes to preheat an outdoor grill. When the fire is ready, spread the coals so that you can cook over the entire grate, not just the center. (Food will cook faster toward the center of the grill, but it's useful to have a few cooler spots toward the side. This way, once your dish is nicely caramelized on the outside, you can place it on the edge of the grate to finish cooking without burning.) Since every grill is different, use the cooking times recommended in our recipes as guidelines, not mandates.

MACERATING

Macerating means soaking fruit or vegetables in liquid or stirring in sugar so that they release their own juices and absorb the desired flavors. It's a particularly effective way of preparing fresh fruit for dessert: just sprinkle it with sugar and let it sit for about 20 minutes until it releases its tasty juices. Macerating can also come in handy when the fruit is not optimal and needs a little intervention. You can macerate fruit in liquors like brandy, but be careful—alcohol might overwhelm the fruit's delicate flavor.

ROASTING AND BAKING

Roasting and *baking* both use the same basic idea: using an oven to provide an enclosed chamber in which food is exposed to dry heat, caramelizing its exterior while cooking through its center.

On average, our wood-fired oven runs at 700°F—hard conditions for the home cook to replicate—so we've adapted many of our wood-fired recipes to work in conventional ovens (though, unfortunately, a conventional oven won't provide you with the smoky flavor of burning wood). For some recipes, especially pizza, we recommend using a baking stone to better simulate the conditions of a wood-fired oven.

REDUCING

Reducing means simmering a liquid until evaporation thickens it; the resulting concentrate will have a much more intense flavor. To reduce, simmer the liquid over medium to medium-low heat. Doing so will allow impurities to rise to the surface, making them easy to skim off with a ladle or brush. Reducing also increases the viscosity of the liquid, giving it a richer mouth feel.

RENDERING

Rendering refers to removing a meat's fat by cooking the meat slowly over low heat. Doing so gets rid of excess grease while leaving the meat brown and crisp. Rendering is most commonly used with bacon, pancetta, duck skin, and pork fatback—all of which are considered flavorful fats, since once they've been rendered they can be reused for sautéing, frying, or making confit.

SAUTÉING

Sautéing means cooking food in a pan over medium-high heat with a small amount of fat. The word comes from the French *sauter*, meaning "to jump"—which refers to how you stir the pan's contents by jerking the pan back and forth and flipping the food quickly in the air. Sautéing is fast; you're trying to achieve a nice color while maintaining a moist interior and fresh flavor. If you're looking for a fast way to prepare food, it's an excellent choice.

SEASONING

Salt and pepper brighten the natural flavors of foods without disguising them, and while we'll often add other herbs and spices to our recipes, they're always our first steps.

We use kosher salt and freshly ground black pepper. Kosher salt is large-grained and additive-free—but be aware that the size of its flakes makes it less dense, so you might find yourself using more salt than you would initially think is necessary. Black peppercorns, native to India and Indonesia, add subtle heat and a hint of sweetness to savory dishes. Freshly ground black pepper-corns have far more flavor than the preground pepper in jars that you find at the grocery store—a statement that holds true for most spices.

It takes a while to learn how to season food to your liking, especially when you're adjusting it before you can actually taste the dish (such as when you're dealing with raw meat). We find that inexperienced cooks tend to under-season, and then start over-seasoning as they learn to appreciate what salt and pepper do to food. But don't worry: one day, it just clicks and you learn what "salt and pepper to taste" looks like on a raw steak.

To help speed your learning process, here are some guidelines:

Seasoning meat and fish: Season heavily right before searing, pan-frying, roasting, broiling, or grilling.

Seasoning salads: Season your salad dressing before tossing it with the greens. Then taste the dressed greens and add more salt and pepper if nec-essary.

Seasoning before toasting or roasting: We like to coat nuts and bread slices with a bit of oil and season them lightly with salt before toasting them. The same concept applies to certain vegetables, like roasted asparagus. You can always add more salt once they're out of the oven.

Seasoning as you go: Throughout our recipes, you'll notice that we recom-mend seasoning each of the components as you go—this is the best way to fully develop the flavors of ingredients that are added to a recipe in different stages. Exercise caution though, and be aware that the amounts of salt and pepper will add up in the final dish. Once all the components come together, taste the preparation as a whole and add more salt and pepper if necessary.

Resources

BIG SUR INSPIRATIONS

Terry Prince's "Hide Sandals" and Rachel Moody's
beadwork are available from their website.
www.bigsur-inspirations.com

BROKEN ARROW RANCH

Free-range, all-natural, truly wild game
meats, like venison, antelope, and wild boar.
www.brokenarrowranch.com

CYPRESS GROVE CHEVRE

Great goat cheese.
www.cypressgrovechevre.com

MICROCOSM MICRO GREENS

Eric Franks and Jasmine Richardson
grow amazing microgreens.
www.enjoyingmicrogreens.com

MONTEREY BAY AQUARIUM

Sea Watch Program, with a seafood guide that
identifies the most sustainable fish.
www.mbayaq.org

OVENCRAFTERS

Alan Scott's family builds wood-fired brick ovens
and has DIY plans on their website.
www.ovencrafters.net

PISONI VINEYARDS & WINERY

Exquisite wines from the Santa Lucia Highlands
by the Pisoni family.
www.pisonivineyards.com

SERENDIPITY FARMS

Jamie Collins sells organic flowers and vegetables,
including a wide variety of heirloom tomatoes.
www.serendipity-organic-farm.com

TLC RANCH

Short for "Tastes Like Chicken," Jim Dunlop's ranch
produces fantastic pasture-raised pork and eggs.
www.tasteslikechickenranch.com

Acknowledgments

To Catherine for taking a year out of her life to translate all of our journals into intelligent-sounding prose; to Sara for taking beautiful pictures, making us laugh, and always finishing the food so it didn't go to waste; and to Katie Jain, Joel Templin, and Shadi Kashefi at Hatch Design for creating such a beautiful book. A special thanks to our editor, Cassie Jones, and the team at William Morrow, including Johnathan Wilber, Jessica Deputato, Mary Ellen O'Neill, Liate Stehlik, David Sweeney, Dee Dee DeBartlo, Paula Szafranski, Lorie Pagnozzi, Lucy Albanese, Lynn Grady, Tavia Kowalchuk, Karen Lumley, Kim Lewis, and Lorie Young—not to mention Judith Regan for discovering us, and Eric Schlosser for his guidance and help. Thank you to Roxana Quiros for testing every recipe in this book. And to Lisa and Charlie Kleissner and Joe and Nancy Schoendorf for their friendship and generosity. Our gratitude goes out to all the servers, bussers, cooks, prep cooks, and dishwashers who keep us alive, and to the greater Big Sur community for their devotion and support. Thank you to the fishermen, hunters, gatherers, raisers, growers, foragers, pickers, and, most important, Wayne, Forrest, and Jim.

Philip: To my mother and father, who always had a hot homemade meal on the table every night. To my sister, Christine, her husband, Dave, and their precious children, Dylan, Julianna, and Ella. To the chefs who mentored me: Peter Roelant, Joe Miller, Josiah Citron, and Mark Peel. To Charles "Chuckie" Eissler, our longest reigning employee and first sous-chef, the NY Boys for making the pizzas for years, Brendan Essons for deciding to become our prodigy, and Orlando and Roberto and their family and friends for keeping us plugged into the workforce. Finally, my thanks go out to my wife, Michelle. She is the driving force behind the Bakery, and without her guidance, love, and grasp on reality, we wouldn't be here today.

Michelle: First and foremost my thanks go to my mother, who's never baked a thing but has supported my culinary career, and my entire life, in every way possible. To my sister for talking to me on the phone endlessly, and to my father for always reminding me that I could work harder. To my Grandma Regan for still making me breakfast in bed when I go home to New Jersey. I love you all! My appreciation goes out to the great chefs I have worked under—George Higgins, Colleen Johnson, Donald Wressel, Nancy Silverton, and Kim Boyce—and to the bakers at the Big Sur Bakery, Dave Laufer and José Martinez, for waking up before the sun comes up to produce beautiful pastries every morning. To Mike for putting up the money and not caring when he made it back as long as the Bakery had great food. Thanks to Emily and Gabrielle for helping me test the pastry recipes. And most of all, I'm grateful to my husband, without whom nothing is possible.

Mike: My heart goes out to my mother and father, both of whom were passionate about the cooking and serving of food and would have been very proud if they could have visited the Bakery. To all who have lifted up the spirits of the Bakery while working there, I thank you. Philip and Michelle, I will always be grateful to you for putting your trust in me. And finally, thanks to my sweet Heather and Daija and my dear friend Terry Prince for sharing the dream.

Index

Note: Page numbers in italics refer to recipe photographs.

G

Garlic

Gravy, 169

Green, Braised, 41

Preserved, 234

Gilson, Mike, 1–5, 126, 129

Ginger Ice Cream, 49

Ginger Sauce, Roasted Duck
Breast with, 226–27, *227*

Graham Cracker Crumbs, 48

Grain(s)

Date and Quinoa Muffins, 23

Hide Bread, 220–21

Nine-, Pancake, 20, *21*

Pearl Barley with Kale and
Butternut Squash, 230–31

Quail Stuffed with Chanterelles and
Foie Gras, with Polenta
and Au Jus, 152–53

Spring Risotto, 60, *61*

Grapefruit

Dressing, Artichokes and Asparagus
with Almonds and, 44–45, *45*

Dressing, Mâche Salad with Citrus,
Avocado, Almonds, and, 222

Pudding, 231

Gravy, Garlic, 169

Greens

Beet, and Goat-Cheese Crostini,
Roasted Beets with, 130–31, *131*

Butter Lettuce with Fennel, Herbs,
Meyer Lemon Dressing, and
Shaved Pecorino, *228*, 229

Field, Salad with Pecans, Croutons,
and Ranch Dressing, 170–71

Grilled Sardines with Frisée and
Whole-Grain Mustard Dressing, 38

Heirloom Tomato Salad with
Microgreens, Burrata, and
Balsamic-Basil Dressing, *132*, 133

Long-Cooked, Turkey Legs
Stuffed with, 167

Mâche Salad with Citrus,
Avocado, Almonds, and
Grapefruit Dressing, 222

Pearl Barley with Kale and
Butternut Squash, 230–31

Ruccola, Endive, and Radicchio
Salad with Pine Nuts and Aged
Goat Cheese, 40

Salmon Trout Wrapped in
Prosciutto, *186*, 187

Seared Ahi Tuna with Mixed
Baby Lettuces and
Seafood Dressing, 184

Grilled Mackerel, 136

Grilled Oysters with Champagne
Mignonette, 188, *189*

Grilled Pork Confit with Chuck's
Barbecue Sauce, 76–77

Grilled Prime Rib Steak with Red
Wine Sauce, 134, *135*

Grilled Ramps, 42, *43*

Grilled Salmon with Meyer
Lemon Dressing, 64, *64*

Grilled Sardines with Frisée and
Whole-Grain Mustard Dressing, 38

H

Hazelnut Flan with Roasted Cherries, 84–85

Heirloom Tomato Pizza, 112

Heirloom Tomato Salad with
Microgreens, Burrata, and
Balsamic-Basil Dressing, *132*, 133

Rice

Nine-Grain Pancake, 20, *21*

Spring Risotto, 60, *61*

Richardson, Jasmine, 57

Risotto, Spring, 60, *61*

Roasted Apricots, 102, *103*

Roasted Beets with Beet Greens and Goat-Cheese Crostini, 130–31, *131*

Roasted Chicken, *150*, 151

Roasted Duck Breast with Ginger Sauce, 226–27, *227*

Roasted Leg of Lamb with Pesto, 39

Roasted Spring Onions, 42

Roasted Striped Bass, 185, *185*

Roasted Turkey Breast, 166–67

Rockfish

Fish and Chips, Big Sur Style, 116–17, *117*

Scampi and Flatbread, 113

Whole, Scored and Charred, 114, *115*

Rolls, Parker House, 172–73

Rose Geranium and Strawberry Shake, 65, *65*

Rose Geranium Ice Cream, 65

Ruccola, Endive, and Radicchio Salad with Pine Nuts and Aged Goat Cheese, 40

Rum

Dresden Stollen, 196–97

Eggnog Ice Cream, 194–95

S

Salads

Butter Lettuce with Fennel, Herbs, Meyer Lemon Dressing, and Shaved Pecorino, *228*, 229

Field Greens, with Pecans, Croutons, and Ranch Dressing, 170–71

Heirloom Tomato, with Microgreens, Burrata, and Balsamic-Basil Dressing, *132*, 133

Mâche, with Citrus, Avocado, Almonds, and Grapefruit Dressing, 222

Roasted Beets with Beet Greens and Goat-Cheese Crostini, 130–31, *131*

Ruccola, Endive, and Radicchio, with Pine Nuts and Aged Goat Cheese, 40

Seared Ahi Tuna with Mixed Baby Lettuces and Seafood Dressing, 184

seasoning, 246

Salmon, Grilled, with Meyer Lemon Dressing, 64, *64*

Salmon, House-Cured, 62, *63*

Salmon Trout Wrapped in Prosciutto, *186*, 187

Sardines, cleaning, 38

Sardines, Grilled, with Frisée and Whole-Grain Mustard Dressing, 38

Sauces

Barbecue, Chuck's, 77

Chocolate, 67

Cranberry, 173

Garlic Gravy, 169

Homemade Mayonnaise, 236

Parsley, 192

Red Wine, 134

Tartar, 116

Tomato, 238

Scallops, Seared, with Cauliflower Purée and Tangerine Reduction, 205

Scones, 16, *16*